PRAISE FOR SANDOR KATZ'S FERMENTATION JOURNEYS

"*Sandor Katz's Fermentation Journeys* highlights the personal anecdotes that ignited his passion for fermentation. We are transported to each remote village through him and introduced to the people behind the recipes he has shared. Fermentation is an important method of food preservation that brings unique textures and flavors to many dishes. Sandor has managed to expose the ancient techniques behind the practice while providing approachable recipes for the home cook."

—**DANIEL BOULUD**, chef/restaurateur, author of *Letters to a Young Chef*

"In his *Fermentation Journeys*, Sandor Katz's life of curiosity-filled travel and exploration elicits a sense of wonder as tastes, sights, and smells leap off the pages to ignite your imagination. This book doesn't simply serve as a near-encyclopedic travelogue to countless ferments from around the world. It cements the grandfather of the fermentation revival as a great naturalist of our time; an enthusiastic adventurer seeking out not giant beasts, but microscopic ones, through friendships, community, recipes, and more-than-human stories."

—**DAVID ZILBER**, chef, fermenter, food scientist, and coauthor of *The Noma Guide to Fermentation*

"Sandor Katz has done it again. This time he learns alongside all of us as we travel the world with him and study centuries-old cultural traditions of all things fermented."

—**DAN BARBER**, chef/co-owner, Blue Hill and Blue Hill at Stone Barns; author of *The Third Plate*

ALSO BY SANDOR ELLIX KATZ

Wild Fermentation:
The Flavor, Nutrition, and Craft of Live-Culture Foods

The Revolution Will Not Be Microwaved:
Inside America's Underground Food Movements

The Art of Fermentation:
An In-Depth Exploration of Essential
Concepts and Processes from Around the World

Fermentation as Metaphor

SANDOR KATZ'S FERMENTATION JOURNEYS

RECIPES, TECHNIQUES, AND TRADITIONS FROM AROUND THE WORLD

SANDOR ELLIX KATZ

Chelsea Green Publishing
White River Junction, Vermont
London, UK

Project Manager: Patricia Stone
Project Editor: Benjamin Watson
Developmental Editor: Natalie Wallace
Copy Editor: Diane Durrett
Proofreader: Angela Boyle
Indexer: Shana Milkie
Designers: subtractor.co.uk and Melissa Jacobson
Front cover photograph: Jessica Tezak, jesstezak.com

Printed in the United States of America.
First printing September 2021.
10 9 8 7 6 5 4 3 2 1   21 22 23 24 25

Our Commitment to Green Publishing
Chelsea Green sees publishing as a tool for cultural change and ecological stewardship. We strive to align our
book manufacturing practices with our editorial mission and to reduce the impact of our business enterprise in
the environment. We print our books and catalogs on chlorine-free recycled paper, using vegetable-based inks
whenever possible. This book may cost slightly more because it was printed on paper that contains recycled fiber,
and we hope you'll agree that it's worth it. *Sandor Katz's Fermentation Journeys* was printed on paper supplied by
LSC Communications that is certified by the Forest Stewardship Council®.

Library of Congress Cataloging-in-Publication Data
Names: Katz, Sandor Ellix, 1962– author.
Title: Sandor Katz's fermentation journeys : recipes, techniques, and traditions from around the world /
    Sandor Ellix Katz.
Description: White River Junction, Vermont : Chelsea Green Publishing, [2021] | Includes bibliographical
    references and index.
Identifiers: LCCN 2021036778 (print) | LCCN 2021036779 (ebook) | ISBN 9781645020349 (hardcover)
    | ISBN 9781645020356 (ebook)
Subjects: LCSH: Fermented foods. | Fermentation. | Katz, Sandor Ellix, 1962—Travel. | LCGFT: Cookbooks.
Classification: LCC TP371.44 .K3698 2021 (print) | LCC TP371.44 (ebook) | DDC 641.4/63—dc23
LC record available at https://lccn.loc.gov/2021036778
LC ebook record available at https://lccn.loc.gov/2021036779

Chelsea Green Publishing
85 North Main Street, Suite 120
White River Junction, Vermont USA

Somerset House
London, UK

www.chelseagreen.com

MIX
Paper from
responsible sources
FSC® C132124
FSC
www.fsc.org

Dedicated to all the amazing people I have met
throughout my life's many travel adventures, and
those who have accompanied me on them, especially
my most steadfast travel companions through the ages:
Todd Weir, Leopard Zeppard/Andrew Williamson,
and Shoppingspree3d/Daniel Clark.

CONTENTS

LIST OF RECIPES

INTRODUCTION

I have always loved to travel. When I think back to some of the travels of my youth, I can see that long before my interest in fermentation began in earnest, traveling primed me to think about fermentation in ways that I likely would not have otherwise. As a 23-year-old, fresh out of college and seeking adventure, I traveled in Africa for several months with my friend Todd Weir. We didn't drink, or even encounter, any alcohol as we crossed the Sahara Desert overland through Algeria for a month, taking buses as far as they went, then hitchhiking. But after we crossed into Niger and the increasingly tropical West African landscape, we began to see beer and locally produced palm wine—the fermented sap of palm trees.

The palm wine we encountered and tried was wonderful, and we greatly appreciated the renewed availability of alcohol. I was struck by the fact that the palm wine was always served from open vessels rather than bottles, and seemed to be a product of cottage industry. The beer that was available was made by national breweries, but the palm wine was all made by people at home, or in very small-scale enterprises. Sometimes we bought it, and other times it was served to us as an expression of hospitality. We were also served home-brewed millet beer and other types of homemade alcohol.

I thought of this often eight or nine years later, after I became interested in fermentation. The literature for hobbyists about home beer brewing and winemaking was so technical. I found it somewhat off-putting in all its emphasis on chemicals to purify the fermentation substrate; sanitization at every step of the process; and special equipment, commercial yeast cultures, and yeast nutrients. All of this made me wonder about the people we had encountered making palm wine and millet beer in remote villages with limited technology and resources. Where were they getting their carboys and airlocks? Where were they getting their tablets of potassium metabisulfite and yeast nutrients? Or, how had they been able to ferment these delicious beverages without all of that? What were the simpler, more traditional ways? Without this experience traveling in Africa, I wouldn't have known to ask such questions. There, as everywhere, fermentation is an essential aspect of how people make effective use of food resources—not only palm sap, but everything from milk, meat, and fish to grains, beans, vegetables, and fruits.

Fermentation is truly a global phenomenon, practiced and of practical importance everywhere, and people in every part of the world make use of fermentation in similar ways. The benefits potentially travel to all the countries I have visited, but if not for my fermentation notoriety, and hosts who share my passion for fermentation, it would have been impossible to find my way to most of the places, people, and practices described in these pages. I feel very lucky to have had the access and entrée that I have been granted, and that makes me feel compelled to share what I have learned. This book is my invitation for you to join me on my adventures, and to learn about the incredible variety of fermented foods and drinks that I have tried and been shown how to make.

I figured I would eventually write a book about the foods and drinks I learned about in my travels, but I was too busy traveling, and had too many places yet to go, to write it. As the COVID-19 pandemic came on, I was teaching in Australia. At the last event before everything was canceled, at Fat Pig Farm in Tasmania, one of the students, a passionate fermenter who showed up with delicious homemade vinegars to share, gifted me with a face mask she had made, which came in very handy. After that, the remaining events I had scheduled were canceled, one by one. I flew back home (wearing her mask). Over the coming weeks, travels that I had planned for the year—to Alabama, Peru, Chicago, Vermont, Yukon, Iceland, Montana, China, and Taiwan—were all canceled. Finally, I had time to write. It took a pandemic.

When I started to write this book, I imagined it organized by geographic region. But at some point, it became clear that my focus was not so much what I saw on a particular trip to China or Colombia (though I have certainly included plenty of that), but on how the different foods I have seen, tried, and learned about relate to one another. In the end, I decided to organize the book by fermentation substrate (simple sugars, vegetables, grains, and so forth) in order to emphasize these relationships.

I spent only brief amounts of time in most of the places I visited. In some countries, my hosts took me on incredible journeys, but frequently I had a full teaching agenda and limited time to explore or learn about local practices. The memories I have of the places I visited, the foods I tried, and the methods I learned, are all highly impressionistic. I do not wish to pass myself off as an expert in the fermentations of any particular region.

Nonetheless, the cumulative impressions from my travels definitely enrich and inform my general understanding of fermentation, and my repertoire of techniques has been multiplied by this broad exposure. My strength as a fermentation writer and educator is in being a generalist. Plenty of people know more than I do about every imaginable realm of fermentation. What my experience offers is less depth than breadth, and organizing the book thematically allows me to better connect the dots.

My intention with this book, and indeed with all my work, is to celebrate and share the ingenuity and diversity of fermentation traditions around the world, and certainly not to exploit, misrepresent, or insult any of them. Cultural diversity is of utmost importance to me, and it motivates me in my work as a fermentation revivalist. Yet I recognize that for me, or anyone, to share other people's cultural traditions can potentially be hurtful, unwanted, inaccurate, incomplete, decontextualized, or worse. My knowledge of any of these specific foods or beverages is superficial compared to that of the

INTRODUCTION

I have always loved to travel. When I think back to some of the travels of my youth, I can see that long before my interest in fermentation began in earnest, traveling primed me to think about fermentation in ways that I likely would not have otherwise. As a 23-year-old, fresh out of college and seeking adventure, I traveled in Africa for several months with my friend Todd Weir. We didn't drink, or even encounter, any alcohol as we crossed the Sahara Desert overland through Algeria for a month, taking buses as far as they went, then hitchhiking. But after we crossed into Niger and the increasingly tropical West African landscape, we began to see beer and locally produced palm wine—the fermented sap of palm trees.

The palm wine we encountered and tried was wonderful, and we greatly appreciated the renewed availability of alcohol. I was struck by the fact that the palm wine was always served from open vessels rather than bottles, and seemed to be a product of cottage industry. The beer that was available was made by national breweries, but the palm wine was all made by people at home, or in very small-scale enterprises. Sometimes we bought it, and other times it was served to us as an expression of hospitality. We were also served home-brewed millet beer and other types of homemade alcohol.

I thought of this often eight or nine years later, after I became interested in fermentation. The literature for hobbyists about home beer brewing and winemaking was so technical. I found it somewhat off-putting in all its emphasis on chemicals to purify the fermentation substrate; sanitization at every step of the process; and special equipment, commercial yeast cultures, and yeast nutrients. All of this made me wonder about the people we had encountered making palm wine and millet beer in remote villages with limited technology and resources. Where were they getting their carboys and airlocks? Where were they getting their tablets of potassium metabisulfite and yeast nutrients? Or, how had they been able to ferment these delicious beverages without all of that? What were the simpler, more traditional ways? Without this experience traveling in Africa, I wouldn't have known to ask such questions. There, as everywhere, fermentation is an essential aspect of how people make effective use of food resources—not only palm sap, but everything from milk, meat, and fish to grains, beans, vegetables, and fruits.

Fermentation is truly a global phenomenon, practiced and of practical importance everywhere, and people in every part of the world make use of fermentation in similar ways. The benefits are numerous. Fermentation is a strategy for safety, producing acids, alcohol, and a range of other by-products that prevent pathogens from growing. It makes many foods more flavorful, and it underlies the beloved flavors of delicacies including chocolate, vanilla, coffee, bread, cheese, cured meats, olives, pickles, condiments, and so much more. Fermentation extends the lifespan of many foods, among them cabbage and other vegetables (sauerkraut and pickles), milk (cheese and yogurt), meat (salami), and grapes (wine). The most widespread form of fermentation is the production of alcohol, from every carbohydrate source imaginable. Fermentation also enhances nutrients and makes them more accessible, and it breaks down many plant toxins and antinutrient compounds. Certain ferments, eaten or drunk raw after fermentation, provide potentially beneficial bacteria, in great density and biodiversity. The process of fermentation confers all these benefits, and more.

We now understand that all the plant and animal products that comprise our food are populated by elaborate microbial communities. There is therefore a certain inevitability to microbial transformation. Cultures around the world have made use of this inevitability, developing techniques that effectively guide microbial

In the rainforest in northern Cameroon with people my travel companion and I met there, 1985.

transformation, not only in the context of food, but also in agriculture, fiber arts, building, and other realms.

Yet far from a unified set of techniques, fermentation encompasses a wide array of distinct processes, and it manifests in different ways in different places, depending upon what foods are abundant, what the climate is like, and other factors. The ferments of the tropics are altogether different from the ferments of the Arctic, starting with the starkly different available food resources, and then the varying climate conditions and practical needs compound the differences even more. This book takes you to both extremes. Even when environmental differences are not so stark, the ways that people work out to make use of microbial activity vary from place to place. Witness the diversity of cheeses, all made from milk, for an easy example. Then, because human migration and the resulting cultural cross-pollination have always been such constants, others' practices and techniques inevitably influence people everywhere. Like seeds, domesticated animals, culinary techniques, or virtually any aspect of cultural practice, fermentation spreads.

Fermentation may be universal, but cultural continuity is not. Around the world, colonization has wiped out entire demographic groups, and displaced others onto unknown landscapes. Indigenous children have been systematically removed from their families, punished for speaking their native languages, and otherwise forced to assimilate into the dominant culture. In our present neocolonial period, the means of oppression have shifted to poverty, social and economic marginalization, and mass incarceration. I have spoken with people who have been unable to find evidence or information about any of their ancestors' traditional fermentation processes because the cultural traditions from which they are descended were destroyed, disrupted, or displaced. Even for those whose cultures have not been subject to such destruction, cultural continuity is frequently disrupted by the allure of certain facets of modern life, such as urbanization, specialization, and mass-produced, mass-marketed food. Cultural practices, knowledge and wisdom, languages and beliefs, are disappearing every year. Like any other manifestation of culture, fermentation practices must be used in order to maintain relevance and stay alive. We must cherish and celebrate the diversity of fermentation practices around the world, and document and share them.

— — —

Who could ever have imagined that my how-to books about fermented foods and beverages would bring me around the world? Certainly not me. Yet that is what has come to pass in the years since the publication of my first book, *Wild Fermentation*, in 2003. At this point, I have taught in dozens of countries and visited a handful more. Everywhere I go, I eat and I learn. I have found myself in remote villages where people mostly subsist on what they can grow and produce, and I learned fermentation methods from them. I have been invited into Indigenous communities to learn their fermentation traditions, as well as the research and development kitchens of some of the world's most renowned restaurants to see and taste their latest fermentation projects. I have met mad experimentalists and people carrying on old family traditions.

I am in quite a unique position. Anyone with the time and the money could potentially travel to all the countries I have visited, but if not for my fermentation notoriety, and hosts who share my passion for fermentation, it would have been impossible to find my way to most of the places, people, and practices described in these pages. I feel very lucky to have had the access and entrée that I have been granted, and that makes me feel compelled to share what I have learned. This book is my invitation for you to join me on my adventures, and to learn about the incredible variety of fermented foods and drinks that I have tried and been shown how to make.

I figured I would eventually write a book about the foods and drinks I learned about in my travels, but I was too busy traveling, and had too many places yet to go, to write it. As the COVID-19 pandemic came on, I was teaching in Australia. At the last event before everything was canceled, at Fat Pig Farm in Tasmania, one of the students, a passionate fermenter who showed up with delicious homemade vinegars to share, gifted me with a face mask she had made, which came in very handy. After that, the remaining events I had scheduled were canceled, one by one. I flew back home (wearing her mask). Over the coming weeks, travels that I had planned for the year—to Alabama, Peru, Chicago, Vermont, Yukon, Iceland, Montana, China, and Taiwan—were all canceled. Finally, I had time to write. It took a pandemic.

When I started to write this book, I imagined it organized by geographic region. But at some point, it became clear that my focus was not so much what I saw on a particular trip to China or Colombia (though I have certainly included plenty of that), but on how the different foods I have seen, tried, and learned about relate to one another. In the end, I decided to organize the book by fermentation substrate (simple sugars, vegetables, grains, and so forth) in order to emphasize these relationships.

I spent only brief amounts of time in most of the places I visited. In some countries, my hosts took me on incredible journeys, but frequently I had a full teaching agenda and limited time to explore or learn about local practices. The memories I have of the places I visited, the foods I tried, and the methods I learned, are all highly impressionistic. I do not wish to pass myself off as an expert in the fermentations of any particular region.

Nonetheless, the cumulative impressions from my travels definitely enrich and inform my general understanding of fermentation, and my repertoire of techniques has been multiplied by this broad exposure. My strength as a fermentation writer and educator is in being a generalist. Plenty of people know more than I do about every imaginable realm of fermentation. What my experience offers is less depth than breadth, and organizing the book thematically allows me to better connect the dots.

My intention with this book, and indeed with all my work, is to celebrate and share the ingenuity and diversity of fermentation traditions around the world, and certainly not to exploit, misrepresent, or insult any of them. Cultural diversity is of utmost importance to me, and it motivates me in my work as a fermentation revivalist. Yet I recognize that for me, or anyone, to share other people's cultural traditions can potentially be hurtful, unwanted, inaccurate, incomplete, decontextualized, or worse. My knowledge of any of these specific foods or beverages is superficial compared to that of the people who grew up eating, drinking, and making them. Words can be taken in ways we never intended. In my enthusiasm to show the broad similarities among diverse practices, I fear that I may sometimes gloss over particular aspects of specific traditions that make them distinctive. I try to be aware and respectful, I welcome feedback, and I'm always interested in hearing from people with intimate connections to any of the foods or traditions that I write about. You can contact me via my website, wildfermentation.com.

While this book is inspired by my travels, the roots of my interest in fermentation are based very much in home and garden. The practical value of preserving garden abundance gave me a reason to learn how to ferment vegetables. And my garden and kitchen still anchor my fermentation practice. Whatever I have learned through traveling, I have put into practice in my own kitchen. My love of food and my relentlessly practical nature ground my passion for fermentation. This is a book of inspiration. It is full of the foods and drinks, processes, people, and places that have inspired me, and that I hope will in turn inspire you in your fermentation adventures.

ONE

SIMPLE SUGARS

I like to start with the simplest of ferments—sweet simple sugars that yeast and bacteria can effortlessly access and metabolize into alcohol and acids. With sugary fruits, plant saps, and diluted honey or sugar, fermentation is a spontaneous phenomenon: utterly unstoppable. Anyone who has ever harvested an abundance of any kind of fruit has discovered that some of it, inevitably, is already fermenting. Squeeze the juice out and it will all start to ferment, quickly. Plant saps readily ferment as well, once you extract them from the plant. Honey does not ferment so long as it remains free of water, but the addition of even small amounts of water enables the yeasts that are always present in raw honey to ferment its sugars and turn it into mead. Even if you are working with honey that has been heated or refined sugar that has surely been cooked, yeasts are everywhere around us and will find their way to any available sugars. The sources of the sugars that people ferment into alcohol and more lightly fermented beverages vary around the world.

As mentioned previously, before I was specifically interested in fermentation, I enjoyed palm wine in West Africa. Many years later, when I was better informed about how it is made, I encountered palm wine again, in a couple of different forms, in Southeast Asia. In Mexico, I learned about the importance of the dryland succulent plant maguey (or agave) and the elaborate cultural traditions around its processing into pulque and mezcal. I've witnessed different methods of fermenting pineapples—into *tepache* and *guarapo de piña*—in Mexico and Colombia. In Italy, I harvested grapes to make wine, and I have encountered passionate winemakers around the world. I have learned about persimmon vinegar (and pickles made from the residue!), mauby, and fruit enzyme drinks. And, of course, I'm still making mead. Wherever there is an abundant carbohydrate source, people likely have a method for fermenting it. In this chapter, I share what I have learned about this realm of fermentation.

Palm Wine

Palm wine, fermented from the sap of palm trees, is a delicious, cloudy white beverage that has always been served to me in simple open vessels, never bottles. Its strength, sweetness, and sourness are quite variable from batch to batch, and these shift over a relatively short timeframe. It is the first fermented beverage I encountered that was not made in a factory (in Niger); I loved it, though I wasn't yet thinking about fermentation and didn't inquire about how it was made.

I have since learned that palm wines and liquors are enjoyed in tropical regions all around the world. In Bagan, Burma (also known as Myanmar), I happened across a toddy drinking hole, recognizing *toddy* as a widespread name for palm wine. I was biking around by myself in the afternoon, meandering and exploring as I made my way toward the hotel where I was staying, when I spotted a simple sign with the word "Toddy," some words written in the beautiful Burmese alphabet, and an arrow. I followed the arrow to a small outdoor café where two young men who were already quite drunk helped me navigate the purchase of a bowl of palm wine. I was glad to have drinking partners, because the bowl was huge and the toddy was strong and already beginning to sour. Toddy, like all palm wines, is highly dynamic; it ferments into alcohol quickly and then passes into vinegar in rapid succession.

Owing to this dynamism, the toddy is frequently distilled into a beverage sometimes known as arak, to concentrate the alcohol enough that it is no longer vulnerable to vinegar-producing organisms and is therefore shelf-stable. (The name *arak* is also used in the Middle East and elsewhere to describe other distilled spirits.) As you will see throughout the book, people all around the world use distillation for this purpose.

I visited a small, rural arak distillery in Bali, and I was struck by the simplicity of the still. It was hand built in place, primarily from earth, with a chamber to hold the fermented toddy above a simple fire chamber. The chamber holding the toddy was plugged tightly, with a tube to carry the vapors into and through a barrel

Toddy in Burma. Quite a large amount was served in the black ceramic vessel, along with coconut shell cups to drink from.

My drinking buddies in Burma.

The arak still we
visited in Bali.

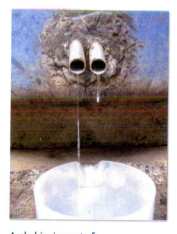

Arak dripping out of
the still.

Coconut sap
fermenting into toddy
prior to distillation.

filled with cold water, causing the vapor to condense and liquefy. The arak then dripped out of a tube on the opposite side of the barrel.

The improvisational nature of this still was especially striking to me at the time because my friend Billy had recently opened the Short Mountain Distillery down the road from my home, and I knew that the gorgeous copper stills he had purchased required a heavy investment. The moonshiners whom Billy originally learned from created improvisational stills not altogether different from what I was seeing in Bali. It's always good to bear in mind that before they were ever elaborated on by industry and engineering, all the basic, transformational processes that turn the products of nature and agriculture into the foods and drinks we love have long traditions of being done with whatever tools and methods that are available.

In addition to the still, I saw the trees whose sap was being tapped. Boys climbed the trees and pinched off just-developing buds, and they attached coconut shells to catch the sap dripping from where the buds were. The boys climbed up the trees every morning and afternoon to collect the sap. Coconut trees produced the sap; coconut shells were used to collect it; and coconut husk fibers (coir) fueled the fire to vaporize the ethanol in the toddy. I tasted the fermenting coconut sap and it was wonderful, though in Bali the tradition is to distill it.

Pulque

In the arid mountains of Mexico, maguey (*Agave americana*), known in English as agave or century plant, thrives. Spiny and slow growing, it flowers only once in its lifetime. Different varieties of maguey take 7 years to more than 20 years to develop; after flowering once, the plant dies. Clever inhabitants of ancient Mexico developed elaborate techniques for harvesting the sap, called aguamiel (honey water), which is extremely delicious and sweet when fresh. Each plant produces hundreds of quarts/liters of it. But aguamiel doesn't stay fresh for long, and it rapidly ferments into the legendary beverage pulque.

Pulque is milky white, slightly viscous, tart, effervescent, and alcoholic. It can be even more wonderful than the fresh aguamiel, though I have discovered that the flavor varies quite a bit from batch to batch and is dynamic over a short timeframe. In addition to being enjoyed as a beverage, pulque is used as a leavening agent for a very special sweet, light bread called *pan de pulque*.

Pulque, like many of the world's indigenous fermented beverages, has been much maligned. Profitable and politically powerful breweries, working with corrupt public officials, orchestrated government campaigns against pulque in the early twentieth century, characterizing it as unhygienic. There were even rumors that pulque was fermented with feces. Factory production of Western beer and Coca-Cola was touted as safer than traditional small-scale pulque production. I heard a similar story in Colombia, where indigenous, ancient *chicha* made by small producers (see "*Chicha*," page 116) was disparaged as unhygienic, and the suggested replacement was modern, hygienic, factory-produced beer and sodas. In spite of the fearmongering, the fact is that fermentation is a strategy that ensures safety, whether for aguamiel, corn, barley, or any other ingredient. In the realm of sweet, carbohydrate-rich substrates, there is no danger beyond the final product becoming too vinegary for most people to find palatable. But the alcohol and acidity from fermentation only make it safer from potential pathogens.

Pouring a glass of bubbly, fresh pulque.

In a field of maguey on his farm, Emilio Arizpe shares pulque with students during a fermentation workshop.

Tlachiquero Don Teo pouring freshly harvested aguamiel into a barrel full of already fermenting pulque.

Pulque is one of the most wonderful ferments that I have had the good fortune to experience in its context: where maguey thrives and little else will grow; where aguamiel is collected twice every day and the pulque fermented. Indeed, pulque is not really available beyond where it is produced. No one has figured out how to completely stop the fermentation without destroying the qualities of the beverage.

I first tasted pulque, and witnessed how the aguamiel is collected, at Villa de Patos, a beautiful, diversified farm in General Cepeda, in the mountains outside of Monterrey in the north of Mexico. Emilio and Sofia Arizpe own the farm, and it is home to huge fields of maguey from which *tlachiquero* Don Teo harvests aguamiel. Tlachiquero means "the one who scrapes" in the Nahuatl language. Don Teo, like the other tlachiqueros I have met in Mexico, learned the harvesting techniques by helping elder family members with the ancient practice.

Fermenting pulque is simple enough. Aguamiel ferments spontaneously very easily. Because fresh sap is harvested twice a day, there is generally some form of backslopping. This involves adding new sap to the already

Don Teo cutting la puerta into a maturing maguey plant in preparation for harvesting aguamiel.

fermenting batch, stirring, and continuing to ferment. The duration of the fermentation varies with the pulque maker and the temperature: from less than 24 hours to several days. At some point, based upon subjective evaluation of smell and flavor, some pulque is harvested, more sap is added, and so on. The harvested portion might be either further fermented or blended with the previous day's harvest.

Beyond evaluating when it is ready to drink, the major skill involved in making pulque is harvesting the sap from the maguey. The tlachiquero's work starts with identifying mature plants that are beginning to develop stalks. Then, to access the center of the plant so they can cut down the developing stalk, they must remove the sharp, spiny edges from some of the outer leaves of the plant, which then allows these leaves to be arched down and secured, thereby creating *la puerta* (the door) to the center. The maguey spines are strong and can pierce deeply, and the sap can be a toxic irritant. Care must be taken to create safe and easy access to the heart of the maguey where all the sap will eventually be collected twice a day for months.

At Villa de Patos, tlachiquero Don Teo had a very specific process that he followed, and the architecture of his cuts was highly stylized. At the very center of

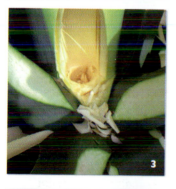

El capazón, or "the castration" of the maguey: Don Teo cuts through the developing stalk (1); pries it off (2); digs a well (3); and covers it with a piece of the removed stalk (4).

the maturing plant is the developing flower bud, but it is shrouded and protected by tight layers of succulent leaves. Don Teo confidently cut through those leaves and removed them. The very lightest (not yet photosynthesizing) central leaves he impaled on the biggest remaining leaves to make it easy to locate this plant for harvesting in the huge field of magueys. Once the growing center of the plant was revealed, Don Teo took firm hold of it in his hand and pulled it downward to the base, where he removed the developing flower bud in a process known as *el capazón*, or castration. He then cut a depression into the base of the maguey—from which the sap would later be collected—covered it with a portion of the removed stalk, and scattered some of the chips left over from creating the well right around it, perhaps ritualistically.

The castrated plant is then left for a few months, during which the wound heals and the bud continues to swell with sap, but the flower cannot develop. When the tlachiquero deems it time, the scabbed-over wound is reinjured—poked, punctured, and mashed—then left for another week or so, after which the fermenting debris is easily removed by scraping the cavity. The cavity (*cajete*) becomes a well from which to collect the aguamiel, and the twice-daily harvesting begins!

Daily aguamiel harvesting involves two main tools. The first is a long, thin gourd called an *acocote*, with a hole at each end that is used to transfer aguamiel from the cajete into a bucket. One end of the gourd goes into the cajete full of aguamiel. The tlachiquero sucks on the hole at the other end like a drinking straw, drawing the liquid (which can vary with the size of the plant and over the course of the harvest, from a cup/250 ml to more than 1 quart/1 liter per plant) into the gourd. A finger is used to cover the hole and keep the sweet sap in the gourd while it is moved to the waiting collection bucket. The finger is removed and the aguamiel flows into the bucket. Finally, the tlachiquero uses a tool to scrape the edges of the cajete and remove any debris, which is collected in a separate bucket to feed to livestock.

Uriel Arellano, another tlachiquero I met, lives in a village called Otumba, overlooking the pyramids of Teotihuacán outside of Mexico City. He does things a little differently. Whereas Don Teo's plants are essentially untouched until he prepares to extract the aguamiel,

Aguamiel in a maguey plant ready to be harvested.

Don Teo with his acocote.

Uriel harvests some of the outer leaves for *barbacoa*, a traditional Mexican style of pit-roasting meat. The maguey leaves are placed atop hot stones in a pit, then topped with the meat and covered with another, insulating layer of leaves to hold in the heat. The succulent leaves keep the meat moist with the sweet steam of aguamiel, and buffer the heat so the meat can cook low and slow. We ate some mutton barbacoa after harvesting with Uriel, at the roadside stand of a friend of his. It was very tender, juicy, and tasty.

Mutton and maguey stand together as mainstays of the local cuisine. Many of the local farmers who grow maguey and make pulque also graze herds of sheep. The sheep generally don't eat the maguey, but they do fertilize the soil. Their meat is cooked on maguey leaves, and the meal is generally enjoyed with pulque. Like pulque, barbacoa is an ancient use of the maguey plant. But between them there is a tradeoff: each leaf removed from a plant results in less aguamiel.

Laura "Lala" Noguera, who calls herself a "cultural activist of agave," brought me and my Mexico City workshop organizer, Galia Kleiman, to meet Uriel. On the slow drive out of Mexico City through heavy traffic, she told us about how she learned to harvest aguamiel and make pulque as a young child from her tlachiquero grandfather. When she hit puberty, her grandfather told her she could no longer be part of the pulque making; her menstrual cycles could disrupt the fermentation. Defying taboo, she continued making pulque without him, and without any problems with the fermentation.

Uriel and Lala between two maguey plants
as we were harvesting aguamiel.

MUJERES MILENARIAS

On my most recent visit to Mexico, Galia and Raquel Guajardo, who together organized a big fermentation event in Oaxaca, took me and other presenters for a drive into the Sierra Madre mountains to visit Mujeres Milenarias, a collective of women pulque makers in a remote village called El Almacén Apazco. It's the only place where Galia and Raquel had encountered women making pulque. We went harvesting with *tlachiquera* Bibiana Bautista. Afterward, because each member of the collective makes her own pulque, we walked from house to house, sampling each woman's pulque. Each was a little different: stronger, sweeter, or sourer. We learned that during drought times, pulque has sometimes been the only hydration available in their community.

On the day we arrived, a community member had found a bunch of beautiful yellow mushrooms, called simply *amarillos*. An older woman roasted the amarillos directly on embers in the fire, then shared them with us. They were incredibly delicious. We bought some pulque to bring back to Oaxaca with us. The pulque was already a little different when we got back a few hours later, and even more so the next day. Pulque is dynamic and constantly unfolding.

When I later exchanged emails about pulque with Galia, she poignantly wrote: "All through Mexican history, from pre-Hispanic times to our days, pulque has been a key reference regarding culture, tradition, and cuisine. If people stop drinking and producing it, we run the risk of losing also the maguey plant and the cultural knowledge related to its cultivation and use." Maguey is not only the source of aguamiel for pulque and leaves for barbacoa, but it is also used by distillers to make mezcal (see "Mezcal") and tequila, has traditionally provided fiber for rope, building, and roofing, and the plant itself prevents soil erosion. Galia argues that continued use of these processes is essential for cultural survival. "Cultures are complex systems of beliefs and knowledge kept alive by the daily activities of the people who express them."

Tlachiquera Bibiana Bautista harvesting aguamiel.

Mezcal

Mezcal is a strong, clear distilled alcohol with deep, complex flavors. Like pulque, it is made from the maguey plant. For making mezcal, however, the maguey's sweetness is accessed in a very different manner. Rather than removing sap from the plant, as is done to make pulque, the starting point for mezcal is the heart of the plant itself, after it has swollen in advance of flowering. When the outer leaves of the maguey are removed, this heart looks something like a pineapple or a pinecone. In fact, it is called *la piña*—the Spanish name for both of those things. La piña is cut out when the maguey matures and develops a stalk, right before it flowers.

My friends Paulina and Daniel, who have a lovely bakery café in Oaxaca called Boulenc and a side fermentation business called Suculenta, took me and a small group of friends for a drive to Santa Catarina Minas, Oaxaca, to visit *mezcaliero* Eduardo Javier Ángeles Carreño, better known as Lalo. He is a fourth-generation mezcaliero who distills under the brand name Lalocura with his family

A stack of freshly harvested piñas ready for roasting.

Me with mezcaliero Eduardo Javier Ángeles Carreño, better known as Lalo.

Chunks of roasted piña for us to taste.

A hole built into the concrete floor and huge wooden mallets for crushing the roasted piñas into a pulp.

Roasted piña pulp mixed with water fermenting in a big wooden tank. Note the cross floating in the center of it.

and a small team of helpers. At Lalo's farm, he and his family grow maguey, then cook it, ferment it, and distill it into mezcal.

La piña is tough and woody. It needs to be pit-roasted for a few days for the fibers to soften and the sugars to caramelize. When we arrived at the farm, freshly roasted piñas had just been dug from the pit. They were still warm, just cool enough to handle. Lalo's niece cut off pieces of one of the succulent piñas and we chewed on them, sucking all the rich, juicy sweetness out of them, then spit out the remaining fibers.

After roasting, the piñas are crushed into a pulp. At Lalocura this was done with direct human power. A rectangular pit built into the concrete floor contained the piña pulp, which was mashed with two massive wooden mallets. Then the pulp was mixed with water and fermented in huge wooden vats. Finally, it was distilled the traditional way, in clay barrel stills.

Tequila is also made from la piña, and it can be regarded as a type of mezcal. Mezcal is made from many different maguey species, while tequila is defined as the product of a single maguey species, *Agave tequilana Weber*. Additionally, for tequila the piñas are typically steamed in ovens rather than roasted in pits, and distilled in copper rather than clay stills.

After seeing how the mezcal was made, we went into the tasting room, where there were dozens of glass carboys—narrow-necked bottles of roughly 5 gallon/20 liter capacity—each filled with a different mezcal. Some of them were distinguished by the variety of maguey they were made from: for example, *espadin* or *tobasiche*. Some were blends. One odd variant, called *pechuga*, involves adding fruit and a raw chicken to the mash being distilled. The building itself was literally a monument to maguey, built of adobe-like bricks made using *bagaso*, the residual maguey fibers left over after distilling mezcal.

Before we could taste each variety, there was a bit of a sensory evaluation ritual. First, a little of the mezcal was poured into a gourd so we could observe small bubbles, *las perlas*, which we were told are a sign of quality. Then, a tiny bit of mezcal was poured into each person's palm, and then we rubbed our palms together in order to feel the texture of the mezcal. Some were definitely more viscous than others. And the flavors were quite varied

Mezcal dripping out of a clay still.

Carboys filled with different styles of mezcal, with bagaso bricks made with maguey fibers behind them.

as well. It was great fun to focus so much attention on each one. I kept track of my favorites, and I bought a few bottles at the end to bring home. But honestly, the accumulation of a dozen tastes left me in no condition to remember each mezcal distinctly.

What was reinforced for me that day was something I already knew: I love mezcal. It has such distinctive and intriguing flavors, and such smoothness. Even more, I love maguey. What an amazing plant, to thrive in such harsh, dry conditions, and to spawn two entirely different ways of processing and two beverages—mezcal and pulque—that each sustain so many people and are so culturally important.

Winemaking in Umbria

In 2006, I was invited to visit a small farm in the countryside of Umbria, in central Italy, by a woman named Etain. I had enjoyed a lively correspondence with Etain about the unregulated underground food market of which she was part, during my research for *The Revolution Will Not Be Microwaved*, a book about grassroots food activist movements. When I finished writing the book, I was ready for a vacation, and the rolling hills of central Italy sounded very alluring.

Etain makes cheese from the milk of her small herd of sheep, as well as other value-added farm products. Until recent years, she had sold her cheese at the farmers market in town. But as European Union mandates came into conflict with customary local practices, she and other vendors found that their cheese and certain other products no longer met the commercial standards. So a group of them started a rotating, word-of-mouth, unsanctioned underground food market.

The barn at Etain's farm, Pratale.

Etain and Jessieca processing vegetables in the courtyard at Pratale.

Arriving at Etain's farm, Pratale, I was struck immediately by the house and the farm buildings—many hundreds of years old, all built from stone. The house had a number of bedrooms and a kitchen, each room opening onto a central courtyard, which at that time of year served as their living room, dining room, and workspace. Etain lives at Pratale with her partner, Martin, and her son. They host a rotating cast of international farm volunteers and visitors, some of whom visit regularly, as I came to learn. When I was there, they had a volunteer from the state of Maine, a man visiting from the Faroe Islands, and a Hakka Chinese woman, Jessieca, who was visiting with her German husband.

The vineyard at Pratale.

One of Pratale's donkeys, Otello, hauling crates full of grapes from the vineyard to the barn.

Martin feeding grapes into the press to crush them into juice.

Wine fermentation barrel with airlock in Pratale's barn.

Etain and Martin use donkeys and horses for plowing and hauling, and they also raise chickens, ducks, and doves. By luck, I was there at grape-harvesting time. This farm is organized around the family's diverse needs rather than production of any specialized crop. They have a vineyard, but it is small. Each of their flocks and herds is small. They have vegetable gardens, which were producing eggplants galore at the time I visited. They have pomegranates, and more figs than I have ever seen; they were eating and preserving as many as they could, but overripe fruits littered the ground around each tree. They also have a small stone and masonry wood-fired oven, and they bake all their own bread in it. The olives were not yet ripe during my stay, but olive trees were all around. Pratale is a back-to-the-land subsistence dream fulfilled.

The most educational part of the week for me was being part of the grape harvest and winemaking. All week long, I enjoyed Pratale's plentiful house wine, so it was satisfying to be able to help replenish the supply. A group of perhaps 8 or 10 of us picked grapes, mixing together different varieties—some green, some dark red. Under Martin's close direction, the donkey, Otello, hauled crates full of grapes from the vineyard to the barn, where they were crushed using a clever old mechanical press. The press had two wooden rollers with interlocking grooves. A hand crank turned the rollers. Above the rollers was a wooden hopper, which we kept filling with grapes. As we cranked the rollers, the grapes passed between them, emptying, crushed, into a vessel below.

The crushing yields a mass of grape skins, stems, and pulp in grape juice. Once the grapes were crushed, we were ready for lunch (accompanied by the previous year's wine, of course). When we returned to the grape juice a few hours later, it was already a bubbling froth. Ripe grapes are so rich, both in yeast and in all the nutrients and conditions that the yeast need to thrive, that vigorous fermentation starts almost immediately. Etain and Martin left the fermenting grapes in open vessels to ferment for the first few frothy days, then strained the liquid, pressed the remaining juice from the solid residue, and transferred the fermenting wine to an airlocked barrel. At a small scale, in a place where grapes grow easily, and with a little bit of special equipment, winemaking is simple and straightforward.

TEPACHE

Tepache is a wonderful, effervescent, lightly fermented pineapple beverage popular in Mexico. It is made from the skins and core of pineapple; you can enjoy the fresh pineapple flesh and also make use of the parts typically discarded in order to enjoy it over a longer period of time.

TIMEFRAME

2 to 5 days

VESSEL

Wide-mouth vessel of at least ½-gallon/2-liter capacity with lid or cloth to cover

INGREDIENTS

for about 1 quart/1 liter

½ cup/100 grams sugar (or more, to taste) ✳

Peel and core of 1 pineapple (eat the rest of the fruit!), cut into 1- to 2-inch/3- to 5-centimeter pieces

1 cinnamon stick and/or a few whole cloves and/or other spices (optional)

PROCESS

Dissolve the sugar in about 1 cup/250 milliliters of water.

Place the pineapple skin and core pieces and the optional spices into the vessel.

Pour the sugar water over the pineapple, then add additional water as needed to cover the pineapple.

Cover with a loose lid or cloth, and stir daily.

Ferment for 2 to 5 days, depending upon temperature and desired level of fermentation. It will get fizzy, and then develop a pronounced sourness after a few days.

Taste each day after the first two to evaluate developing flavor.

Once you are happy with the flavor, strain out the solids.

Enjoy fresh or refrigerate for up to a couple of weeks.

If it gets too sour, do not despair! After straining out the solids, leave it with its surface exposed to airflow and it will become pineapple vinegar after a week or two.

✳ ideally piloncillo, panela, or another unrefined sugar, but any type of sugar will work

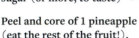

Guarapo de Piña

Guarapo de piña is another fermented pineapple beverage, which I tried in Bogotá, Colombia, after seeing how it was prepared at the Bogotá Fermentation Festival by a man named Pacho, who was from an Indigenous group in the Colombian Amazon called the Matapi.

Guarapo de piña is deceptively simple. Grate ripe pineapples (skin and all), let the mash spontaneously ferment, then strain and drink. It requires an abundance of pineapples, and it is made only where they grow. Pictured here are some of the tools Pacho used to make it. Beyond the drink itself, it was especially interesting to learn about the ceremonial context in which guarapo de piña plays an important role in the Matapi culture.

The ceremony was explained to me by Esteban Yepes Montoya, my Colombian host. According to Esteban, each season, at a time dictated not by a calendar or a celestial body but by biological developments such as the emergence of cicadas or frogs, the Matapi gather in their *malocas* (big ceremonial lodges) for a ceremony marking the passage of the season. The ceremony celebrates reciprocity with other life forms and involves the use of several especially sacred plants: tobacco, coca, and pineapples. For days, participants dance and sing, foregoing all food and beverage except for guarapo de piña. As Esteban described it to me, this brings them into a trance state, in which they "surrender to the here and now of the season" and "bow to the sacred essence of the pineapple." As in many Indigenous traditions around the world, it is a product of fermentation that embodies sacred interconnectedness.

Left, removing the grated pineapple flesh from the grater.

Middle, the guarapo grating tool, called a *jualapa* in the Matapi language.

Right, a *totuma* (gourd cup) of guarapo de piña.

MAUBY/MABÍ

When I visited the Caribbean island of St. Croix, I knew to be on the lookout for mauby—*mabí* in Spanish—a lightly fermented soft drink made from the bark of the mauby tree (*Colubrina elliptica* or soldierwood) and enjoyed in many Caribbean lands. Mauby is bitter, sweet, and very bubbly due to the saponins in the bark. People flavor it with different spices: cinnamon, nutmeg, mace, star anise, ginger, and beyond.

Years earlier I had made a couple of batches as best I could, without ever having tasted it before, using bark and instructions that were mailed to me by a Puerto Rican reader of *Wild Fermentation*. The only problem was, she didn't know how I would be able to start the mauby, which is typically started by backslopping from a previous batch. I improvised using water kefir, with great results. My experience is that starters—especially in the realm of lightly fermented sweet beverages—are largely interchangeable.

At the Saturday morning farmers market in St. Croix, I was very excited to find a woman selling her homemade mauby. It was bottled in reused plastic beverage bottles, bulging with the pressure of fermentation. The cold mauby was delicious and refreshing in the hot weather there! I managed to bring a small bottle home with me to use as a starter, and I've kept a little (in the refrigerator) from each batch I've made since then, backslopping continuously for a decade now.

Dried mauby bark.

TIMEFRAME

3 days to 1 week

VESSEL

Crock or another vessel with at least 1-gallon/4-liter capacity

Reused plastic soda bottles or other sealable bottles. Plastic has the benefit of allowing you to feel how pressurized the bottles of mauby are becoming, so you can refrigerate bottles to avoid explosions.

INGREDIENTS

for 1 gallon/4 liters

1 cup/40 grams mauby bark, loosely packed ✳

Small amounts of roots such as licorice and/or ginger, and/or spices such as cinnamon, star anise, clove, and/or allspice (don't be afraid to experiment!)

Pinch of salt

2 cups/400 grams sugar (to taste) †

1 cup/250 milliliters of a previous batch of mauby, water kefir, ginger bug, or other active starter, or even a pinch of yeast

PROCESS

Simmer the mauby bark and any additional roots or spices in about ½ gallon/2 liters of water for at least ½ hour, or as long as 1 hour or more, to make a flavor concentrate.

Strain the mauby and spice decoction into the fermentation vessel.

Add the salt and sugar, dissolving in the hot liquid.

Add cold water to bring total volume to 1 gallon/4 liters. (It will take more than ½ gallon because some of the original ½ gallon you started with will have evaporated or absorbed into the bark and spices.)

Add the starter. Stir well, cover to protect from flies, and ferment for a few days.

Stir a few times each day.

Once it seems to be getting bubbly (generally faster in a warm climate or with a vigorous starter), bottle it. Be sure to save some in a jar that will become the starter for your next batch! Transfer the rest into sealable plastic bottles so you can feel the pressure and gauge the level of carbonation.

Ferment the starter jar and plastic bottles overnight or for a couple of days, until the bottles feel pressurized.

Refrigerate the mauby and enjoy cold.

Starter can be stored in the refrigerator for a year or longer.

✳ available in Caribbean markets and via the internet

† ideally in a less-refined form such as panela or jaggery, but any sugar is fine

PERSIMMON VINEGAR

I love persimmons! My favorite ones are North American persimmons (*Diospyros virginiana*)—small, soft, juicy, and caramelly. In the woods where I live in Tennessee, we pick ripe persimmons from the forest floor from September into December. Each tree's persimmons are distinctive, and I have a few special favorite trees, though all the fruit is delicious. You learn to spot the signs that they are fully ripe; unripe fruits are horribly astringent. You can make this vinegar with American persimmons or any of the more widely available Asian varieties.

I learned about this wonderful and simple method for making persimmon vinegar from my one-time student and Australian tour organizer Sharon Flynn, who includes it in her beautiful book, *Ferment for Good*. Sharon says she first knew of it from Korea, then saw a recipe in Nancy Singleton Hachisu's amazing book, *Preserving the Japanese Way*.

Beyond the pleasing sweet-sour persimmoniness of this vinegar, one of the most appealing rewards is that the persimmon pulp by-product can then be used as a pickling bed (Persimmon Pickling Medium, page 24).

The only ingredient for this vinegar is persimmons. Any kind of persimmons. Nancy Singleton Hachisu recommends using them while they are still firm, or "baseball hard." She uses a mix of Fuyu (the ones that are sweet even when the fruits are firm) and Hachiya (the ones that are tannic until they get soft). If you use indigenous North American persimmons, try to use fully ripe fruit, but don't worry if you get some underripe ones. The fermentation should break down the tannins. This recipe is intended for long, slow fermentation starting at persimmon harvest time in the autumn and continuing into winter.

TIMEFRAME

About 3 months,
in a cool environment

EQUIPMENT

Ceramic crock, bowl, or
another nonreactive vessel

Cloth to cover vessel, and string
or rubber band to secure it

Strainer and muslin or other
finely woven cloth to line it

Sealable narrow-neck bottle(s)
for bottling

INGREDIENTS

*for roughly 2 cups/
500 milliliters*

2 pounds/1 kilogram of fruit

PROCESS

Remove the calyx, the non-pulpy crown, from each persimmon.

Place the persimmons in a vessel big enough that you can stir the persimmons from the bottom.

Cover the vessel with a cloth and secure with string or rubber band to keep flies out of the persimmons.

Ferment for a few days. "Set the crock in a sunny spot and let nature take its course," advises Nancy.

Look them over after a few days. If molds started to develop on any of the skins, trim them away. Stir the persimmons around a little. They should be getting softer and starting to get juicy.

Stir them every day or two as they get juicier and juicier. The juice will get bubbly as it ferments. Taste the juice and enjoy experiencing its transformation from sweet to alcoholic.

Once the bubbling subsides and it starts to taste a little vinegary, leave it be for a few months, covered with the cloth to allow it to breath while protecting it from flies.

Taste the evolving vinegar every week or two. A mother may or may not develop on the surface. Don't worry either way.

You can enjoy persimmon vinegar young, as a light drinking vinegar, or ferment it for 2 or 3 months for higher acidity. Definitely harvest before hot weather arrives.

When you are ready to harvest the vinegar, strain it through a fine strainer lined with muslin or other finely woven cloth. Let the persimmon mash drain on its own for a few hours, then fold the corners of the cloth into the center and use a moderate weight, such as a bowl or pot (potentially with some other weight inside it), to press further liquid from the pulp. After this pressing, gather the remaining pulp into a ball in the cloth and squeeze with your hands to extract as much juice as you can.

Store the vinegar in full, well-sealed bottles.

Use the pulp as a pickling medium, as described in the following recipe, Persimmon Pickling Medium.

PERSIMMON PICKLING MEDIUM

One of the most exciting aspects of making persimmon vinegar is using the by-product as a pickling medium to carry the pulpy-seedy residue, still rich with persimmon flavor, into acidic pickled vegetables. As we explore in later chapters, by-products of one fermentation process are often used as the starting point for another. Japanese pickles, collectively known as *tsukemono*, are made in an unusually wide array of styles and make use of incredibly diverse mediums—many of them fermentation by-products—such as sake lees (see "*Kasuzuke*" on page 80) or these persimmon pickles.

TIMEFRAME

A few days

VESSEL

Small crock, wide-mouth jar, or other nonreactive container with a capacity of at least 1 quart/1 liter.

INGREDIENTS
for ½ pound/250 grams

About ½ pound/250 grams vegetables, such as daikon, other radish, turnip, carrot, or cucumber, or experiment with others

1 or 2 tablespoons coarse salt

Roughly 1 pound/500 grams residual pulp from Persimmon Vinegar, page 22

PROCESS

Dry root vegetables in the sun for several days before submerging them in the pickling medium. This makes them pliable, lowers their water content so they do not water down the pickling bed, and allows the vegetables to absorb more of the persimmon flavor.

Chop the vegetables into chunks big enough to find and retrieve easily.

If you are using cucumbers, salt the chunks and leave them in a colander to drain for a couple of hours before burying in the persimmon mash. Then rinse and dry.

Rub the edges of the other vegetable chunks with coarse salt before submerging them (to scratch the surface and facilitate faster transfer of flavors and nutrients).

Bury the vegetable chunks in the persimmon mash so that they are not touching one another and all the surfaces are touching the mash.

Ferment the vegetables in the mash for 2 or 3 days, then remove them, along with the persimmon mash that sticks to them. Slice and serve.

You can reuse this bed once or possibly twice, but by then the flavor will wane and it will become excessively sour.

Fruit Enzymes

I've met people across Asia who are getting excited about fruit enzymes. I cannot say why it is the enzymes people get so passionate about rather than the organisms; in fact, all ferments involve enzymes—proteins produced by cells, including microorganisms—which enable the cells to digest nutrients. The enzyme enthusiasm revolves around two different preparations. One is for drinking. It's more or less young country wine: fruit, brown sugar, and water, fermented for a few weeks. The other, which uses fruit and vegetable scraps, is for cleaning as well as agricultural and bioremediation applications.

In Yunnan, China, my travel companions and I were told by our friend Jared, who lives in Dali, that there was an enzyme "cult" there, and we were curious. He arranged for us to visit and have dinner with a lovely and earnest group of enzyme believers who live collectively and follow a vegetarian diet. The group were followers of a Malaysian enzyme promoter, Dr. Joean Oong, who learned from Dr. Rosukon Poompanvong in Thailand.

The enzyme promoters perhaps start to tread into cult territory with their insistence that enzymes are the solution to everything, from cleaning up polluted waters, to restoring the ozone layer, to regenerating soil. I found lots of information in English about Dr. Rosukon's methods and ideas on her website, Enzymesos (www.enzymesos .com). A chart in their brochure shows two contrasting future possibilities: "Global Warming: The Feverish Earth" versus "Eco Enzyme: Cooling Down the Earth." Elsewhere, they state: "Making Eco Enzyme is an easy but effective way to save the Earth." I wish it were so simple!

A few weeks after visiting the enzyme enthusiasts in Dali, I visited Kyoto, Japan. Tomoko Ogawa, a Japanese woman whom I had met a few years earlier, took me to a café called Hakko Shokudo Kamoshika. Tomoko translated Hakko Shokudo as "Fermentation Diner." I started with a delicious cocktail consisting of a fermented-fruit enzyme drink mixed with *shochu* (a Japanese spirit) and carbonated water. I then had a simple and delicious dinner with soup from homemade miso and pickles,

Chinese enzyme enthusiast opening a bottle of the drinking enzymes for us to taste.

Drinking enzymes in different fruit flavors.

Enzymes used for cleaning in process.

served with fermented brown rice. When I went to wash my hands, in place of soap I found fruit enzyme. Then I noticed that there was fruit enzyme promotional materials (in Japanese) everywhere. The people working at the café didn't seem to know about the Malaysian or Thai gurus but said they were part of a Japanese enzyme association. Encountering these enzyme preparations repeatedly in different locales convinced me that interest in them is widespread, and gave me a reason to learn how to make them.

Here's the basic process for drinking enzymes: Start with about 2 pounds/1 kilogram of any kind of fruit. Chop or slice the fruit (unless they are grapes or berries), along with any edible skins. Layer the fruit with about 2 cups/400 grams of unrefined or brown sugar (or honey or other sweetener) in a 1-gallon/4-liter-size jar or crock, then cover with dechlorinated water, leaving some air space in the vessel. Cover loosely and ferment for about 2 to 3 weeks, stirring frequently. After fermentation subsides, strain out the fruit and enjoy.

Cleaning enzyme is sometimes called garbage enzyme because you can use fruit and vegetable scraps. By weight, combine about 3 parts fruit and vegetable scraps (including citrus peels) with 1 part sugar and 10 parts water. Ferment in sealed buckets or plastic bottles, leaving some air space. Release pressure frequently in the early period, stirring and pressing the floating solids down into the solution. Let it ferment for at least 3 months before use. Filter out the solids and use the liquid, generally in diluted form. Store at room temperature. My friend Mara Jane King, who traveled with me to China and appears in later chapters, has made and used cleaning enzyme for years. "It is excellent for cleaning," she enthuses. "It kills mold in bathrooms, whitens tile, and is great for cleaning up pet potty accidents."

Mead and Honey

Honey is one of the most widespread and readily accessible sources of sugar. Because of this, fermented honey, or mead, is widely thought to be the first intentional ferment. I think this is highly speculative, although I must say fermenting honey was one of my gateways into wild fermentation. My earliest winemaking experiments were guided by the mainstream literature for hobbyists, and it involved Campden tablets to kill the native yeast on the fruit, then introducing yeast and yeast nutrients that I had bought. As I was doing this, I recalled the palm wine and other local ferments I had tried in remote villages in West Africa. How had they been able to ferment such delicious beverages without all that technology? What were the simpler, more traditional ways?

The first clue that I found was also African: a recipe for *t'ej* in an Ethiopian cookbook. It was appealing in its simplicity: Dissolve one part honey in four parts water; add botanical flavorings; stir daily for two to three weeks;

James Creagh, in protective gear, catching a swarm.

then drink. No added chemicals, yeast, or yeast nutrients. No cooking the honey. And it worked! I've made tasty meads this way for almost 30 years, though I now ferment much longer for a stronger and drier mead, and I age it further in the bottle (Turmeric Mead, page 30).

During my travels, beekeepers everywhere have gifted me with beautiful honeys. Bees are incredible creatures, with fascinating lives and complex social organization. Their importance in ecological as well as economic systems cannot be overstated, thanks to the pollination they accomplish. When they move from flower to flower, they spread pollen as they harvest nectar to feed on and "dry" into honey.

When I travel to Australia, which I have now done for three workshop tours, my first stop is always the rural New South Wales home of my old friend James Creagh, who is a beekeeper (among his many other pursuits). On my latest visit, there was a swarm of bees clustered on a branch while I was there, and I watched in awe as James, in full protective gear, shook the swarm, with their queen, into a box to establish another hive.

I've been keeping bees and I find it mesmerizing to observe them in and around the hive. I built my own top-bar hive, and twice I've had my bees abscond. That's the word beekeepers use when a hive of bees packs up and leaves. Maybe they are fleeing some danger; maybe they've received news of greener pastures. Nobody seems to know for sure. This year, I introduced new bees to the hive, and they are multiplying in number, producing lots of honey, and appear to be thriving.

The Terra Madre
honey tasting area.

One of my favorite memories from Terra Madre is the showcase of honey diversity, experienced visually and through tasting. It was stunning to see hundreds of honeys from so many different parts of the world, in every shade of a color spectrum that ran from clear to black. It was possible to taste as many as you wanted, and I tasted a lot! I was struck by the dramatic differences in texture and flavor, generally associated with the specific flowers the nectar for the honey came from.

Honey is rarely fermented alone, although it can be. Typically, meads include botanical enhancements. Certain traditions use very specific plants, but my own experimentation and tastes of other people's concoctions has led me to the conclusion that you can use virtually any edible part of almost any plant as an element of a mead. Mead is a perfect way to share the flavors, aromas, and other powers of plants. Meads are also enriched by the additional yeasts and often complementary nutrients that the plants contribute.

I have tasted so many meads—many sublimely delicious, some not as much. Thanks to a culture of mead-sharing circles that has emerged, especially among herbalists, foragers, and other botanically minded people, I have been exposed to a great variety of meads, from simple herbal and fruit infusions to thematic or esoteric herbal or spice infusions. Personally, I usually like to keep it simple. This next recipe is a tasty and beautiful mead that I've been making since I started growing turmeric.

TURMERIC MEAD

Flowering turmeric plant.

Turmeric mead fermenting.

I just learned a couple of years ago that I can grow turmeric where I live. It is a beautiful plant; in a single growing season each plant produces an impressive mass of rhizomes, and with heavy mulching, the rhizomes can overwinter. And I love turmeric mead. It has a beautiful, balanced flavor and a lovely warm color. I add a little black pepper, too—a subtle flavor accent that is also said to increase our ability to absorb curcumin, turmeric's anti-inflammatory compound.

Typically, I ferment mead for at least a full year before bottling. Six months in the original vessel, then six months more after it has been strained and siphoned into another. You can certainly enjoy it much sooner than this, any time after about a month. But if you decide to drink it young and sweet, don't try to bottle it for long-term storage. For long-term bottling and aging, be quite certain that the fermentation is complete.

TIMEFRAME

1 month for a very sweet, young mead; 1 year for a dry mead that can be aged

PROCESS

Cover turmeric rhizomes with water. Rub them vigorously with a brush or your hands to remove loose skins, then rinse.

Slice the turmeric rhizomes crosswise into thin slices, then place them in the smaller, wide-mouth fermentation vessel. Add the black peppercorns if desired.

EQUIPMENT

1-quart/1-liter (or larger) ceramic crock or wide-mouth jar

1-gallon/4-liter glass jug (the kind you can buy apple juice in)

Airlock and carboy bung (from beer and wine supply shop for a few dollars; these are helpful but not necessary)

Bottles and corks, or other sealing tops, of any size, totaling 1 gallon/4 liters (if you wish to age mead past fermentation)

INGREDIENTS

for 1 gallon/4 liters

About 8 ounces/250 grams turmeric rhizomes

1 to 2 tablespoons black peppercorns (optional)

3 cups/1 kilogram honey (raw if available)

Mix the honey with the turmeric and stir. You could go ahead and add water at this stage, as directed in the next step, but I like to infuse the turmeric in honey first. The little bit of juice that the honey pulls from the turmeric is enough to start fermentation. I like to stir or shake the turmeric-honey mixture once a day for a couple of weeks, until it's nice and bubbly.

Once the turmeric-infused honey is good and bubbly, transfer it to the jug. Have a little more than 3 quarts/3 liters of dechlorinated water on hand to add. Pour a cup or so of the water into the original vessel and shake it to get all the honey residue from the edges, then add it to the jug. Add another quart/liter of the water to the jug and shake to dissolve the honey. Finally, fill the jug with dechlorinated water to the point where the neck narrows, leaving just about 2 inches/5 centimeters of air space in the neck of the bottle. Mix well, until the honey is thoroughly dissolved.

Cork with an airlock if you can, or improvise with a balloon, condom, or any jar lid that can rest on it loosely and slow airflow without holding pressure in.

Ferment for several months, until all signs of bubbling stop. You can enjoy it now, though it will still be quite sweet and relatively low-alcohol. Or you can continue to ferment it.

Strain out the turmeric slices and enjoy them as a tasty snack or cooking ingredient.

Drink it now, or bottle and store in the fridge or in bottles that get off-gassed; bottling for aging at this stage is typically premature and can result in popped corks or explosions.

If you wish to continue fermenting, siphon the strained mead back into the jug. Siphoning aerates the liquid and gets a "stuck" fermentation unstuck. You'll lose some volume from the turmeric and lees left behind during the siphoning. Top it off with honey water as needed, adding about 4 tablespoons of honey for each 1 cup/250 milliliters of water. Cork again with an airlock if you can, or improvise. Ferment for several more months, until all signs of bubbling stop. Siphon fully fermented mead into bottles to age.

TWO

VEGETABLES

Fermenting vegetables was my gateway into fermentation. I typically recommend it as a first fermentation project because the process is so straightforward and intrinsically safe; because you can enjoy results relatively quickly; because we all need more vegetables; and because fermented vegetables are so delicious, nutritious, and rich in probiotic bacteria. Ever since that first batch of sauerkraut decades ago, I have had vegetables fermenting in my kitchens. Over the years, I have experimented with different styles and continued to learn about new approaches. Though the basics of the process are extremely simple, fermentation is versatile and can be varied in nearly infinite ways.

All the historical tales of sauerkraut and its origins point to China as the source of fermenting vegetables in salt. When I traveled to China, learning about the Chinese roots of my ancestral pickles was my most specific interest. In this chapter,

I share what I was able to learn there about Chinese methods for fermenting vegetables. This chapter also investigates vegetable fermentation traditions in other regions of the world that I have had the opportunity to learn about, such as the method of fermenting whole heads of cabbage in southeastern Europe, along with stuffing fermented whole cabbage leaves (*sarma*) and fermented grape leaves (*dolma*). I bring you along on my visit to the town of Kiso in Japan, where residents carry on a tradition of fermenting vegetables without any salt, backslopping each batch with juice left over from the last one, continuously for more than 200 years. Some people I have met whom I regard as masters of their craft share some of the things they've learned, including recipes for a perpetual turmeric pickling medium, *kasuzuke* (vegetables pickled in sake lees), and a very special beet kvass. Finally, this chapter explores experimental approaches to dehydrating vegetable ferments.

Me in my garden.

Growing and Preserving Abundance

It was my garden that gave me a practical reason to learn how to ferment vegetables in the first place, and the rest of my journey has followed from that. One of my misgivings about all the travel I do is that it means I neglect my garden, which I always miss. So whenever my travels take me to farms, where many of my favorite workshops through the years have been held, I feel a sense a familiarity and camaraderie, and I get ideas and inspiration for my garden.

The farm where I have taught most frequently is Long Hungry Creek Farm in Red Boiling Springs, Tennessee, which is farmed by my friend Jeff Poppen. I first met Jeff more than 25 years ago, when he was giving away greens at an organic gardeners and farmers event. Whenever I have seen him out and about since then, he has been giving away vegetables. Over the years, he has given me and my friends literally tons of vegetables, which we have (mostly) fermented. He doesn't give away all the vegetables he grows, though; Jeff sells many through his community supported agriculture program, and some to restaurants. But it seems like his greatest pleasure comes from creating abundance and sharing it freely.

Every year for at least 15 years, I've done an autumn harvest workshop at Jeff's farm. I teach a vegetable fermentation workshop, then return home with about 500 pounds of vegetables to ferment and share. Jeff hosts the workshop, promotes it, and makes his annual small batch of kimchi. But actually, the workshop is a relatively small part of the day. For me, the focus of the day is harvesting.

Jeff's vegetable patches are spread around his sprawling farm, so he and his helpers pile hay bales on an open trailer bed for people to sit on, and they pull the trailer around the farm with his truck. Another truck follows, which we fill with the veggies that I bring home. Each year's weather and conditions determine which veggies Jeff has in abundance. It's always some combination of radishes, napa cabbage, and/or bok choy. This year, it was mostly

Jeff Poppen talking with students in a field of daikons.

watermelon radishes and bok choy, and the big batch (53 gallons/200 liters) of kraut that I made with the harvest is hot pink. Some years it's been mostly daikons, other years napa cabbage. It's always a mix, based on abundance: the ultimate motivator of and incentive for fermentation everywhere.

For at least the last 10 years, I've scheduled the five-day fermentation residency program I host at my place to overlap with my trip to Jeff's farm, and I also invite local friends to come along. So I typically show up there with as many as 20 people, and about that many are usually there from Jeff's own network. We load everyone onto the hay bales and drive into Jeff's dispersed fields. At each of several stops, Jeff talks a little about how he farms and answers questions, and then we spread out and harvest. Jeff uses biodynamic methods, and he speaks passionately about his primary crop being soil microbes. As the group disperses to harvest root vegetables, Jeff pleads with us to remove soil from the roots and leave it on the farm. He's happy for us to leave with hundreds of pounds of the vegetable manifestations of his farm's fertility. But the soil, the basis of that fertility, is far more precious to him.

I look forward to this event every year because it is so very fun. Everyone's spirits are uplifted by the sense of abundance—the size of the vegetables and the expanse of rows that go on and on; and the speed at which we fill our arms, bushel baskets, and the bed of the pickup truck. We could pick twice as much, three times as much, four times as much, and still there would be more.

Students with a truckload of daikons and other radishes we have just harvested at Jeff's farm.

Chinese Fermented Vegetables

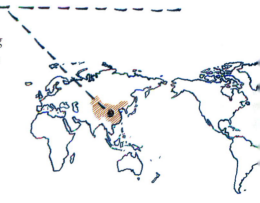

In 2016, I traveled in China for a couple of weeks, hoping to learn more about fermentation practices there. Above all, I was interested in how people ferment vegetables. Every historical account of sauerkraut repeats the idea that the nomadic peoples of central Asia brought the Chinese methods for preserving vegetables through fermentation westward into Europe. Although there is abundant information on certain Asian traditions of fermenting vegetables—notably those of Japan and Korea—there has been little written in English about Chinese methods. So, at least in part, my trip to China was a search for the historical roots of sauerkraut.

I traveled with three Chinese speakers: my one-time student and friend Mara Jane King, raised in Hong Kong; her mother, Judy King, a lifelong resident of Hong Kong and extremely well traveled and knowledgeable about food; and our Italian videographer friend Mattia Sacco Botto, who learned Mandarin through studying, living in China, and working on Italian reality television shows there. Throughout this book, I share stories of things we

PEOPLE'S REPUBLIC OF FERMENTATION

Our travels in China were well documented in eight short (roughly 10 minutes each) videos, each focusing on a specific realm of fermentation. In them you will see many of the people, events, and processes that you read about in this book. The videos were shot, directed, and edited by the very talented Mattia Sacco Botto, an Italian filmmaker with a focus on traditional foods, who is fluent in Mandarin. The videos are fast-paced, beautifully photographed, and were recognized by *Saveur* magazine as the best food video blog of the year that they came out (2017). You can find the videos on YouTube by searching for "People's Republic of Fermentation."

Markets in China were full of really beautiful vegetables in great abundance and variety.

Crock stall at a market. Traditional fermenting crocks are widely available in China.

saw and learned about in China. I would have understood nothing there without this wonderful team.

Truth be told, I never actually encountered the sauerkraut method (dry-salting shredded vegetables) during my short time in China. Nonetheless, I encountered many different styles of fermented vegetables there. I saw ginger, chilies, garlic, and scallions, each fermented alone in brine to be used as stir-fry ingredients; brined whole vegetables and bamboo shoots galore; red-hot, spicy, mixed shredded vegetable ferments; crunchy pickled vegetables tossed with fermented bean pastes and/or peanuts, sesame seeds, and chili oil; and even Jerusalem artichokes in a lovely, bright, elusively spiced *pao cai*. There was a plethora of choices at the market pickle stalls and also the private homes and restaurant kitchens into which we were invited.

It's no wonder there were so many varieties of fermented vegetables in China, because the abundance, diversity, and quality of vegetables at the markets everywhere was mind-blowing. People there eat a lot of vegetables, which is how I like to eat, too. In addition to the availability of vegetables themselves, fermentation vessels are also widely available at markets—an indication that home fermentation remains at least somewhat widespread.

I'm sure that in every region of China there are different styles of fermenting vegetables. The following recipes are a few that I learned about in my short time in the southwestern part of the country.

MRS. DING'S PAO CAI

A bowl of pao cai Mrs. Ding served to us, which featured Jerusalem artichokes.

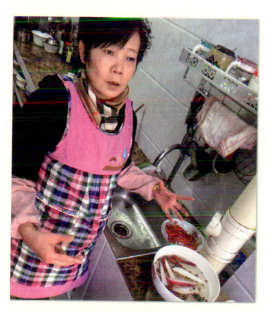

Mrs. Ding in her kitchen generously sharing her pickling methods with us.

We had not made any plans for our first day in China. As we wandered around the neighborhood where we were staying in Chengdu, to get our bearings, I noticed some sausages hanging to cure outside a street-level apartment window, and I stopped to photograph them. Mrs. Ding saw me photographing her sausages and came out to talk to us. She ended up inviting us for lunch, showing us all her fermentation projects, and teaching us how she makes them.

Pao cai is a Chinese style of fermenting vegetables. Its most distinctive feature is that it involves a perpetual brine. My first exposure to pao cai was in Mrs. Ding's home. Her pao cai brine was years old. Once the brine is mature, veggies ferment in it very quickly. She told us that the ones she fed us, which were complex and delicious, had been in the brine for only about 12 hours. However, the first batch with a fresh brine takes much longer to develop its flavor—from one to two weeks, depending on the environment.

The following recipe is a guideline to get you started. However, every batch we tried was a little different, so feel free to experiment by omitting or adding ingredients. I've been adding a little dried licorice root to my brine, which is great and really different.

MRS. DING'S PAO CAI

TIMEFRAME

1 to 2 weeks to develop the brine and pickle the first round of vegetables, then ongoing

VESSEL

2-quart/2-liter jar or another vessel

INGREDIENTS

for 2 quarts/2 liters

1 tablespoon salt

1 tablespoon sugar

3 slices fresh ginger (to taste)

2 teaspoons Sichuan peppercorns (to taste)

5 dried chilies (to taste)

2 black cardamom pods (to taste)

1 teaspoon dried or shredded licorice (optional)

About 1 pound/ 500 grams veggies for pickling, cut into medium-sized chunks †‡

PROCESS

Start with about 5 cups/1¼ liters of water. Mrs. Ding suggests boiling the water first. I love my spring water, so I ignore that with fine results. I just boil about a cup of the water for ease of dissolving the malt sugar, then dilute with fresh water.

Combine the water with the salt and sugar in your vessel.

Once the brine has cooled, add the spices and the vegetables for pickling.

The first batch of vegetables should take 1 to 2 weeks to ferment, at which point they will have a crisp texture and mildly sour and richly spiced flavor. Taste periodically to monitor the evolving flavor.

Once you deem the pickles ready, remove them from the brine whenever you want to eat some. When they are gone, add more vegetables for a shorter fermentation of a day or two. The more seasoned the brine, the faster the pickling time.

Over time, the salt, sugar, and spices in the brine will diminish as they infuse the vegetables that are removed. Evaluate the flavor by tasting, and add more salt, sugar, and spices as needed.

If the brine develops a yeast layer on the surface, Mrs. Ding's technique is to add a tablespoon of strong distilled alcohol.

* Mrs. Ding uses a specific type of malt sugar called *ding-ding tang* (see *"Ding-Ding Tang"* on page 41), but maltose, malt syrup, or granulated cane sugar work fine

† one or any combination of the following: radish, cabbage, onion, carrot, or cucumber, or try others

‡ big enough to easily find and remove from the brine, but with enough surface area to allow the brine to quickly penetrate

DING-DING TANG

Mrs. Ding was emphatic that the sugar to use for pao cai is a type of sugar known in China as *ding-ding tang*. It looked to me like Turkish Taffy, because if you pull it apart it stretches and stretches. To cut off a piece, you must strike it hard and break it. Because of these strange properties, Mara describes it as having a "non-Newtonian texture."

Ding-ding tang is actually a form of malt sugar, derived from malted (sprouted) grains. Its name has nothing to do with Mrs. Ding; it refers to the sound that street vendors make as they walk the streets, making their presence known. The vendors use a chisel and hammer to break off pieces to sell, and they strike their tools together as they walk. For some reason, this sugar seems not to be available at markets, only from these vendors who ply the streets.

Once we saw the sugar and heard the story, we listened for the ding-ding clanging. One day we heard it, in Guiyang, and bought some from the vendor. He had blocks of the taffy-like sugar in a basket fitted with straps that he carried on his back as he walked and clanged his tools together. He used his chisel to indicate where to cut, then when he had the amount we wanted, he placed the chisel on the block of sugar, struck it with his hammer to break off a chunk, and wrapped it in a plastic bag. I have been unable to find ding-ding tang outside of China, but barley malt syrup (available in many natural foods stores) and maltose (available in many Asian markets) are the closest substitutes. Granulated cane sugar or other forms (or none at all) can be used with fine results.

Ding-ding tang malt sugar from a street vendor in Guiyang, China.

YANZI AND CONGE'S PAO CAI

Yanzi and Conge in front of their yurt in the rural outskirts of Dali in Yunnan province, China.

Vegetables drying in the sun before pickling.

Even though we lucked out in meeting a home fermenter in a huge city on our first day in China, traditional practices such as fermentation are being carried on by fewer and fewer people as China urbanizes. Fewer people subsist from the land; fewer people have space or time; and products of fermentation (as well as other convenience foods) are widely available for purchase. The same is true almost everywhere, for the same reasons.

It made me very happy to meet Yanzi and Conge, a couple who I would describe as Chinese back-to-the-landers. They had grown up and met in Wuhan, but (like me) decided to leave the big city to pursue a different kind of life. They live in a yurt, garden and preserve vegetables, and homeschool their kids on the rural outskirts of the charming countercultural crossroads of Dali in Yunnan province. It was so exciting to meet people in China who are part of a demographic wave so similar to my own, because it shows that amidst China's rapid urbanization, there is a countervailing social movement seeking connection to nature and the land that recognizes the importance of once-ubiquitous processes like fermentation. Throughout our journey in China, we encountered fermentation mostly among older generations, or in traditional village settings. It was great to meet young people who are reconnecting to traditional practices. Yanzi and Conge showed me a book that had inspired them—a Chinese translation of *Living the*

Yanzi pouring water over the vegetables she has placed in her pao cai.

Good Life, by the iconic, pre-hippy New England, back-to-the-landers Helen and Scott Nearing. They also showed us how they make pao cai.

A distinctive feature of Yanzi and Conge's method is to sun dry some of the vegetables for a day before fermentation, to keep the pickles crunchy. When we arrived at their place, mustard greens were hanging from the clothesline and spread over baskets and crates to bask in the sunshine.

TIMEFRAME

At least 1 week

VESSEL

Wide-mouth vessel with at least a 2-quart/2-liter capacity

INGREDIENTS

for 2 quarts/2 liters

6 cloves garlic (to taste)

3 slices ginger (to taste)

3 whole chilies (to taste)

2 teaspoons Sichuan peppercorns (to taste)

2 tablespoons salt

About 2 pounds/1 kilograms vegetables, washed, sun-dried for a few hours if possible, and cut into large chunks *

PROCESS

Place the seasonings and salt at the bottom of the vessel. Unlike Mrs. Ding, Yanzi and Conge add no sugar to their pao cai.

Add the vegetable chunks and cover completely with water.

Taste the brine the next day to determine if the salt level is right. Add salt or water as necessary.

Ferment at least a week, or longer if desired. Enjoy vegetables directly from the jar; you can refrigerate it if you don't want them to continue fermenting.

The brine may be reused indefinitely. Add more veggies, as well as more salt and spices as needed.

* mustard greens, napa cabbage, daikon, carrot, or others

RICE WATER PICKLE

We learned about these from a woman we met in a Guizhou village called Xi Mi Cun. When I got home and followed her instructions, I loved these pickles! Starchy rice water gives them a wonderfully distinctive flavor. The longer you ferment them, the better they get.

TIMEFRAME

1 week to 1 month, or even longer

VESSEL

1-quart/1-liter wide-mouth jar, or a small crock

INGREDIENTS

for 1 quart/1 liter

½ cup/115 grams uncooked sticky rice ✳

About 1 tablespoon salt

About 1 pound/500 grams vegetables, cut into chunks †

A few cloves of garlic (to taste)

A few slices of ginger (to taste)

2 or 3 tablespoons mijiu or sake (optional)

PROCESS

Toast the sticky rice in a dry, heavy pan over medium heat, stirring frequently, until the rice becomes fragrant and develops a golden color.

Boil about 3 cups/750 milliliters of water and add the toasted rice to it. Simmer the rice for about 10 minutes.

Pour the pan's contents through a strainer over a bowl or a pot to remove the rice (which you can enjoy separately), and cool the starchy cooking water to room temperature.

Salt the vegetables and place them in the fermentation vessel. Add the garlic and ginger.

Cover the vegetables with the cooled rice-cooking water.

Add the *mijiu* (or sake), if using. Stir everything to combine.

Ferment at least a week, or as long as you like. If it's sealed in a jar, loosen the lid every day to release pressure from carbon dioxide production, especially in the early days. In cool weather, the taste just keeps getting better.

✳ also called sweet rice or glutinous rice

† any kind of cabbage, mustard greens, daikon, carrot, onion, or others

TRADITIONAL AND IMPROVISATIONAL FERMENTATION VESSELS

In the mountains of Sichuan province, a couple of hours from Chengdu, Mrs. Zhang, the elderly mother of the farmer who hosted us, showed us her pickles. Her pao cai was in a glass vessel in the classic Chinese design: a collar around the opening of the vessel is filled with water, like a moat, to protect the ferment from air, and the lid fits into the collar. But Mrs. Zhang's chilies and bamboo shoots were fermenting in repurposed plastic packaging. In China, as everywhere, people improvise with available resources.

Mrs. Zhang shows us her pickles.

Chef Guan's Pickle Shack

Chef Guan of Pixian Red Star Restaurant, a huge (more than 500-seat) restaurant in Pixian, an hour from Chengdu, took us to his pickle shack down the street. There, under a shed roof without walls, he had rows of huge, ceramic, potbelly-shaped crocks. Each crock had a capacity I'd estimate at about 20 gallons/75 liters. The scale of the pickle shack was impressive, and in the feast we enjoyed at the restaurant, pickles were well represented. There was a tasty array to enjoy with the meal, and they were also integrated as ingredients in many of the cooked dishes.

None of the crocks in the pickle shack were labeled, and they all looked identical. Chef Guan specifically wanted to show us his fermenting long beans, but he opened a half dozen other unmarked crocks before he found the one he was looking for. Chef Guan pulled various vegetables out of the crocks. From one, he pulled a giant daikon radish. From another, he pulled a whole pickled head of bok choy. Another was full of small chilies. Eventually he found the long beans.

The brine in each crock had a little bloom of kahm yeast on the surface, which Chef Guan mixed right in without giving it a thought. I was struck by his unselfconsciousness about this, despite our cameras and rolling video. Surface growth is one of the biggest worries for many Western people who start fermenting vegetables. People are fearful about microbes and don't always know what is really dangerous versus what isn't. A lot of pickles and sauerkraut have been unnecessarily discarded for developing the same growth that Chef Guan was so casually mixing in. To the people most intimate with the process, surface kahm yeast growth is just an inevitable part of fermenting vegetables—nothing to worry about.

Chef Guan of Pixian Red Star Restaurant shows us a fermented whole head of bok choy as my travel companion Mara Jane King looks on.

Sunki

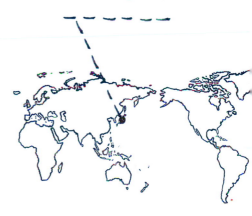

While most traditions of fermenting vegetables involve salt, there are some that omit this ingredient. Kiso, Japan—located in a mountain valley a few hours west of Tokyo—has historically had little access to salt. Because of this, the people of this region developed a technique for fermenting vegetables without any salt.

I visited Kiso with Yuri Manabe, whom I had met in the United States some years prior when she photographed me for a Japanese magazine. Yuri is an out queer Japanese woman, and she was very interested in the rural queer community of which I am part. We stayed in touch, and when I told her I was coming to Japan, she invited me on a trip with her.

Yuri wanted the trip to be educational for me. She reached out to Misa Ono, the author of multiple books about *shio-koji* and other ferments (*Shio-koji*, page 156), and the two of them decided to bring me somewhere with a really atypical fermentation tradition—something unique in Japan. That place was Kiso, where their tradition of fermenting turnip greens without salt, called

Kiso.

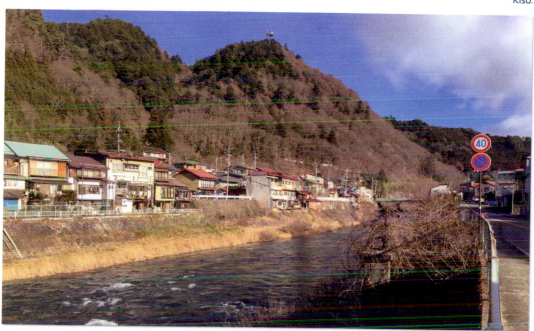

Fermented sunki draining before packaging, to preserve juice for next year's batch.

Sunki crowns.

Me looking out from the sunki-making kitchen.

sunki, involves a starter of fermented juice from the previous year's batch. Misa knew another young fermentation enthusiast, Aya Tsuzuku, who moved to Kiso to work at a regional research institute with a small museum and cultural center; Aya made arrangements for us and served as our guide.

The sunki are delightful! They are sour, bright, and surprisingly firm and crispy. We ate lots of them just as they were, but they were also featured in a broad array of dishes: an incredible sunki soup with soba, a sunki omelet, rice porridge with sunki, and a sunki salad dressed with bonito flakes and soy sauce. In fact, we were served sunki everywhere we ate. They are a local specialty, integrated into the culture, identity, and economy of the valley.

Sunki is made with the tops and crowns of locally grown Kaida turnips. (The turnip roots are pickled in other ways.) The vegetables are cleaned, chopped (in the old days they were left whole), and briefly cooked in moderately hot but not even simmering water (140°F/60°C). My guess is that this process denatures the enzymes that soften vegetables—a process that salt typically slows—but can make salt-free ferments mushy and unappealing. After the brief cooking, the vegetables are cooled with a quick rinse, and then they are covered with juice saved in cold storage from the previous year's batch (added at a proportion of about 20 percent of the weight of the vegetables).

The sunki makers call the juice from the previous year the mother. It is deliciously sour; I could drink it by the glass. I think of this as backslopping: using a previous batch of anything to start the next batch (generally in a fermentation context, such as when making yogurt, sourdough, vinegar, or beer, but I've also seen it done with stock). This backslopping is key to the quality of the sunki. The sunki makers said the backslopping has been continuous for more than 200 years, and no one knew where the original mother came from. Origins are always elusive. The turnip tops and mother juice are left to ferment at warm ambient temperatures for just 24 hours, then they are stored in a cool spot to eat throughout the winter. The excess juice is drained off before packaging and is saved for the following year.

The sunki makers were all older women. They worked in a shared commercial kitchen space, where we also

Aya shows us a Kaida turnip, the kind used to make sunki, that she has just harvested in a Kiso hoop house.

witnessed *mochi* making and other small-scale food-processing enterprises. The women seemed to enjoy their work, and each other's company. When we were there, they were sitting together at a table, packaging sunki by hand while talking and laughing.

Interestingly, there is a style of salt-free fermented radish in Nepal with an almost identical name: *sinki* (see *The Art of Fermentation*). Yuri was very excited to hear about Nepalese sinki, because, she told me, there is a history of ancient visitors to Japan from a faraway land in the Bhutan region, which is very close to Nepal. Could the similarity in the names suggest some ancient cross-cultural influence, or is it a mere synchronicity?

For our journey, Misa brought tofu and eggs that she had cured in shio-koji (*Shio-koji*, page 156). Aya, who moved to Kiso out of an interest in learning about and helping to preserve the special fermentation traditions there, brought along six different varieties of her homemade miso. They were all delicious, and each one was unique. Misa and Aya are revivalists like me: learning, experimenting, and sharing skills in a society where food traditions are rich and abundant, but no longer very commonly practiced.

Aya telling me about all the different styles of miso she makes.

ADAM JAMES'S TURMERIC PASTE PERPETUAL PICKLING BED

Adam James is a former student of mine who started his own fermentation business, Rough Rice, in Hobart, Tasmania, after extensive travel to explore different fermentation traditions. We stayed in touch, and he invited me for a visit when I came to Tasmania in early 2020. Adam served me a very memorable lunch. The meal was conceptually simple: rice, fresh sea urchins he had harvested while diving, and lots of different pickles and fermented condiments.

The most novel items from the pickle plates were a flavorful, bright yellow fermented turmeric paste and daikons that had been pickled in it, absorbing the turmeric's color and flavor. Adam was using the turmeric paste as a pickling medium, and both the pickles and the paste it was pickled in, a condiment in its own right, were gorgeous and flavorful. On a small deck outside his apartment sat a row of big ceramic crocks, each with a capacity of more than 100 liters. One of them was filled with the bright

Adam James on the deck outside his Hobart, Tasmania, apartment, with his crocks full of fermenting goodies.

One of Adam's big crocks filled with turmeric-garlic paste, which he uses as a perpetual pickling medium.

Turnips pickled in Adam's turmeric-garlic paste.

yellow-orange turmeric paste—the paste was actually turmeric blended with garlic and turnips—and vegetables buried within. It turned out that the paste was a couple of years old, and Adam was using it as a perpetual pickling medium—adding vegetables, removing them days or weeks later, and adding more, like pao cai or *nuka* (the Japanese style of pickling in a rice bran medium). Adam generously shared a recipe for his turmeric paste, which appears here. I've had a batch going ever since in my kitchen, with turmeric, garlic, and turnips from my garden, and I've enjoyed a wide range of vegetables pickled in it. My current favorites are onions, cut in half, and celery. When the paste inevitably gets watery (the salt draws water from the vegetables), I remove flavorful liquid using a small ladle and use it in dressings, marinades, and sauces. Here's how Adam describes it:

This is undoubtedly one of my favorite and most-used condiments. It is an incredibly delicious combination and has seemingly endless applications. Its flavor is tart, earthy, layered, and zingy, and it has an intensely vibrant hue. I started this when a farmer friend had a glut of turmeric and garlic, and I've kept it going for more than four years now. Adding Hakurei turnips toned down the intensity and added some body. I've experimented with other paste combinations: turmeric and garlic with chili, ginger, coriander root, and lime leaf—kind of like a yellow curry paste; fermented chili sauce; and beetroot, turnip, cumin, and nigella for a "borscht" medium. With the turmeric paste, I stir it regularly, feed it intermittently with turnips, top it up with salt as needed, and once a year I add some more turmeric and garlic.

TURMERIC PASTE BY ADAM JAMES

TIMEFRAME

About 1 month for paste; at least 1 week for fermenting vegetables

EQUIPMENT

Food processor or immersion blender

Jar or crock with at least a 2-quart/2-liter capacity, with an interior and/or exterior lid

INGREDIENTS

for about 1½ quarts/ 1½ liters of paste

14 ounces/400 grams turmeric root

10 ounces/300 grams garlic cloves, peeled

14 ounces/400 grams Hakurei or other small, tender turnips

3 tablespoons salt (roughly 4 percent weight of turmeric, garlic, and turnips)

About ¾ pound/350 grams vegetables (daikons, turnips, carrots, celery, or others) to pickle once the pickling medium is mature

PROCESS

Using a food processor or an immersion blender, grind the turmeric root, garlic cloves, Hakurei turnips, and salt with just enough water (roughly 2 cups/500 milliliters) to form a thick paste.

Ferment the paste in a jar or crock for about a month, stirring periodically. For best results, protect the surface of the paste from air with an interior lid or a layer of plastic.

After a month or so, the paste should be active enough to start using as a fermentation medium. Simply submerge the whole vegetables. Turnips and daikons work really well since they are not too dense.

Depending on the temperature, the size and density of the vegetables, and how vigorous the medium is, the vegetables should be fermented in about a week; however, I often leave mine for a month or even longer. The resulting pickles take on the intense yellow (another reason why white vegetables are good), shrivel slightly due to water loss, and have a wonderful acidic and earthy crunch.

This paste itself can be used on its own: as a condiment (great with mussels and oysters); as a base for a salad/vegetable dressing (thin with olive oil, water, and a dash of rice vinegar); as an excellent addition to fire ciders and fermented hot sauces; or made into my possible all-time favorite curry paste, by simply cooking it down with fresh puréed ginger, then adding a tin or two of coconut cream and some good (preferably homemade) fish sauce and fresh lemon or lime. I also use it as a base for brown rice congee that I serve at the farmers market. It's also a fantastic addition to shio-koji for an intense, "fresh" hit of zingy umami.

Croatia

"To me, revealing the richness of our store room is kind of entrusting you with our top secrets :)," wrote Miroslav Kis, a Croatian man who was reading my book, *The Revolution Will Not Be Microwaved*. He and his partner Karmela were avid gardeners, and he excitedly told me about Karmela's fermentations and other food preservation endeavors. Miroslav also told me about Croatian delicacies, such as a cheese called *kajmak*—made by layering the creamy, rich skins that form on scalded milk—and cured sausages called *cevapcici*. "In a word, it is still a rich tradition," he wrote.

Yet Miroslav was worried about trends he was seeing: "All these things are still alive, but much less than before. Some of the practices disappeared into factories, but much more was strangled by import business." He feared that Croatia's rich food traditions were being replaced by cheaper imported foods. A lively correspondence ensued, and in 2008 I visited Miroslav and Karmela at their home in Istria, the province in Croatia that is closest to Italy.

Miroslav and Karmela were wonderful hosts. They took me to see beautiful and interesting sights, and they introduced me to some of their friends. One day we hiked to an old, abandoned water-powered flour mill. Another day we visited a friend of theirs who lives in Motovun, a stunningly well-preserved medieval walled city with narrow cobblestone streets. But more than anything, what I remember from that trip is all the delicious food Karmela cooked.

One food that Karmela introduced me to—which I absolutely loved and have eaten frequently since that visit—is *ajvar*, a rich and bright condiment spread (not typically fermented) made from roasted sweet peppers and eggplants. Karmela also introduced me to the technique of fermenting heads of cabbage whole rather than shredded, and using the big fermented leaves as

Karmela and Miroslav.

the basis for sarma, stuffed cabbage. Sadly, Miroslav died in 2016. But Karmela and I keep in touch, and she generously shared her recipes for ajvar, whole cabbage sauerkraut, and sarma.

An old abandoned water-powered flour mill Karmela and Miroslav took me to see.

TERRA MADRE KRAUT-SHARING

When I visited Karmela and Miroslav in Croatia in 2008, I was en route to Torino, Italy, for Terra Madre, the biennial international Slow Food event. Brussels fermentation activist Maria Tarantino came to Terra Madre, too, along with a team of fellow fermenters and kilos of various fermented vegetables vacuum-packed in their luggage. My favorite of the krauts they brought was made from parsley root, which I had never tried before. The Brussels fermenting friends were making and distributing their ferments not commercially but as educational tools to empower people with skills to produce healthy food and revive and reinvent tradition. My people!

My favorite part of Terra Madre that year, by far, was serving kraut to people. Tasting samples were abundant, but they leaned heavily toward rich animal foods such as meat, cheese, and fish—all of which I love— along with breads, candies, oils, vinegars, wines, and beers—which I also love—but very little in the way of vegetables. Many people were ready for some tasty fermented vegetables after too much of the heavier samples.

I had great conversations with people from all over the world, including José Antonio, who was part of a small storefront institute in Havana, Cuba, teaching fermentation and other food preservation skills. As we served fermented vegetables, we started to compile a list of words to describe them in different languages. Sharing food is always a great icebreaker.

The 2008 Terra Madre occurred against the backdrop of the global financial crash. On my way home, I wrote: "As the global financial markets crumbled around us, speaker after speaker contrasted the disappearing fictional wealth of speculation on abstractions with the core foundation of economic security: the sustainable production of food." I still believe this to be true. Every community and region of the world would do well to increase its capacity to produce food in sustainable ways. Decentralized food production is foundational to any real security.

Brussels fermentation activists Maria Tarantino and
Sabina Terziani offering tastes of fermented vegetables
at Terra Madre, 2008.

AJVAR

This is Karmela's recipe for ajvar, a roasted pepper and eggplant spread, which I have adapted to share with you. Ajvar is not fermented, but it is so delicious!

TIMEFRAME

A few hours

EQUIPMENT

Food processor or meat grinder

Sealable jars

INGREDIENTS

for about 1½ quarts/1½ liters

4½ pounds/2 kilograms sweet paprika peppers (substitute with some chili peppers to make ajvar hot)

2¼ pounds/1 kilogram eggplant

1 garlic head (to taste), peeled

2 teaspoons/4 grams salt

5 tablespoons/75 milliliters vegetable oil

PROCESS

Grill the whole peppers. This can be done on a hot barbecue, directly on the flames of a gas range, or in a hot oven or broiler. Turn the peppers frequently to distribute the charring of the surface. Grill until the peppers are soft.

Place the grilled whole peppers together in a bag or another enclosure to allow them to steam as they cool. Once cool, remove the skins and seeds.

Bake the eggplants in a 450°F/235°C oven for about 45 minutes, until soft. Then cut them in half, scoop out the soft flesh, and discard the skins.

Grind the peppers, eggplants, and garlic using a food processor or meat grinder.

Combine the mixture with the salt and oil in a large pot.

Bring the mixture to a boil, then reduce the heat. Cook for about an hour, until thickened. Stay with it while it slowly bubbles, and stir often. The process is messy! Expect ajvar to splatter all over the kitchen as it cooks.

Transfer the hot ajvar to jars and seal. Once it has cooled, store in the refrigerator.

Enjoy ajvar as a condiment, spread, or dip.

CROATIAN WHOLE SOUR CABBAGES

Cored cabbages, with the cores.

Cabbages are typically fermented whole not only in Croatia but throughout the Balkan states of southeastern Europe. This renders a more intense, funkier flavor. If some of the fermented cabbage is to be eaten shredded, it is shredded just before it is served.

The recipe Karmela gave me was for 55 pounds/25 kilograms of cabbage, fermented in a big barrel. I've scaled it down to 18 pounds/8 kilograms of cabbage, which can be fermented in a 5-gallon/20-liter crock or plastic bucket. Karmela does it the contemporary way, inside a plastic bag that lines the barrel. The bag is sealed, thereby preventing airflow and thus funky aerobic surface growth. In Croatia, large food-grade plastic bags are commonly available for this purpose. In many places, these may be hard to find. Moreover, some people prefer to avoid plastic. "In the past they did it without plastic bags, in a barrel where they used to skim the top," writes Karmela. If you try this without a plastic bag, surface growth may develop; if so, skim it off. Karmela further adds: "In the old-fashioned way they also added some pepper grains and dry corn grains (probably to help the fermentation)."

Whole cabbages are best fermented in cool weather. Karmela suggests starting the fermentation at a warm indoor temperature for about two weeks, then moving it to a cooler cellar or outdoor location to continue fermenting more slowly for another month.

Use for the recipe *Sarma*, page 62;
use leaves as wraps; or shred fermented
cabbages for sauerkraut.

CROATIAN WHOLE SOUR CABBAGES

TIMEFRAME

6 weeks or longer

EQUIPMENT

Crock or plastic bucket with
a 5-gallon/20-liter capacity

Large food-grade plastic bag
(optional)

Object to weigh down cabbages

INGREDIENTS

for 18 pounds/8 kilograms

18 pounds/8 kilograms cabbage

10 ounces/300 grams salt

Peppercorns (to taste,
optional)

Small handful of dried
whole-grain corn (optional)

PROCESS

Remove the outer leaves and cores from the cabbages. Use a sharp
knife to remove the entire conical core, which extends about
halfway up the cabbages. This enables the brine to reach the center
much faster than if the cores are left intact.

Fill the holes in the cabbages (where the cores were) with the salt.
If there is leftover salt, dissolve it in the water (see the step below).

Pack the cabbages tightly in your vessel with the salt-filled cavities
facing up. Depending on the size of your cabbages and the size of
your vessel, it may be tricky to fit them in. Something I have done
to make them fit is to cut one or two of the cabbages into wedges
that can fit among the whole cabbages. Sprinkle peppercorns and
kernels of corn among the cabbages, if using.

Cover the cabbages with dechlorinated water. This should take
roughly 2 gallons/8 liters of water.

The water should cover the cabbages, but if it doesn't quite cover
them, don't panic. You can add a little more water if need be;
however, the salt will draw more water out of the cabbages over the
first few days, so the cabbages will shrink a little and the volume
of water will increase. Be patient, and try to keep the exposed
cabbages weighed down. If you are using a plastic bag, close the
bag tightly over the submerged cabbages once they are covered,
removing as much air as possible and securing by tying the bag or
using a rubber band or string. If you are using a crock or bucket,
use a weight (a plate may suffice) to hold the cabbages under the
brine. If you are using a plastic bucket, secure the top.

Ferment for about 2 weeks at room temperature, then continue
outside or in an unheated cellar for another month. If you are
using the plastic bag method, do not open the bag until you are
ready to eat some of the sour cabbage.

Romanian Whole Sour Cabbages

This process is similar to that of Croatian Whole Sour Cabbages (page 59) but relies on salt and heavy weight alone to draw juice from the cabbage without the addition of water. I have not been to Romania, but a reader of my books (who prefers not to be named) sent me photos and a description of the process, as he observed it in Romania. "The best fermented cabbage I've ever had by far," he wrote. "I ate so much of this the months I spent there."

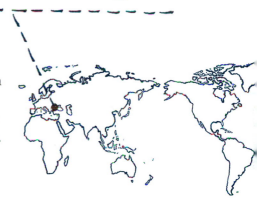

The cores of the cabbages are removed, then the cavities are packed with coarse salt. Seasonings are added: horseradish and quince, along with whole kernels of dried corn.

The cabbages are weighted under wooden slats and a big heavy rock, then covered with a lid. As brine collects at the bottom, some is drained out and poured over the top of the cabbages. If undissolved salt crystals collect at the bottom, they too should be recirculated to the top.

SARMA

This is Karmela's method for stuffing the leaves of the fermented cabbages. It is so delicious! "Sarma is traditionally done in wintertime, in a large amount, and reheated," she says. "The more you reheat it, the better it is. If there is not enough sauce, during the reheating you can always add tomato paste mixed with water."

TIMEFRAME

About 1 hour of prep and 3 hours of cooking

EQUIPMENT

Large pot with a heavy bottom

INGREDIENTS

for 20–25 stuffed cabbage leaves

1 or 2 soured cabbages (Croatian Whole Sour Cabbages, page 59)

2 pounds/1 kilogram ground beef

1 cup/200 grams uncooked rice, rinsed and drained

1 teaspoon salt

1 pound/500 grams smoked bacon

2 quarts/2 liters canned tomatoes or tomato juice

PROCESS

Carefully separate the leaves of the cabbages for stuffing. (Don't use the smallest leaves in the center; save the centers to add into the pot to cook with the stuffed leaves.) On the back (outer side) of each leaf, trim away the heaviest part of the spine so it becomes possible to fold it over without breaking it.

Rinse each leaf to remove slime and excess salt.

Prepare the filling. Mix the raw ground beef, rice, and salt. Karmela says some people use a mixture of pork and beef. She doesn't pre-cook any of the stuffing ingredients, and she doesn't use any seasonings in the stuffing. "Some people do it differently, this is the way we do it in our family," she explains. Add some minced onion or other seasonings, vegetables, or other grains if you like. I like to experiment.

Prepare the pot. Spread a couple of the largest outer leaves of the cabbages, or any that tore as you separated them, over the bottom of the pot. As the sarmas are stuffed, they will be stacked in the pot, layered with the bacon.

Stuff the prepared leaves. Use 2 to 3 tablespoons of stuffing per leaf, depending on size. Don't stuff them too full, because the rice will expand as it cooks. Secure the stuffing within each leaf by folding in from each side toward the center, then rolling from the base of the leaf toward the end, tucking the end under the weight of the roll as it is stacked in the pot. "Put a layer of stuffed sarma," says Karmela. "Add some pieces of bacon, and repeat." You can also layer in the leftover centers of the cabbages. Generally, Karmela fills the pot about halfway.

Cover the sarma with canned tomatoes or tomato juice, mixed with water as needed.

Simmer the covered pot of sarma gently for about 3 hours.

Enjoy! "Usually sarma is served with mashed potatoes," according to Karmela.

Reheating: I concur with Karmela that sarma gets better every time it is reheated. "I make a big pot and reheat it 4 or 5 times," she says. Reheat over low heat, adding more water and tomato as necessary.

DOLMA

This is very similar to sarma, except that rather than stuffing fermented cabbage leaves, we are stuffing smaller fermented grape leaves. Interestingly, both sarma and dolma are Turkish words, dolma meaning "filled or stuffed thing," and sarma meaning "wrapped thing," though in this case any distinction between stuffed and wrapped seems like splitting hairs. The technique for using the leaf to wrap (or be stuffed by) the filling is almost the same.

I make small batches of cucumber pickles all summer, and I use a handful of grape leaves in each. As I eat the pickles, I collect the grape leaves and garlic in a jar, keeping them covered with brine. I like to drink residual brine or use it in chilled summer soups, salad dressings, and other culinary applications. The pickled garlic I eat as is, or I use it in cooking. And the grape leaves become delicious dolma. I've always eaten dolma at room temperature or chilled, but I understand that some people like to eat them hot. According to Claudia Roden's *The New Book of Middle Eastern Food*, hot dolma is generally made with a meat stuffing; cold dolma, without. I've only eaten them without meat. As with sarma, you can experiment with incorporating different grains, vegetables, herbs, or flavorings. I first learned to make dolma from Roden's recipe in the afore-cited book, which she says is her Egyptian mother's recipe. The stuffing features rice, tomato, onion, parsley, mint, cinnamon, allspice, salt, and pepper. A beautiful book I have on Iraqi cuisine, *Delights from the Garden of Eden* by Nawal Nasrallah, has a dolma recipe that includes chickpeas, garlic, dill, pine nuts, and currants in the stuffing. Vary the stuffing as you like, and feel free to experiment.

TIMEFRAME

About 1 hour of prep and 1 hour of cooking

EQUIPMENT

Heavy-bottomed cooking pot

PROCESS

Pick through the grape leaves and separate out any that are ripped or partial. These will be used to line the pot. Taste a grape leaf and evaluate saltiness. If it tastes excessively salty, cover the grape leaves with boiled water and soak for 15 minutes to remove salt; if they do not need it, skip this step. If you are using fresh rather than brined grape leaves, blanch them for a few seconds in boiling water to wilt them.

INGREDIENTS

for about 25 dolma

25 (plus a few extra) fermented grape leaves (or you can use fresh ones)

1 cup/200 grams uncooked rice

1 or 2 tomatoes, finely chopped

1 onion, finely minced

A few tablespoons fresh parsley and/or dill and/or dried mint, finely chopped (to taste)

2 tablespoons currants, raisins, or pine nuts (to taste, optional)

A pinch of ground cinnamon and/or allspice

Salt and pepper

A few whole garlic cloves, peeled

½ cup/120 milliliters olive oil

Juice of 1 lemon (to taste)

Boil about 2 cups/500 milliliters of water and pour it over the rice, stirring well to make sure there are no pockets of dry rice. Then rinse under cold water and drain.

Mix the tomatoes, onions, and fresh herbs into the rice.

Add the currants, raisins, and/or pine nuts (if using), spices, and salt and pepper to taste, and mix the stuffing well to combine ingredients.

Prepare the pot by lining it with damaged grape leaves, tomato slices, or the outer leaves of a cabbage. This layer functions as something of a buffer to protect the dolma as they cook.

Stuff the leaves. Lay out a leaf, vein side up. If a leaf is torn, lay a second on top of it; if a leaf is particularly small, lay a second overlapping to expand it. Place a teaspoon or two of stuffing (varying with the size of the leaf) in the center of the leaf. Fold the stem and base of the leaf up, then the two sides toward the center. Finally, roll the stuffed center over onto the top of the leaf. Gently squeeze the stuffed leaf in your hand to shape the roll, and place it in the pot, outer edge down and sealed side up.

Repeat until all the stuffing is used and/or all your leaves are stuffed. As you complete each layer in the pot, start another layer on top of it. Intersperse whole cloves of garlic in the gaps among the stuffed leaves.

Mix the olive oil and lemon juice with about ½ cup/120 milliliters of water, and pour this liquid over the stuffed grape leaves until covered. If the stuffed grape leaves are not covered by the olive oil and lemon juice, add a little water to cover them.

Find a small heat-tolerant plate that fits inside the pot and can rest atop the stuffed leaves to prevent them from unraveling while they cook.

Cover the pot, place on medium heat, bring to a simmer, and gently simmer for about an hour, adding water if necessary to keep dolma covered.

Cool the dolma in the pot, and enjoy at room temperature or cold.

KRAUT FACTORY IN THE SWISS MOUNTAINS

One thing I appreciate about Switzerland is that you can take the trains anywhere, even to the smallest towns, such as Burgistein. Burgistein is about a half hour from Bern, and it was the location of a talk I gave at a small on-farm sauerkraut factory called Mäder Sauerkrautfabrik. I spoke to a group of food-curious professionals and aficionados who meet at different places every month or so to learn how various foods are produced, or about other food topics of interest. Before we began, the owners of the factory obliged us with a tour. Their contemporary vessels are huge plastic tanks, each with a capacity of thousands of liters, and they shred and mix the cabbage with machines. But in another building, they showed us the rectangular concrete tanks and the huge wooden mallets that were used in an earlier time, until about 50 years ago.

Me standing in front of a contemporary plastic sauerkraut tank at Mäder Sauerkrautfabrik.

The previous generation's sauerkraut tank at Mäder Sauerkrautfabrik.

Heavy wooden mallets that were used for pounding the cabbage before Mäder Sauerkrautfabrik switched to machine processing.

SAUERKRAUT CHOCOLATE CAKE

Many people seem shocked at the idea of a chocolate cake made with sauerkraut. But it is quite delicious and moist, and the sauerkraut blends into the sweet cake just like the shredded carrot in a carrot cake or the zucchini in a zucchini bread. The sourness of the kraut is mostly neutralized as it reacts with the alkaline baking soda, and the reaction between them is part of what rises the cake.

Sauerkraut chocolate cake was first served to me at a wonderful fermentation-themed feast in Amery, Wisconsin, where the dessert course was prepared by pastry chef Leigh Yakaites. Leigh told me her grandmother, from Fond du Lac, Wisconsin, used to make sauerkraut chocolate cake when Leigh was young, though "she of course didn't tell the kids it had sauerkraut in it until we had eaten it."

Leigh didn't follow a family recipe, but she directed me to one published online by Canadian food blogger Bernice Hill, on her website Dish 'n' the Kitchen (dishnthekitchen.com). Because I am constitutionally unable to follow a recipe, I have adapted hers, and I offer this as a guideline for you to adapt further.

Spread jam between the layers; I thought marmalade worked especially well, but any fruity jam would be great. Leigh served it covered with a fantastic chocolate balsamic glaze—her recipe for that is included. A simple chocolate icing or whipped cream would be fine as well.

As for the sauerkraut, I recommend a very simple and plain kraut without a lot of additional ingredients beyond finely shredded cabbage and salt.

TIMEFRAME

About 2 hours including cooling time

EQUIPMENT

Two 8-inch/20-centimeter round cake pans

Parchment paper

Whisk or electric mixer

INGREDIENTS

for two layers of an 8-inch/20-centimeter round cake

¾ cup/170 grams butter, room temperature

1½ cups/300 grams sugar

3 eggs

1 teaspoon vanilla extract

2¼ cups/380 grams white flour

½ cup/75 grams cocoa powder

1 teaspoon baking soda

1 teaspoon baking powder

½ teaspoon salt

1 cup/160 grams sauerkraut, drained and squeezed of excess juice, and very finely shredded

½ cup/65 grams cacao nibs (optional)

½ cup/120 milliliters jam of your choice to spread between the layers

INGREDIENTS

for the Chocolate Balsamic Glaze

⅔ cup/160 milliliters balsamic vinegar

3 tablespoons sugar

1.5 ounces/45 grams bittersweet baking chocolate, grated or cut into small pieces

PROCESS

Preheat oven to 350°F/175°C.

Prepare two 8-inch/20-centimeter round cake pans: Rub butter on interior surfaces, dust with flour, and line bottoms with parchment paper.

Cream the butter and sugar together, using a whisk or electric mixer, until smooth.

Add the eggs one at a time, mixing each one in until smooth.

Add the vanilla and mix until smooth.

In another bowl, combine the dry ingredients, then sift them slowly into the butter-sugar-egg mixture, mixing well with a spoon or spatula. Add 1 cup/250 milliliters of water, a little a time, as you stir it into a smooth batter.

Add the sauerkraut and cacao nibs (if using), and stir to mix them in thoroughly.

Pour the batter into the two prepared pans.

Bake for 30 minutes, then stick a toothpick or fork into the center of one of the cakes to see if it comes out clean. If so, remove the cakes from the oven; if not, bake for another 5 minutes.

Allow the cakes to cool on a rack until they are cool enough to handle. Then remove from the baking pans and peel the parchment paper from the bottoms of the cakes.

For the glaze, combine the balsamic vinegar and sugar in a saucepan, whisking them together and heating until it is hot but not boiling. When the sugar is fully dissolved, remove from heat and whisk in the chocolate until it is melted.

Place one layer of the cake on a serving plate or cake stand, spread jam on top of it, then place the second layer on the jam. Pour the glaze over the top and sides of the cake.

Enjoy!

MEXICAN-INSPIRED KIMCHI

Corn, pinto bean, and quinoa tempeh.

For the 2019 Ferment Oaxaca event, my presentation was "Cross-Cultural Fermentation: Kimchi, Dosas, Koji, and More Using Corn and Other Local Ingredients." In preparation, I experimented at home using corn in all of these ferments and more, with great success. One of the best was tempeh made with corn, pinto beans, and quinoa, as pictured here.

I arrived in Oaxaca a few days before the summit. I had always heard intriguing things about Oaxaca, and I was excited to finally see and experience it. The morning after I arrived, I went to Mercado Benito Juárez, a vast indoor food market. The market is a maze in the center of the city, filled with hundreds of small vendors. My mission was to assemble ingredients for a Mexican-style kimchi. The major concept I had premeditated was to use fresh masa dough (ground nixtamalized corn) as the

PEANUT BUTTER AND KIMCHI SANDWICHES

When I was served peanut butter and kimchi sandwiches for the first time, I was quite surprised. Although the combination was not an obvious one to me, I shouldn't have been surprised, because peanut butter can pair well with almost anything. Peanut butter is a perfect contrasting base for kimchi, and together they make a delightful sandwich. I generally make open-faced sandwiches on whole grain bread, and it's one of my favorite snacks. Try kimchi with other nut and seed butters as well. You can't go wrong.

basis for a spice paste. It was easy to find that in the market; it was also easy to find the spices we wanted, and the veggies. *Chapulines*—crunchy, spiced grasshoppers that are widely eaten in some parts of Mexico—and pineapple were both abundant at the market, and they more or less suggested themselves. We bought some of each, the chapulines being almost exactly analogous to using tiny dried shrimp in some Korean kimchi.

I offer this not so much as a recipe to be followed but rather as an example of how to substitute what is available and abundant for ingredients that are more typically used. After I made the chapulín kimchi, I visited my friends Daniel and Paulina at their business, Suculenta, and they gave me a taste of their delicious kimchi made with *chicatana* ants.

My Oaxacan kimchi with chapulines and pineapple.

My friends Paulina and Daniel's kimchi with chicatana ants.

MEXICAN-INSPIRED KIMCHI

TIMEFRAME

A few days to 1 week

VESSEL

Crock, wide-mouth jar, or another vessel with a capacity of at least 2 quarts/2 liters

INGREDIENTS

for 2 quarts/2 liters

3 pounds/1.5 kilograms cabbage and/or radishes and/or other vegetables

6 tablespoons salt

A few chilies, any type, fresh or dried, for moderate spice; more for spicier

About 4 tablespoons/ 70 grams masa

1 garlic head (to taste)

4 tablespoons grated fresh ginger (to taste)

1 pineapple

1 large or 2 small onions and/or bunches of scallions, coarsely chopped

4 tablespoons/20 grams chapulines (to taste, optional)

PROCESS

Coarsely chop the vegetables and place in a bowl or pot. Salt the vegetables generously as you shred them.

Add just enough water to cover the vegetables, then set a plate on top of them to keep them submerged. Leave the vegetables submerged in brine on the kitchen counter for about 24 hours.

If you are using dried chilies, rinse them and cover them with a little water to allow them to hydrate for at least a few hours (or up to 24 hours). When you are ready to make the spice paste, remove the chilies from the soaking water, and use the soaking water as some of the water for the next step. If you are using fresh chilies, skip this step.

Make the paste. In a small saucepan, mix the masa with about 1 cup/250 milliliters of cold water (including any chili-soaking water). Stir well to break up the masa in the water, then gently heat at a moderate temperature, stirring constantly to prevent burning. Cook for a few minutes as the mixture thickens into a starchy, gooey paste. It should be thick, but still runny. If it seems too thick, add a little more water and stir well. Remove the masa paste from the heat and leave it to cool.

Mince the chilies with their seeds. Peel and coarsely chop the garlic.

Mix the chilies, garlic, and ginger into the masa paste and stir until well combined.

Drain the brine off the vegetables. Really let it drain, and even press lightly to force water out. Taste the vegetables for saltiness. That initial salting mostly pulls water out of the vegetables, but not much of it absorbs into them. If you cannot taste salt, add 1 to 2 teaspoons salt to the spice paste. In the unlikely event that the vegetables are too salty, rinse them.

Prepare the pineapple. Remove the peel and core, reserving them for tepache (*Tepache*, page 18). Cut the sweet, tender flesh into small pieces.

Combine everything together. Place the drained vegetables in a large mixing bowl. Add the spice paste and mix to distribute it. Add the onions, pineapple, and chapulines, if you are using them. Mix everything together well.

Pack the kimchi into the vessel. Pack it tightly, pressing down until the paste or liquid rises to cover the vegetables. Weigh down the vegetables to keep them submerged. If you're using a jar, leave a little space for expansion.

Ferment in a visible spot in the kitchen. If you are using a sealed jar, be sure to loosen the top to relieve pressure each day for the first few days. While you are there, use your (clean!) fingers to push the vegetables back under the brine, and after a few days taste the kimchi. As the days pass it will be less sweet and more sour. When making a kimchi with fruit, I like to eat it while the fruit still has some sweetness, so I can enjoy all the contrasting flavors. In this case, I would ferment it no longer than a week—probably less.

Once it tastes ripe to you, move it to the refrigerator.

INSECTS AS FOOD

Grasshoppers and ants are tasty and nutritious, as are many other insects. I am not all that adventurous when it comes to eating insects, especially compared to a handful of very actively curious people I have met, and only once have I captured insects (cicadas) myself to prepare and eat. Still, in my home kitchen and in my rural queer extended community in Tennessee, as well as in travels in Africa, Mexico, China, and even once at a highway rest area in the Netherlands, I have eaten many different kinds of insects. As I was working on this book, my partner found some cave crickets under the house, killed and stored them in the freezer, and cooked them up for a delicious dinner. You really can't go wrong with spicy, crunchy exoskeletons.

Western civilization largely deems eating insects to be barbaric. Westerners who are not big food adventurers typically respond to the idea with a dramatic show of disgust. I think this disgust is learned rather than innate. Colonialism could be justified only by dehumanizing Indigenous peoples for their traditional practices, which often include using insects as a food source. "The people who eat such disgusting things are not fully human," the convoluted reasoning goes. "Civilized people would never eat such things." The food itself, no matter how tasty, nutritious, and practical it may be, becomes a way of dehumanizing the people who eat it.

Yet in every part of the world, insects are a traditional food source. As a practical matter, in a time when there is great concern about feeding the rapidly growing population of the world, insects have huge potential. Food traditions are about turning environmental abundance into sustenance, and many of the insects that can drive us mad with their abundance are nutritious and can be prepared in appetizing ways. I just recently learned, from a book, that tomato hornworms are delicious to eat. I wish I had known that a few months ago when I was picking them off the tomato and pepper plants in my garden! Next year I'll eat them before they devour my plants.

Here are a couple of books with practical information on eating insects:

Stefan Gates, *Insects: An Edible Field Guide* (London: Ebury Press, 2017).
David George Gordon, *The Eat-A-Bug Cookbook, Revised* (Berkeley, California: Ten Speed Press, 2013).

Chapulines, roasted grasshoppers.

POLISH KIMCHI

One person I met during my travels, who impressed me with his bold experimentation, is the Polish chef Alexander Baron. Chef Baron wrote a book in Polish about fermentation, and he hosted a workshop for me at his small restaurant, Solec 44. In contrast with some of the restaurants I've written about that have separate research kitchens, this restaurant was, itself, the lab, filled with shelves of fermenting vegetables, herbs, and fruits. These ferments were incorporated into delicious, down-to-earth food and fun drinks, alcoholic and not. I loved his "Polish kimchi," featuring bolete mushrooms, horseradish, sweet peppers, herring, and other regional delicacies. Solec 44 has closed, but Baron's current venture, Baron the Family, is both a restaurant and a retail shop selling their ferments and other preserves, including fermented baba ghanouj. There is no end to the foods that can be enhanced by fermentation!

Alexander Baron poses with his book and mine in front of shelves of his fermentation projects in his restaurant.

Cultured Pickle Shop

In my travels, I have had the opportunity to visit many small- and medium-sized fermentation businesses. Whether they are making kraut or working in other realms of fermentation, the people behind these enterprises are fermenting for their livelihood, day in and day out. I always learn from them.

I have watched quite a few small businesses start and succeed. Some have stayed small—just one or two people, or a few employees—while others have expanded into national brands, then sold their brands to bigger companies. I have seen businesses start with great dreams, then crash beneath the weight of harsh regulatory and financial realities. I have seen privately owned enterprises transition to worker-ownership. And I have met some people who are committed to being artisans more than business people; people without grander entrepreneurial ambitions who simply want to earn a living with their skill.

I have come to admire so many different producers, at different scales, almost everywhere in the world I have visited. I mean none of them any disrespect by highlighting the small producer I have visited most frequently (for well over a decade now, every time I go to the San Francisco Bay Area): the Cultured Pickle Shop in Berkeley, California. It is a tiny storefront and workshop located far from the bustle of Berkeley's busy commercial strip. There, Alex Hozven, her husband Kevin Farley, and a small team of part-time helpers make some of the most delicious and distinctive ferments I have encountered anywhere.

Alex and Kevin make wonderful sauerkraut, kimchi, and brine pickles, but they specialize in unique single batch seasonal creations. The parade of fresh vegetables and fruits in California is never ending, and they work with a wide array of fresh ingredients. They also use extremely varied techniques, many drawn from the broad palette of pickling mediums used in Japanese tsukemono.

One year when I visited them, the back window of their shop was full of daikon radishes hanging to dry in the sun—tops and all—for *takuan*, one of my favorite Japanese pickles. Another time, I arrived to the same

Brandon Jones, head brewer of the Embrace the Funk sour and wild beers program at Yazoo Brewing Company in Nashville, Tennessee, shows me his new *foeders* (giant barrels) for aging beer.

Cultured Pickle Shop ferments. *Top row*: asparagus kimchi; celtuce fermented with jalapeño and dill; *rakkyo* scallions fermented in the style of *umeboshi*. *Middle row*: takuan; Tangerine-Scarlet Queen turnip kombucha and lemon–bee pollen–mint kombucha; watermelon rind with chili and hyssop. *Bottom row*: carrots in a ginger and turmeric brine; kabocha squash in *kasu*; Tokyo turnip kasuzuke.

Me with Alex and Kevin and their team in the Cultured Pickle Shop, 2011 in a photo collage created by artist Douglas Gayeton as part of his Lexicon of Sustainability.

window full of persimmons hanging to dry. In my fridge, I recently found the months-buried remains of a jar of their kasuzuke, or vegetables fermented in *kasu*, the Japanese name for sake lees, the solid by-product of sake making (see "*Kasu*" on page 151). The kasuzuke in my fridge is celeriac, sliced paper-thin and bathed in a paste of sweet-salty kasu, earthy from a year of slow enzymatic breakdown. (See "*Kasuzuke*" on page 80 for Alex and Kevin's guidance for preparing it.)

AIR DRYING DAIKON
This is the first step in creating "Takuan," a traditional Japanese rice bran pickled daikon named after the monk Takuan Soho (1573–1645)

TONIC KRAUT
(herbal formula meant to nourish the system)
Siberian ginseng, astragalus root, schizandra berries, tumeric, reishi mushrooms, Celtic sea salt.

...TATION
...convert sugars into lactic acid.

...AN ENVIRONMENT IS CREATED TO ACTUALLY ENCOURAGE THE GROWTH OF CERTAIN TYPES OF BACTERIA

Cultured.
Berkeley, CA

Alex and Kevin's creations are playful and visionary. They blend sometimes unexpected vegetables, fruits, herbs, seasonings, and pickling mediums, consistently producing ferments with flavors and textures that are compelling and well balanced. From watching them, talking with them, and tasting with them in the shop, it is obvious how much attention they pay to that most import-ant fermentation variable: time. Frequent tasting is part of their routine, and they maintain an ongoing dialogue about the devel-opment and readiness of in-process batches. They sometimes harvest part of a batch and leave the rest fermenting to see how it develops further. I've tasted some very earthy, very aged ferments they had squirreled away.

Beyond vegetables, Alex and Kevin make excep-tional kombuchas. They leave tea and herbs in the fermenting kombucha, so their mothers have lots of other botanical ingredients bound up in them. Then they mix fresh-pressed fruit and vegetable juices in with the kombucha for a secondary fermentation. A turnip juice kombucha I tried there was perhaps the most delicious kombucha I have ever had. In recent years, they have transformed the shop into a tiny restaurant with Rice & Pickles lunch service on the weekends, showcasing their pickles with their impeccable pairing sense and design aesthetic.

Kasuzuke

By Alex Hozven and Kevin Farley

We've been producing kasuzuke at the Shop for nearly 15 years now. We are uniquely situated to do so. Takara Sake, one of the larger sake producers in the country, is located just blocks away from our shop. They produce an organic *junmai* sake using rice grown in California. The kasu is light-colored, mild-flavored, and moist enough that it comes to us as a paste rather than in dry-pressed sheets.

We had no experience with the pickle or the process before we started producing it. In researching traditional Japanese pickling methods, we found some guidance on the process. After a couple of years of tweaking, we landed on 10:3:1 as the ratio of kasu, sugar, and salt, respectively, for our standard kasu mix. We use an unrefined cane sugar and fine sea salt for the mixture.

We begin by salting the vegetables at 6 percent of their weight with a fine sea salt, then press for two days under weight. The salt press removes a fair amount of liquid from the vegetables, which serves two functions. The first is to aid with texture preservation, and the second is to minimize vegetables crashing out (releasing their liquid) when they are put into the salty kasu medium, changing the viscosity from a paste to a slurry and possibly altering the balance of the ferment. Though it is possible to ferment any vegetable in kasu given our salt and sugar proportions and fermentation time (9 to 18 months on average), we prefer sturdy root vegetables such as beets, turnips, and burdock. Pumpkin and kabocha squash, as well as whole spring onions and red jalapeños, also work well for us. More delicate vegetables, such as salad greens and mushrooms, will likely lose their textural integrity. Most of the vegetables we use are left whole, but larger vegetables such as winter squash or large beets are broken down. After the two-day salt press, we rinse the vegetables and allow them to air-dry for the day. At the end of the day, we layer the vegetables and the kasu mixture in a vessel in an approximately 1:1 ratio, then cover with plastic wrap (to protect the surface from airflow) and a lid.

As preservers, we are in essence pickers of moments. First, we must find and choose that moment in the vegetables' life—in its taste and texture and color—that we want to preserve. Then, after the vegetable is processed, we must observe and capture a moment when the flavors and textures of the vegetable have been preserved and enhanced by the technique: a moment of balance between preservation and transformation. Good sourcing is vital to our work. The preservation techniques we use are not meant to cover up flaws in the source product; rather, they are meant to preserve and enhance their best qualities.

With our proportions of salt and sugar, the pickle is unbearable for many months. The salt is aggressive and forward on the palate, the sweetness cloying. As the yeasts living in the lees metabolize the sugar, the alcohol can skyrocket and must evaporate off and mellow. So it is typically somewhere around month nine before a balance starts to be struck within the vessel. The salt softens and rounds out. Although we would consider this a sweet pickle, the sugars are metabolized out to a palatable sweetness, and the alcohol has mellowed back to its original gentle sake-ness. The vegetables are fermented clean through, with no raw parts in the center, yet they retain much of their essential vegetable quality. The texture retention is remarkable—a slight initial give when you bite, then a snap of freshness. The flavor echoes the textural qualities, as the soft caramelization from the long braise gives way to the flavor of the fresh raw vegetable. This is the point at which we choose to harvest, package, and refrigerate, wanting to showcase the transformative qualities of the medium while preserving the color, flavor, and texture of the source product. If allowed to continue fermenting, the pickle ages quite beautifully, but loses the flavor of the vegetable and takes on the flavor of the aging medium. The vegetables take on a light to dark caramel color and flavor during the second and third years, then a range of chocolate during the fifth to seventh years. After seven years, flavors of licorice, blackberry, and tobacco dominate, and any vestige of the original vegetable flavors are long gone.

BUBONIC TONIC BEET KVASS BY FAB FERMENTS

Another small producer whose products I really appreciate is Fab Ferments of Cincinnati, Ohio. Jennifer De Marco and Jordan Aversman, the couple who own and operate Fab Ferments, came to my residency program long ago, and brought me to Cincinnati to teach once, but I have run into them semi-regularly on the conference circuit, as their product promotion has overlapped with my teaching. When I'm traveling, it is fortifying for me to eat fermented vegetables as much as I can along the way, as well as drink them. I am not at all picky and almost always enjoy them, but sometimes they are just extraordinary and special.

Every time I see Jenn and Jordan, I drink as much as I can of their beet kvass, a wonderfully sour fermented beet beverage, something like beet pickle juice. Fab Ferments makes a few different flavor variations of beet kvass. My favorite is the one they call Bubonic Tonic®, with a strong horseradish-ginger-garlic flavor. It got its name because it was inspired by traditional immune-supporting tonics "used for fighting everything from colds to plagues," as Jenn explains. She encourages experimentation. "Try incorporating different beet varieties, herbs, spices, and other nourishing ingredients to create your own probiotic tonic," she says. "We're just adding additional ingredients based on inspiration!"

"Beets, water, and salt lay the foundation," according to Jenn. "Water is key. The best results have been achieved using water that is free of chlorine, chloramines, and fluoride."

TIMEFRAME

2 to 3 weeks

VESSEL

1-quart/1-liter jar

INGREDIENTS

for about 3 cups/750 milliliters

¼ pound/125 grams
(or more) beetroots ✳

¼ pound/125 grams cabbage

¼ pound/125 grams altogether
of a mix of onion, ginger, garlic,
horseradish, and jalapeño

About 1 tablespoon sea salt

PROCESS

Coarsely chop the vegetables and mix in the jar.

Dissolve the salt in 2 cups/500 milliliters of lukewarm filtered or spring water (lukewarm to help dissolve the salt). Pour the cooled brine over the vegetables and add additional water as needed to nearly fill the jar. Screw the lid on only loosely so pressure won't be trapped in the jar.

Ferment for 2 to 3 weeks at about 72°F/22°C; it goes faster if warmer, slower if cooler. (If it's too hot, beet kvass can become goopy or stringy.) Shake up the jar every few days and gauge the developing bubbliness. Tighten the lid for shaking, but don't forget to loosen it so pressure won't be trapped in the jar.

"Ferment until the kvass develops a sour zing!" says Jenn.

Strain the liquid from the solids. Store the liquid in the refrigerator and drink. Enjoy residual vegetable pieces as pickles.

✳ with skins is preferable but not essential

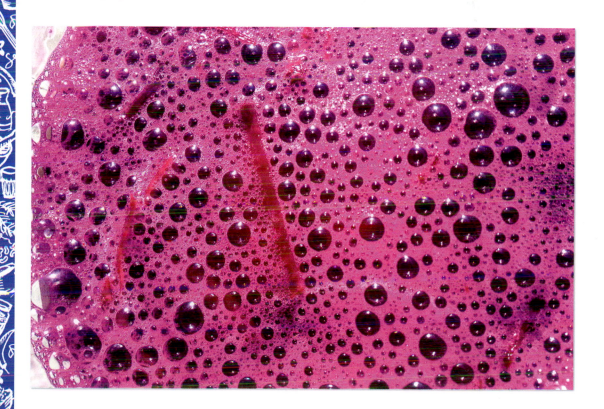

LAHPET BURMESE PICKLED TEA LEAVES

A vendor at a market in Burma selling lahpet, fermented tea leaves.

Burmese cuisine is unusual in its use of tea as a food as well as a drink. The tradition there is to ferment tea leaves, then eat the sour-bitter pickled tea leaves in salads with lots of contrasting flavors and textures; they probably appear in other dishes, as well. The pickled tea leaves are readily available at markets there, directly from small-scale producers. My impression is that most people in Burma (Myanmar) do not make lahpet themselves at home, but rather buy it from local producers. Pickled tea leaves are also packaged and exported. I have found lahpet sporadically in immigrant groceries in the US, or on the internet, but often it has been elusive.

I had eaten and written about lahpet before I visited Burma, so I knew to be on the lookout for it in markets there. It was easy to find. I could also see (and smell) fermented fish and shrimp pastes, incredible dried fish, lots of pickled vegetables, fermented tofu similar to what I had seen in China, natto-like fermented soybeans, and dried disks of fermented beans (*Tua Nao*, page 213). But so much of what I saw at the Burmese markets was inscrutable to me. I visited as a tourist, with a friend from home, not with a team who spoke the local language, as had been the case in China, Japan, and elsewhere. I was able to find people who helped me glean some information, but it was difficult to get detailed answers to detailed questions without a translator.

As I roughly understand it, the process for lahpet starts with fresh tea leaves.

Generally, young and tender leaves are selected for eating, while the older leaves are for drying and drinking. The tea leaves are steamed, packed tightly into clay or bamboo vessels, then fermented for months. I've never tried it myself, owing mostly to the fact that fresh tea leaves are generally not available outside of tea-growing regions. But I was inspired to try my hand at a version of lahpet from dried green tea leaves. I learned about this method not far from home, at the Tennessee Local Food Summit in Nashville, where I attended a presentation by immigrant and refugee gardeners organized by the Tennessee Immigrant & Refugee Rights Coalition. One of the speakers was a young woman from Burma, who shared her adapted version of lahpet that uses dried tea leaves.

TIMEFRAME

2 days

EQUIPMENT

Small food processor

Jar with a capacity of at least 2 cups/500 milliliters

INGREDIENTS

for about 2 cups/1 pint

2.5 ounces/70 grams whole-leaf green tea

Juice of 1 lemon

3 garlic cloves, peeled and chopped

1 jalapeño pepper, chopped

1 to 2 tablespoons fresh ginger, peeled and minced or grated

1 teaspoon galangal, peeled and minced or grated (if available)

1 teaspoon salt

2 tablespoons vegetable oil

PROCESS

Sort through the tea leaves and pick out any twigs.

Steep the tea in a quart/liter or more of hot water (not quite boiling) for 10 minutes or longer, to leach bitterness from the leaves.

Drain off the water, pick out any hard stems you can find, and rinse.

Soak the tea leaves in a quart/liter or more of fresh, cold water for 1 hour, then drain, pick out any additional hard stems you can find, and rinse again.

Squeeze out any excess liquid.

In a small food processor, add the tea leaves, lemon juice, garlic, jalapeño, ginger, galangal (if using), salt, and oil. Pulse until you have the consistency of pesto.

Pack into a jar and seal. Ferment at room temperature, out of direct sunlight, for 2 days or more.

Enjoy in salads, on sandwiches, and as a delicious condiment. Store pickled tea leaves in the refrigerator, where they will continue fermenting much more slowly.

Olives

I came to appreciate olives relatively late in life. Well into adulthood I avoided eating them whole, though increasingly I accepted them minced in or on other foods. Now I love them, especially certain styles. One of the most memorable settings for a workshop was the town of Valldemossa and a nearby farm called Son Moragues, on the Spanish island of Mallorca. Son Moragues has a vast hillside of ancient olive trees.

The workshop was organized by Ana de Azcárate, a Venezuelan woman living in Madrid—part of a vast diaspora of Venezuelans, fleeing a dire situation, whom I have encountered in Europe, North America, and throughout Latin America. Ana invited me to come teach a workshop at her cousin's farm on Mallorca.

The day we were preparing for the workshop, Ana's cousin Bruno Entrecanales gave me a tour of his farm. First, he showed me previous generations of olive oil presses. The ones he uses now are stainless steel and hydraulic. In another building, he preserved a nineteenth-century mechanical press with steel cogs and a much older stone press. The old pressing room has channels built into the floor to carry the oil.

Then he took me out to see the olive trees. The terrain was rugged, and he drove me in a two-seated, open, all-terrain vehicle. We drove up, up, up on an ancient stone-paved road, through stone terraces, past a vast expanse of olive trees, some hundreds of years old and gnarled. The farm grows other products (tomatoes, onions, lemons, quince, other fruits, and more), but it's mostly olives—lots of them—for olive oil and curing. When we reached the top of the hill, I wasn't prepared for what was there: a cliff overlooking the brilliant blue waters of the Mediterranean Sea.

Nineteenth-century mechanical oil press at Son Moragues, now replaced by hydraulic technology.

An earlier stone press for olive oil.

The stone road
around the farm.

View of the Mediterranean
Sea from the top of the
hill at Son Moragues.

FERMENTED OLIVES WITH LEMON

Nerea's fermented olives.

Nerea Zorokiain Garín is a fermentation educator based in the Basque city of Pamplona in Spain. Nerea runs a small school there, has brought me to Pamplona for workshops, and has published a book on fermentation in Spanish called *Fermentación*. Nerea ferments a lot of olives, since they are so abundant in Spain. This is her recipe, a simple and delicious way to ferment olives. There are two steps to the process: first, debittering the olives by lightly crushing them, soaking them in water, and changing the water each day; then, fermenting them in a seasoned brine.

"Olives in brine are one of the best-known ferments in the Mediterranean," says Nerea. "It's one of the best ways to preserve their nutrients and fatty acids, not to mention their fiber." She points out that her method is just one way to ferment olives. "There are as many ways to prepare them as there are families, since each family has their own inherited recipe." You can experiment with other aromatic ingredients. Nerea's book is full of gorgeous olive marinade variations.

TIMEFRAME

A week to several months

VESSEL

Jar or crock with a capacity of at least 1½ quarts/1½ liters

INGREDIENTS

for 2 pounds/1 kilogram

2 pounds/1 kilogram olives

5 tablespoons/70 grams salt

2 lemons, halved

3 garlic cloves (to taste)

2 sprigs of rosemary (to taste)

1 bunch of cilantro (to taste)

2 cayenne peppers (to taste)

PROCESS

TO DEBITTER THE OLIVES

Start by splitting the olives: Crush them until they begin to split. You can use the bottom of a bottle, or the wooden handle of a kitchen knife. You want to see that their juice is beginning to seep out once you have crushed them.

After you split each olive, place it in a container with water so that they don't oxidize and turn brown. Use unchlorinated water or water from the most natural source possible. Traditionally, they are prepared using rainwater.

Let them soak for 5 to 20 days, changing the water every day. After the first few days, you can start tasting them to see if they have lost that characteristic bitter taste. Continue this process until you like the way they taste. Keep in mind that later on in the fermentation process, they will continue to lose more of their bitterness, but I recommend you be patient in order to get good results.

Once they are debittered, they will be put into the brine with the rest of the ingredients.

TO BRINE THE OLIVES

To prepare the brine, combine 1 quart/1 liter of water and the salt in a container and stir well so the salt dissolves completely.

Marinate the olives. Put the olives together with the halved lemons and other remaining ingredients, which can be whole, cut into chunks, or finely chopped, however you prefer.

Add the brine until everything is covered. Place a weight on top so that the olives are covered well and protected from oxygen.

In just a few days you can enjoy them, and they will continue to preserve over several months.

If you don't eat them every day, keep in mind that it's normal for a white layer to form and float on top. It's a natural thing called the mother of the olives. Just move it aside to get olives out, and try to put it back, as it will protect them.

PICKLE SOUP

This delicious pickle soup recipe, created by Chef Kristi Kraft, is from a restaurant called Coppa in Juneau, Alaska. Although they use curried kelp pickles—made by Barnacle Foods, another Juneau business that makes an array of tasty kelp-based foods—you can make this recipe with dill pickles if (like me) you don't have access to kelp pickles. It is no less delicious.

TIMEFRAME

About ½ hour

EQUIPMENT

Cooking pot of at least 2-quart/2-liter capacity

Whisk

INGREDIENTS

for 4 to 6 servings

1 medium-sized onion, diced

2 tablespoons canola oil

1 carrot, chopped

1 cup pickles, drained and finely chopped ✱

5 cups/1¼ liters vegetable stock

3 medium-sized potatoes, cubed

1 teaspoon salt

¼ teaspoon black pepper

1½ teaspoons curry powder (if using curried kelp pickles)

¼ cup/60 milliliters sour cream

1½ tablespoons flour

¼ cup/60 milliliters pickle juice

¼ cup fresh dill, chopped (if using dill pickles)

PROCESS

In the pot, sauté the onion in oil until translucent.

Add the carrots and pickles, and sauté until coated in oil,

Add the stock, potatoes, salt, pepper, and curry powder (if using), and simmer until potatoes are soft, about 15 minutes.

While the potatoes are simmering, whisk together the sour cream, flour, pickle juice, and dill (if using) in a separate bowl.

Once the potatoes are soft, stir in the sour cream mixture and simmer for a couple more minutes to thicken slightly.

Serve and enjoy!

✱ dill pickles, curried kelp pickles if you can find or make them, or others

Dehydrating Fermented Vegetables

Fermented vegetables can be delicious when dehydrated. In some regional traditions, such as *gundruk* and sinki in the Himalayas, vegetables are routinely sun-dried after fermentation for longer storage (as described in my earlier books). Dehydration can be a strategy for extending the shelf stability of fermented vegetables, as well as for salvaging vegetables that have become soft and mushy during fermentation. They can be transformed into crispy snack foods or toppings.

The amount of time necessary for dehydration varies. More finely diced vegetables have greater surface area and less thickness; therefore, they dry faster. Drying is also a matter of degree. You can dry fermented vegetables partially—rendering a chewy texture and concentrated flavor—or you can dry longer for a crispier result that is more shelf-stable. If you use an electric dehydrator, keep the temperature below 115°F/46°C to maintain probiotics.

Fully dried fermented vegetables can be ground into powder for a wonderful seasoning. Matteo Leoni, an Italian chef I met in Switzerland, pulverizes his dehydrated fermented vegetables with koji "for an extra umami result."

I have also had great success making crackers by dehydrating fermented vegetables with whole flax seeds. To make crackers, mix one cup each of minced fermented vegetables, flax seeds, and water (or juice from fermented vegetables). Allow the liquid to absorb into the flax seeds for a few hours, until it all becomes a slimy, mucilaginous mass. Then spread it out as thinly as possible on a silicone sheet or a lightly greased cookie sheet. Dehydrate below 115°F/46°C, or in an oven at its lowest setting—several hours in a dehydrator, less in an oven. When dry enough to lift crackers off the sheet, flip them over to expose the bottom sides, and continue until the crackers are crisp and dry.

Dehydrated Brine Salts

Sasker Scheerder runs the Manenwolfs food lab in Rotterdam, Netherlands. At the Rotzooi festival in Amsterdam, he offered me tastes of his crystalized dehydrated brines. This was my first encounter with brine salts. They are amazing—crystals of salt emboldened by the acidity, flavors, and funk of fermented vegetables: so delicious! Sasker had a few different salts, each dehydrated from a brine with different vegetables and seasonings. Each, in turn, had a very distinctive flavor and color. A salt made from the brine of fermented chili peppers retained the chili flavor, and so on. He called them *pekelzouten*, which roughly translates to "pickle salts," except that, as he explained, "*Zouten* typically refers to the coarse salt that is used to keep the road and driveways free from ice during the winter."

Sasker's methods have evolved as he has learned from his experiments. His first experiment was with the brine of a batch of fermented chili peppers:

Salt crystals dehydrated from fermented chili brine.

I poured the brine onto a flat silicone tray and dehydrated this at a low temperature (somewhere in the range of 35–40°C/95–104°F) over a couple of days. The outcome was pretty amazing. Where all water had evaporated, all the other molecules in the brine had turned into a sticky, but highly tasty, mess. It was salty and spicy of course, but there was also acidity (from the lacto-fermentation), sweetness (the slow dehydration caramelizing the prefermented carbohydrates in the brine), and more surprisingly umami,

Salt crystals dehydrated from fermented daikon brine.

Salt crystals dehydrated from a variety of fermented brines.

and lots of it. Apparently, a high-enzyme activity had transformed free amino acids into glutamate-containing peptides—the ones we call umami. Yes, I was pretty excited about this crazy cocktail of flavours, and I repeated this dehydration-reduction-ripening process with many other ferments, leading to extremely different outcomes in texture and taste. Still, this wasn't salt. Sometimes salt crystals would appear, but mostly it would be a sticky paste.

Sasker developed a technique for increasing crystal formation: He adds salt to the brine to saturate it so there is a greater concentration of salt relative to plant particulates and all the various fermentation by-products. When I asked him how to gauge how much salt to add, he replied that it's hard to say, as it involves many variables:

If it were a plain salt solution it would be easy to measure with high school chemistry, but the fermentation messes things up, releasing all kinds of soluble, sometimes nonsoluble particles into the brine. The variables are so different in every type of ferment—ratio of vegetable to brine, brine strength, duration of fermentation—that it is pretty hard to predict. But by dissolving more sea salt into the brine after the fermentation, a button was created with which to manipulate the texture.

Sasker has also experimented with evaporating in deeper vessels versus shallower ones. In a deeper vessel, it is possible to hang strings, which can enhance crystal formation. I mentioned to Sasker that I remembered doing this as a kid—hanging strings in a sugar solution to form rock candy.

Dehydrated brine as
sticky paste.

Dehydrator with
different brines
dehydrating.

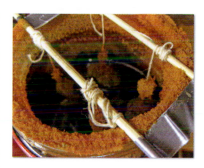
Crystals forming
on strings.

"Yes, same process, and just as fun as when we were kids!" He went on to explain:

When the water level drops, the dissolved salt solution becomes unstable and seeks anything it can cling to—other salt molecules—thereby forming crystals. The string (or anything) works as a catalyst. I started out doing it in that way. It makes beautiful crystals but it takes ages; therefore, I started evaporating on a flat surface. The deeper the mass, the bigger the crystals, but also the longer the process. This is also the part of the process where vibrations can disturb the formation of salt crystals, so easy does it.

Brines can be dehydrated faster at higher temperatures. Sasker advocates low-temperature dehydration to preserve probiotic properties. "Not all, but there are some lactic acid bacteria types that are salt-tolerant enough to survive," he says. "This pekelzout can then be used in its turn to kickstart another fermentation, adding both probiotics and flavor."

Sasker notes that pekelzout continues to ripen after dehydration: "Sometimes, for instance in the case of daikon radish, the original flavor of the salt can be pretty unappealing, but after some weeks it starts to mellow down and deepen, and it is actually one of my favorites."

BRINE CONCENTRATES: EAU DE KRAUT AND KRAUT TAR

Because of my off-the-grid solar electrical setup, running an electric dehydrator 24 hours for multiple days is just not feasible, so I concentrate extra brine leftover from big batches of kraut by cooking it down. The cooking brine has an intense aroma that fills the house! I cook it down for 6 to 8 hours to reduce it, and I reserve a little raw brine to add back in for probiotics. I call the concentrated brine Eau de Kraut, and I use it frequently as a salty, sour, funky, and all-around delicious seasoning! If you keep cooking it, the concentrated brine thickens and the flavors intensify. I've cooked it into a sludge that I call Kraut Tar, a sensory explosion; and I've experienced a failure, in which the brine became so thick that it began to burn.

THREE

GRAINS AND STARCHY TUBERS

In most regions of the world, grains and starchy tubers are dietary staples. Fermentation unlocks and enhances nutrients in these foods, accents their mild flavors, lightens their textures, and can turn them into alcohol. Some traditional grain and starchy tuber ferments involve growing molds on the substrate; these more specialized processes are covered in chapter 4.

For most people in the West, grain fermentation primarily means bread and beer. I am very devoted to both of these, but I touch on them only tangentially here because they are so thoroughly covered in more specialized books. However, I do include a bread recipe that uses a little of the foamy yeast from beer or sake brewing or other vigorous alcohol fermentations as a starter, illustrating the intimate connection between bread and beer; and another recipe for salt-rising bread, a traditional Appalachian food that involves a unique fermentation process. But grain fermentation goes far beyond bread and

beer—in every place I have traveled or read about, fermentation is applied to grains and starchy tubers in myriad ways.

In this chapter, we start with the basics: the simplest ferments, which involve merely soaking grains in water. Then we return to China, learning two rice fermentation methods from the village of Qinfen—one for rice alcohol, or mijiu (our exploration of rice alcohol continues in the next chapter as we address growing molds), and another for the starchy water left over from rinsing rice. Next, I take you with me to South America for a deep dive into chicha, which describes a surprisingly wide range of fermented beverages. I also explain how to make *yuca podrida*—tortillas of fermented cassava—and *tucupí*, a fermented Amazonian condiment made from the bitter, toxic juice of cassava tubers. We begin with the milling of grains, since the availability of technology dictates what people can and cannot do with grains, and with how much effort or ease.

Grain Milling

In our mass-production world, most flour is milled in huge factories, and most of us never see the process. The tradeoff for this convenience and efficiency is that we consume old, oxidized, nutritionally diminished, and sometimes rancid flour; and the supply chain is vulnerable to disruption. Some food-obsessed people (like me) have small home mills. But these mills are rare, and good ones are expensive. However, one of the things I have witnessed in my travels is community-scale, intermediate milling technologies.

Grinding nixtamal into masa at a mill in General Cepeda, Mexico.

Water-powered grain mill in the village of Kalap in India; in exchange for using it, community residents would leave a small share of the grain they had milled.

Fresh oil being pressed from toasted rapeseeds in a storefront in a small town in Sichuan province, China.

I had a wonderful experience at a workshop at Villa de Patos farm in Mexico (see "Pulque" on page 4), after we nixtamalized some corn under the guidance of a couple of local women who work at the farm. Nixtamalization is the process of briefly cooking corn with calcium hydroxide (also known as cal) or wood ash in order to loosen and remove the tough skins on each kernel while simultaneously enhancing the flavor, digestibility, and nutritive content of the corn.

The next morning, after the corn had cooled, we scrubbed it to remove loose skins and rinsed off the caustic cal. We then took a short walk into town with the whole kernel nixtamal to use the services of the local mill. We arrived at a small storefront with a single electric mill—just the right tool for fast, easy grinding. It was not some huge industrial machine, but it was still much too big for any single household: Its intermediate size was perfect for the town's combined households and small businesses that rely upon it, enabling them all to enjoy the freshest, tastiest, most nutritious food possible. The mill provides a few jobs as well as a small community gathering spot, and it fills an important niche in the local food system.

In India, I visited a water-powered community flour mill in a remote Himalayan village without electricity, where villagers left a share of their flour in exchange for using the mill. In China, an aroma lured me into a little oil-pressing shop in a small market town, where I bought the freshest, most delicious oil I have ever tasted.

I am inspired by places like this. Huge centralized factories or the opposite—everybody processing food ingredients for themselves, by hand—are not the only possibilities. Let us reinvigorate, everywhere, the traditions of not only growing most of our food locally and regionally, but also supporting local and regional processing at a modest scale, using intermediate technologies. Local- and regional-scale food processing is a vital economic sector that is ripe for resurgence. It is a path to fresher, more flavorful, more nutritious food, as well as local jobs and food security.

KISIEL

- ●

The most fundamental technique for fermenting grains is extremely simple: soak them. Bacteria and yeasts are naturally present on dry grains, but they are dormant in the absence of water. This is true whether the grains are whole, cracked, or finely ground, so long as they are raw. As soon as the grains are soaked, the dormant organisms awaken and begin metabolizing nutrients and reproducing.

Porridges and gruels are among the most widespread applications of grain fermentation, found across all civilizations born of grain agriculture. Unfortunately, these traditional grain ferments have long been waning in popularity, eclipsed by baby foods, sugary cereals, and other processed foods that render porridges and gruels comparatively unappealing to kids, in spite of their vastly superior nutritive content.

At the University of Gastronomic Sciences (UGS) in Pollenzo, Italy, I was excited to meet Andrea Pieroni and hear about his ethnobotanical field work studying traditional foods of the Balkans. He subsequently sent me some of his papers to read, which were fascinating and informative, but also sad, insofar as one of the major objectives of his work is to document disappearing traditional practices. In one journal article, Andrea and a team of co-investigators include a list of the "most uncommon (and endangered) recorded preparations" among Eastern European traditional practices, with "gruels and sour beverages made of cereals" heading the list. "Fermented oat (*Avena sativa*) dishes were a popular component of the Eastern European diet," they write, "but now are strongly declining."[1]

I love oat porridge and gruel. Porridge is thicker and more substantial; gruel is more watered down—thinner and soupier. They both feel so wholesome and deeply nourishing for me—all the more so when they have been fermented. Their nutritional profile contrasts sharply with the processed breakfast cereals that have become staple foods in the Western world and beyond, which are nutritionally deficient, high in sugar, and potentially harmful over time. These processed cereals are also high-profit products through which we transfer wealth to a few vast multinational grain-processing corporations, relying upon them and the infrastructure that enables them to exist for one of our most basic daily necessities, which they satisfy poorly.

Fermented oats have many different regional names. In Estonia, write Andrea and his collaborators, a beverage called *kile*

> was made of oat flour mixed with water; it was let to stay in warmth for a night. This filtered sour beverage was consumed instead of sour milk on the side of the meal. If the filtrate was boiled, it became a kind of gruel, which was also called kile, *but also* kiisel *or* kisla, *and eaten hot with butter or fat or later, as a cold jelly. The boiling procedure took a long time at slow heat and required constant mixing; it had*

to meet an exact standard of sourness, otherwise it would not produce the required result. Similar gruels (also similarly named) were prepared from rye or from rye and potatoes. In Belarus, lacto-fermented gruel was called kisiel, but also a semi-liquid fermented dish from the oat flour was called by the same name. It was eaten with poppy or cannabis milk and is now, as in Estonia, recognized as a historical use only.[2]

Inspired by this description, I began experimenting. And because my maternal grandparents, Sol and Betty Ellix, came to the United States from Belarus, I adopted the Belarussian name *kisiel* for this sour oat milk and porridge. Both the oat milk and the porridge that this simple fermentation produces are compelling in their deliciousness.

TIMEFRAME

2 to 5 days, depending upon temperature and taste preference

INGREDIENTS

for 1 quart/1 liter of oat milk and porridge for 4 to 6 servings

About 2 cups/200 grams oats, rolled, cracked, or milled into flour

Pinch of salt

PROCESS

Soak the oats in about 1 quart/1 liter of water, in a loosely covered container.

Stir, smell, and taste the soaking liquid daily to monitor the evolving flavor. I've gone as long as 5 days, at which point I detected notes of coconut.

When you decide it is ready, strain the soaking liquid from the solids.

Enjoy the flavorful and nutritious oat milk raw.

Transfer the soaked oat solids to a pot, cover with 4 cups/1 liter of fresh water, and add a pinch of salt. Bring to a boil, then gently simmer over low heat, stirring frequently to prevent burning on the bottom of the pot, until liquid thickens.

Enjoy your porridge with sweet or savory seasonings, as you prefer. (I love mine savory, with butter, peanut butter, miso, and garlic.)

WHOLE GRAIN BREAD FROM FERMENTING BEVERAGE STARTER

It's fun to use the froth from a vigorously fermenting beverage as starter for a loaf of bread. It takes just a tiny bit to make a great loaf, without having to maintain a starter. Even a by-product such as kasu (sake lees) can be used to rise dough. This recipe is for a hearty bread, the way I like it, with some whole grains in it. You can use the froth from a vigorously fermenting beverage as a starter for pretty much any style of bread you like.

TIMEFRAME

2 to 3 days, depending upon temperature

EQUIPMENT

2 loaf pans for easiest process described here (or you can use dough for basket rising or other methods)

INGREDIENTS

for two loaves

¼ cup/60 milliliters active foamy alcohol in process, or kasu; Try anything in its vigorous stage: beer, mead, cider, pulque, chicha, *doburoku* (unfiltered sake), or *jiu niang* (unfiltered Chinese rice alcohol)

About 7 to 8 cups/1.1 kilograms flour, two-thirds or more wheat (whole and/or white), up to one-third other flour if you like; or try it with your favorite gluten-free mix

PROCESS

Make the starter. Mix the frothy alcohol with ½ cup/120 milliliters of lukewarm water and about ¾ cup/100 grams of the flour. Leave to ferment in a warm spot, loosely covered, overnight or longer, stirring occasionally, until it gets nice and bubbly.

Soak the whole grains. At the same time as you prepare the starter, soak the whole or cracked grains of your choice in at least 2 cups of water.

Mix the dough. Once the starter gets foamy, it's time to mix the dough. Drain the soaking water off the grains, and let them drip for a few minutes. In a mixing bowl, measure about 6 cups of the flour (reserving the remaining flour to add later as needed). In a well in the center of the flour, combine the foamy starter with 2½ cups/625 milliliters of lukewarm water, salt, and the soaked and drained grains. Mix everything together with your hands until all the flour is incorporated into a cohesive dough. It will probably still be very sticky. Keep adding flour slowly until it is smooth enough to fold. Fold the dough over itself a few times, turning a few times, folding from each new direction. Cover and let it rest in a warm environment if possible.

Continue to fold the dough every half hour, or as you can, as the dough ferments. After a few hours, you will notice the dough

1 cup/200 grams rice, rye berries, wheat berries, oats, barley, millet, quinoa, grits, or other whole or cracked grains

1½ tablespoons/25 grams salt

Butter or vegetable oil for greasing loaf pans (if using)

getting lighter. After the dough starts to feel lighter, continue folding for one or two more intervals, then divide the dough in half to form two loaves.

Prepare the loaf pans. Brush melted butter or vegetable oil over all the interior surfaces, especially the corners.

Form the loaves. Flatten one of the masses of dough; fold each side into the center, then roll it into a loaf shape and place in a greased loaf pan. Repeat with the second loaf.

Final rise. Cover the loaves to protect them from drying out, and leave them to rise for a couple of hours in a warm environment, until they expand noticeably.

Preheat the oven to 400°F/205°C.

Bake the loaves for 30 minutes, then lower the heat to 350°F/175°C and bake for 15 minutes more. To test for doneness, remove a loaf from its pan and tap on the bottom of the loaf. If it sounds hollow, like a drum, remove the breads from the oven. If not, bake for 5 or 10 minutes more and test again.

Cool the loaves on a rack.

SALT-RISING BREAD

Salt-rising bread is a very distinctive bread, risen not by yeast or salt, but by the bacteria *Clostridium perfringens*. Some may recoil with fear at the idea of eating a food fermented with this notorious bacteria, certain strains of which are associated with digestive illness, but microbiologists investigating salt-rising bread have found that the starters contain none of the toxins or genes associated with illness. The starter for this style of bread is not perpetuated; it is made fresh for each batch. It involves very warm temperatures (ideally 104–110°F/40–43°C, but somewhat lower temperatures may work, too, only more slowly and less reliably), and a little bit of baking soda, not for its rising power but for its alkalinity. As the bacteria flourish in that warm, alkaline environment, the starter develops a strong cheesy smell, bordering on putrid at full vigor. But the putrid notes disappear in the baking, and the bread is very tasty indeed, especially toasted.

Most of my information on and guidance for salt-rising bread comes from the excellent book *Salt Rising Bread: Recipes and Heartfelt Stories of a Nearly Lost Appalachian Tradition*, by Genevieve Bardwell and Susan Ray Brown. Their book is full of practical information about different ways to make salt-rising bread, but their greatest devotion is to the people carrying on this tradition, and their stories. "Without exaggeration, we can say that in the universe of breads, it stands alone," they write.

There is nothing else remotely like it in terms of flavor, personality and technique. There is mystery about it in the wild microbes that cause it to rise. It has attitude and holds tantalizing secrets that have never been fully revealed. Sadly, very few people are alive today who know how to make this delicious yeastless bread the authentic way. That is the reason that we took it upon ourselves to be the chroniclers and preservers of this nearly lost tradition.[3]

They report that similar processes are also found for breads made in Greece and Sudan.

The salt-rising fermentation process consists of three distinct steps: preparing a starter, expanding it into a sponge, then expanding it further into firmer dough and forming it into loaves. I followed the basic outline of Pearl Haines's recipe that Genevieve and Susan documented. Her method (described in detail below) calls for scalded milk poured over a mix of cornmeal, flour, and a tiny bit of baking soda. Other variants include potatoes (always peeled and with green flesh removed), sugar, salt, and boiling water rather than milk.

Genevieve and Susan offered a few tips for making salt-rising bread. They both emphasized the importance of temperature. "One of the biggest challenges, but also very important in making salt-rising bread, is keeping your starter at the right temperature (104–110°F/40–43°C)," explained Susan. "If it is too cool or too warm, the starter will not be successful."[4] I've used the oven with the pilot light lit as my incubation chamber, with great success. This is the same temperature range necessary for making yogurt, so any yogurt-making setup could be used, or a heating pad.

Salt-rising bread can take time. One batch I made was not active the morning after I started it, and I wondered whether something had gone wrong. A couple of hours later it was foaming. "You must pay attention, and you cannot hurry it along," according to Pearl Haines, the elder whose starter recipe I followed.[5] Though it cannot be rushed, the starter and sponge cannot be forgotten too long. "Use them while they are still active," advises Susan. "If they go too long, they will lose their rising power and then your bread will not rise."[6]

TIMEFRAME

Less than 24 hours, generally

EQUIPMENT

2 loaf pans (roughly 8½-by-4½-by-2½ inches/ 21-by-11-by-6 centimeters)

INGREDIENTS

for two loaves

FOR THE STARTER

½ cup/120 milliliters milk or water

3 teaspoons cornmeal

1 teaspoon flour

⅛ teaspoon baking soda

FOR THE SPONGE

1 cup/135 grams flour

FOR THE DOUGH

1½ tablespoons/25 grams salt

7 to 8 cups/1.1 kilograms flour ✳

Melted butter or vegetable oil for greasing pans and the tops of the breads

PROCESS

Heat the milk. Stir the milk as it heats; until tiny bubbles are forming, nearly but not quite at a boil. Then remove from the heat. If using water, bring to a boil.

Mix together the cornmeal, flour, and baking soda in a small bowl or jar. Pour the hot milk or water onto the dry ingredients while it is still hot, and mix well. Most of the yeast and bacteria are killed by the hot liquid, but the *Clostridium* bacteria we are aiming to cultivate can survive the heat. If you use water rather than milk, add an extra teaspoonful of either cornmeal or flour.

Loosely cover the starter to allow for gas exchange. I rest a small plate on it; if you use plastic or foil, poke a hole in it. Leave the starter in your warm incubation environment to ferment about 12 hours, until vigorously foamy.

Prepare the sponge. In a large mixing bowl, combine the foamy starter with 1 cup/250 milliliters warm water in the same incubation temperature range and 1 cup/135 grams flour. Leave the sponge in the warm incubation space to ferment about 2 to 3 hours, until foamy.

Prepare the dough. Add to the sponge 2½ cups/600 milliliters incubation temperature water, salt, and 6 cups/900 grams of the flour, reserving about 1½ cups/200 grams. Mix well, then add more flour, a little at a time, until the dough is easy to handle. Add as little of the remaining flour as necessary to reach this point.

✳ white, whole wheat, a mix of flours, or a gluten-free flour mix

Knead the dough for a few minutes, then divide into two.

Prepare the loaf pans. Brush melted butter or vegetable oil over all the interior surfaces, especially the corners.

Form the loaves. Flatten one of the masses of dough, fold each side into the center, then roll it into a loaf shape and place in a greased loaf pan. Repeat with the second loaf. Brush melted butter or vegetable oil over the tops and exposed sides of the loaves.

Final rise. Leave the loaves to rise for 2 to 3 hours in a warm environment (but not quite as hot as the starter or sponge, ideally about 100°F/38°C). Give them the time they need until you can see a substantial rise.

Preheat the oven to 400°F/205°C.

Bake the loaves for 30 minutes, then lower the heat to 350°F/175°C and bake for 15 minutes more. To test for doneness, remove a loaf from its pan and tap on the bottom of the loaf. If it sounds hollow, like a drum, remove the breads from the oven. If not, bake for 5 or 10 minutes more and test again.

Cool the loaves on a rack.

Salt-rising starter vigorously bubbling.

Rice Alcohol in China

On my very first day in Chengdu, China, when Mrs. Ding and her family invited us for lunch (see "Chinese Fermented Vegetables" on page 37), I experienced the incredibly generous Chinese hospitality that includes copious drink as well as food. The beverage was *baijiu*, a distilled alcohol made from rice, and sometimes sorghum or other grains. Baijiu is widely available at market stalls, and commonly produced in homes in rural villages. Distillation, which is another process altogether, requires its own specialized equipment. We found simple, well-engineered wok-top stills at market houseware stalls everywhere we traveled in China. Here's how they work: The porridge-like fermented rice, with water added, fills the wok. As the wok heats, the still apparatus is placed above it, and the outflow chute is channeled to a collecting vessel. The top of the still is filled with cold water. Ethanol vaporizes at a lower temperature than water; when the ethanol vapors from the heated rice hit the cold top of the still, they condense into liquid form. The water atop the still must be kept cool so water flows into it and out.

Distilling alcohol offers distinct advantages. Whereas fermented beverages are dynamic and can degrade over time or transform into vinegar, distillates are much more stable. Additionally, off-flavors that can develop in fermented beverages are left behind as alcohol vapors separate from the rest of the ferment. Along with these advantages comes a potential disadvantage, which is the possibility of concentrating another "higher" alcohol, methanol. The most important general rule for distilling is that you want to discard the "heads," the first distillate that concentrates. The reason for this is that methanol, the alcohol that can blind and kill, vaporizes at an even lower temperature than ethanol. Typically, there are traces of methanol in fermented alcoholic beverages—so small as to be insignificant, until you concentrate them. In high enough concentrations, they can kill. A more common scenario, if the distiller fails to discard enough of the heads, is that the drinker develops

Stills like these, that sit atop woks, are widely available in China. In Qinfen, the rural village we visited in Guizhou, they are heated by wood fire.

Judy King, our connection to Qinfen.

The Qinfen school Judy helped to start.

a terrible headache. Most home-distilled alcohol I have encountered has been wonderful and left me with warm feelings of grateful appreciation. My travel companions in Qinfen—Mara Jane King and Mattia Sacco Botto—and I were there as guests of Mara's mother Judy King. Judy is a lifelong resident of Hong Kong, where Mara was raised. In order to explore China's diverse textile traditions, she has traveled extensively, visiting ethnic minority villages in rural areas. She forged friendships with residents of Qinfen, and she has visited there regularly over the past few decades, becoming deeply involved in the life of the village. Many of the Qinfen adults speak the local language, Dong, but not Mandarin. They wanted to hire a teacher for the village so the kids could start to learn Mandarin before they left the village to go to school away from their families. Judy helped raise money for the village to hire a teacher, so she was celebrated there.

When we arrived in Qinfen, we were greeted with big smiles all around, ushered into the schoolteacher's home, and seated on low stools around semicircular tables. The village children were giddy with the excitement of visitors to their remote home that sees few, watching us as they laughed and played. Food started to appear, all served family-style. A big bowl of leafy greens in a delicious broth; rice, of course; and *an yu*, or whole carp fermented in a bright red paste made with rice and lots of spices. The an yu was lightly warmed, and we used scissors to cut off chunks of fish. Each plate of an yu was a bit different, though they were uniformly scrumptious. An yu is something that every household has fermenting in a crock, and the various plates were each family's contribution to the feast. There was a bowl of scrumptious, crunchy sautéed crickets. There was chicken and pork and vegetables, all in great abundance. I was raised to eat all the food I am served, but in China that was not possible. In fact, finishing all the food you are served can be seen there as a request for more. Leaving some food in your bowl is a way of saying, "I am satisfied, thank you."

We were given drinking bowls and served baijiu, as well as wonderful mijiu, a fermented beverage made from sticky rice (*Nuo Mijiu*, page 114). People kept refilling our bowls any time they were getting low. I was feeling very lightheaded as the baijiu kept flowing. The only phrase of Mandarin I picked up on my own was *gou le*, "Enough!"

Our Qinfen welcoming feast.

Crickets served at our welcoming feast.

Qinfen.

Almost everyone in Qinfen was either a child below the age of 10 or an adult over 50. The older kids boarded at a school in a bigger town, while the younger adults were off working in cities, earning money to support their children and their parents back home. Judy's closest friend there, Xiao Luo, lives part of the time in Beijing, where she sells hats and other elaborate handicrafts made by women of the village. Xiao Luo was our translator into Dong. When I wanted to ask questions of the people who spoke only Dong, one of my three Mandarin- and English-proficient travel companions would translate my English into Mandarin, then Xiao Luo would translate it into Dong, and vice versa.

The news had spread that Judy's daughter and her friends wanted to learn about fermentation in the village. In fact, we had timed our end-of-November visit to coincide with prime fermentation season, when the villagers were putting up food for winter. Once the feast was over, no sooner had we brought our bags to our rooms than we received word that a neighbor was fermenting rice alcohol, if we'd like to see. Off we went . . .

Everything we saw cooked in the village was prepared in a wok heated by wood fire. Every house had a kitchen that featured a built-in, vented firebox with a circular hole over the fire to hold a big wok. When we arrived at the neighbor's house, the wok was full of cooked rice, still hot but cooling. Our hostess was multitasking, on to another labor-intensive project—grating and

Serving homemade mijiu at our welcoming feast.

pounding taro to cook into a thick paste, then cool into gelatinous donut disks (*yu tou gao*) that would be hung for storage and sliced as needed into noodles! I wish I understood her taro processing enough to explain it fully, but I only glimpsed it. It reminded me how much work sustenance takes, and how wide-ranging the skills and knowledge it demands.

Her process for making the rice alcohol was simple. She mixed the still-warm but cool-enough-to-handle rice with a commercial starter, called *jiu qu*, from a plastic bag. Jiu qu is a generic term that describes various alcohol starters made from rice or wheat. They are created using different methods and result in different forms, such as the Chinese yeast balls I use in *Nuo Mijiu*, page 114, or any of the molded starters discussed in chapter 4. We noticed that our hostess used a lot of starter, much more than was called for on the bag's instructions. She mixed it in thoroughly, then packed it firmly into her vessel, a plastic bucket.

Most notable was a ritualistic touch at the end: She took a stem with a few dried whole chili peppers attached and waved it around above the rice-filled vessel, then set it atop the rice. At first, I imagined this was a general protection ritual to ward off evil spirits. However, I learned that its purpose was more specific than that: to keep away pregnant women, whose presence is believed to potentially spoil the ferment. This was not the first time I had heard of prohibitions on pregnant or menstruating

Mixing jiu qu into rice.

Chilies ritually placed atop rice in fermentation vessel.

Mara covering the rice for its fermentation.

women coming into close proximity with a ferment (see "Pulque" on page 4). However, I have never seen any validation for the suggestion that pregnancy or menstruation might impact fermentation. Furthermore, in most of the places where I have heard such ideas, I have also met women who disregard them, with fine results.

Our hostess covered the rice with a cloth and left it to ferment for several weeks in the cool, late-autumn temperatures. She didn't add any water at the beginning of the process (as I have come to do), but suggested adding some to the partially liquefied rice after fermentation, before distilling. After pressing, the leftover rice solids (*jiu niang*) are enjoyed either as desserts or in a number of different ways, just like sake lees (see "*Kasu*" on page 151).

FERMENTED RICE STARCH WATER

The Dong women of the small villages we visited in Guizhou have the most extraordinary hair! It is extremely long and thick; a deep, dark, uniform black; and hangs straight as can be, except they generally wear it elaborately tied atop their heads, held in place with decorative combs. Several of them attributed their luxuriant hair to frequent rinsing with fermented rice starch water. I've been using it regularly, and while it hasn't restored my gray hair to its former dark color, it looks and feels great.

To ferment the starchy water from rinsing rice, leave it sitting for several weeks, until it is sour. Then use it to rinse your hair.

Alternatively, you can add ginger, Sichuan peppercorns, salt, and other seasonings to the same rice starch water, and ferment it for several days to enjoy as a summer soup.

The Dong women we met have long, thick black hair (generally worn tied with combs), which several of them attribute to rinsing with fermented rice water.

NUO MIJIU

This recipe is for a sticky rice alcohol,
inspired by what I saw and tried in Qinfen.
It's easy to prepare, delicious, and strong.

TIMEFRAME

About 2 weeks

EQUIPMENT

Steamer

Crock with at least a
1-gallon/4-liter capacity

Fine mesh bag or cloth
for straining

INGREDIENTS

for about 3 quarts/3 liters

2 pounds/1 kilogram
uncooked sticky rice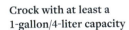

1 (if fresh) or 2 Chinese
yeast balls

PROCESS

Rinse the rice and soak it overnight.

Steam the rice, held above water as it cooks. Use at least twice as much water by volume as rice. I use a bamboo steamer for this, lined with cotton cloth. If the steamer is above a wok, be sure to check the water level as it boils and add additional hot water as necessary. Steam the rice for about half an hour, until it is fully cooked and soft.

Allow the rice to cool to body temperature; to speed this process, remove the rice from the steamer onto a tray or in a large bowl and break it up into clumps.

Crush the yeast ball(s) into powder, using a mortar and pestle, bowl and spoon, or mechanical grinder.

Mix the crushed yeast ball into the cooled rice. Because the rice is so sticky, wet your clean hands first, then squeeze the rice and stir with your hands repeatedly, in order to make sure yeast ball enzymes and yeasts get well distributed.

I like to mix in about 2 quarts/2 liters of water at this point. I have found that without adding any water (as I saw it done in Qinfen), the rice can dry out, impeding the process. When I did a side-by-side controlled experiment, the batch with added water fermented much faster than the batch without, though both fermented. (If

* also called sweet rice or glutinous rice

you decide to forgo adding water now, I would recommend adding it at the end of the fermentation, prior to straining.)

Ferment in a crock or bucket, covered to protect it from drying out and from flies, for about 2 weeks. Stir it, smell it, and observe it periodically. At first, the rice will absorb the added water and swell. As enzymes break down complex carbohydrates into sugars, it will smell sweet. As it sweetens, yeasts will begin to metabolize sugars into alcohol. As the rice breaks down, it partially liquefies, but the carbon dioxide created by the activity of yeast and koji enzymes lift the solid remains so they float on the liquid. As the days turn into weeks, there will be more liquid and less solids, and the sweetness will yield to the taste of alcohol as it accumulates. The temperature, humidity, and potency of your yeast ball are all factors influencing the rate of fermentation, though ultimately, how long to ferment is a highly subjective, personal decision. As time passes, more of the sugars are converted into alcohol, but if you let it go on for too long, another stage of fermentation may take hold, fermenting the alcohol into acetic acid, or vinegar.

When mijiu tastes ready to you, strain it through a fine mesh bag or cloth to separate liquid from solids, then press to remove as much liquid as possible. Enjoy the solid residue as a flavoring or leavening (similar to "*Kasu*," page 151).

If you bottle and store mijiu, be aware that fermentation may continue in the bottle. Release pressure periodically, even if storing in the refrigerator.

Chicha

Chicha describes a broad range of South American beverages, generally (but not always) fermented, and most commonly made from corn, but also from other grains, tubers, fruits, honey, sugar, and more. In *Wild Fermentation*, I describe chicha as South American corn beer. My Colombian host, Esteban Yepes Montoya, took issue with that. We drank a good bit of chicha together during my visit, always drinking from totumas, drinking gourds. "I think it's not good to call chicha South American wine or South American beer," he told me, and he's absolutely right. Its Indigenous South Americanness is what defines it as chicha, so why try to describe it with comparisons to beverages from elsewhere? We don't want the familiar comparison to eclipse what is unique about the unfamiliar food or beverage.

An elder sharing a big totuma of chicha at the Bogotá Fermentation Festival.

Ceramic fermentation vessels for making chicha at the Bogotá Fermentation Festival.

Chicha is actually an accidental name, arising from a linguistic misunderstanding on the part of Spanish colonizers, who erroneously called a fermented beverage that was served to them (known to its makers as *fabkua*) chicha. As Esteban recounted the legend to me, the fabkua had given the newly arrived Spaniards diarrhea, for which *chicha* was the local word. The Spaniards mistook *chicha* as the name of the beverage, and used it to describe other similar fermented beverages they encountered. *Chicha* has come to encompass such a wide variety of indigenous beverages that Esteban regards it as central to "the ancestral ethnogastronomy of the Americas." Chicha is used primarily as a beverage for celebrations and rituals, but its makers also use chicha in the kitchen, using it in meat marinades, stews, and sauces. Esteban calls it a "primordial ingredient." Like any fermented alcohol, chicha becomes vinegar after a time, opening it up to an expanded set of kitchen applications.

Chicha making becomes a life-long relationship for the women who are its traditional makers. Chicha is traditionally made in clay pots, or in other cases gourds, that are not washed between batches. These vessels are passed through the generations, so the pots themselves become a means of perpetuating the chicha. "Knowing that they have been fermenting in the same container for so long, so it still has all the yeast and all the bacteria, for generations, is so magical and mystical to me," reflects Esteban. He continues:

> Grandma has been taking care of this living being for her entire life, and she has this intimate relationship with it. There are songs for the chicha, there are poems for the chicha. . . . It's so very different how a commercialized, more industrialized, tourist-business chicha tastes, compared to the chicha from neighborhoods where grandmas are still fermenting them in old clay pots and taking care of them as living beings.[7]

Back when I was researching for *Wild Fermentation* in 2001, I read about a style of chicha that involves chewing the cooked corn. This was fascinating—a low-tech alternative to malting, or molds such as koji, that uses salivary enzymes to break down complex carbohydrates into simple sugars that can be easily fermented into alcohol. With much help, I made a couple of batches of

A bottle of home-made chontaduro (palm fruit) chicha.

Alfredo Ortiz of the Bogotá Chicha Museum serving quinoa and amaranth chicha.

chewed-corn chicha, rather enjoying the strange ritual of chewing corn without eating it, instead forming it with our tongues into balls of saliva-saturated corn mush, then spitting them out. It was fun to recruit friends and do this together (though according to Esteban, in some traditions, only the saliva of virgins can be used), and this style of chicha is delicious. I developed a recipe, Chicha (Andean Chewed-Corn Beer), which is included in *Wild Fermentation*.

Chewing corn is definitely an ancient way of making chicha, and it reportedly persists in some places. But all the corn chicha I have encountered, and the vast majority of that which I've heard about in stories from around South America, has relied upon malting or added sugar and/or fruit (for one exception that relies on molds, see "Bribri *Chicha*," page 182). I have sampled many different corn-based chichas in my travels, and a recipe follows for *chicha de jora*, *jora* being malted corn, sweetened by amylase enzymes that develop during germination. Thinking expansively about chicha, as Esteban encourages, I suppose the Tarahumara *tesgüino* and the Cherokee *gv-no-he-nv*, two fermented corn beverages that I wrote about in my earlier books, can also be viewed as relations on the chicha family tree, as can many other corn-based fermented drinks of the Americas.

I have also encountered many chichas made from base ingredients other than corn. I drank delicious *chicha de chontaduro* in Colombia. *Chontaduro* is the Colombian name for a small orange fruit from a palm tree (*Bactris gasipaes*), known as peach palm in English, and as *pejibaye* in some other Spanish-speaking lands. This bright orange chicha de chontaduro, made by a friendly young woman named Rosane, who I met at the Bogotá Fermentation Festival, was sweet and pulpy. Rosane blended the fruit pulp with water and panela, added some active chicha as a starter, and fermented it just a few days. It was bubbly, still sweet, and had developed just a little bit of alcohol. At the same festival, I also drank a wonderful quinoa and amaranth chicha, sweet, earthy, and very low-alcohol. Esteban even told me about a style of chicha made from peas, *arveja de firavitoba*.

In the pages that follow you will find recipes for a few different styles of chicha. An internet search will yield many further variations.

EL TALLER DE LOS FERMENTOS

My visit to Colombia was organized by Esteban Yepes Montoya and his enthusiastic, energetic, and fun team of young collaborators at El Taller de los Fermentos, a workshop space producing fermented foods and beverages, providing fermentation education, and documenting indigenous fermentation traditions. I appreciate how deeply engaged they are in indigenous networks, and the extensive outreach they did to invite Indigenous groups spanning the country's incredible geographic and cultural diversity—from the Amazon basin to the mountain highlands—to the Bogotá festival and our other fermentation events in Colombia.

At the festival, Indigenous elders shared sacred chicha from a huge totuma (drinking gourd), accompanied by drumming, singing, incantations, and ceremony. Agustina Yolanda Tumiñá, a Namuy Misak woman from Silvia, in Colombia's mountain highlands, took part in the workshops all week. The young Fermentos called her *abuela* (grandmother). When one of the students began to cough and feel ill, Agustina shared a bit of her Namuy Misak tradition's fermentation wisdom. She peeled an onion, carved out a little well in the center, and filled it with panela (unrefined sugar) and herbs I did not recognize. By the following morning, the panela had drawn juice from the onion, diluting it into a syrup already bubbly with fermentation. After a couple of spoonfuls, the ill student started to feel better.

Kimchi-making workshop at La Minga retreat center in Choachi, Colombia.

To celebrate my arrival in Colombia, the Fermentos had buried some surprises. After reading about the idea in my books, Esteban and his collaborators had buried jars of fermenting vegetables a couple of weeks prior to my arrival. Together we dug up about five different flavors, one with mango in it—yum!

Next, the Fermentos surprised me with a *pachamanca*, which is a South American pit roast. All sorts of different foods, including lamb, whole squashes, whole pineapples, plantains, potatoes, sweet potatoes, and other starchy tubers, were buried in a big pit in the yard, along with rocks that had been heated for hours in a fire, big leaves from *bijao* and banana plants, and aromatic herbs. Everything was covered with layers of the bijao and banana leaves, then soil to insulate it so the food in the pit stayed hot and roasted for hours, the flavors and aromas intermingling.

Digging out the pit was exciting! The first task was removing the layer of insulating soil with shovels. Then people took turns getting into the pit.

Agustina Yolanda Tumiñá with a medicinal ferment she made from panela and herbs in an onion.

Esteban showing Agustina a jar of fermented vegetables that he had just dug up.

They lifted the last of the soil away on the banana leaves, which had wilted into a mat, until the first roasted foods were revealed. The whole roasted pineapples were soft and juicy, and they smelled so sweet. Pieces of lamb were wrapped in banana leaves, and as they were unwrapped we could see how tender and moist the meat was. Whole tubers and plantains emerged looking luscious. Everything was delicious beyond belief.

The young organizers liked to party, too. There was late-night music, dancing, singing, drinking, and much merriment. But there was seriousness, too, as Agustina led us in a ritual of grieving and release for Esteban's mother, who had passed not long before. All of this, along with workshops in venues as varied as a science museum in Medellín and a farm on the outskirts of town, made my visit to Colombia one of my favorite trips ever. Esteban continues to be an inspiration to me; he has helped me enormously with this project, and he frequently steers me to interesting new information and perspectives.

Removing our roasted feast from the pachamanca pit.

CHICHA DE JORA

This is an Ecuadorian style of chicha. Jora is malted corn. You may be able to purchase some at a Latin American market or on the internet. If you can't find any jora to purchase, you'll have to germinate the corn yourself. See the sidebar "Making Your Own *Jora*" for guidance on how to do that.

This is my adaptation of a recipe from Michelle O. Fried, whom I met when she attended one of my workshops in Ecuador. Michelle was born and raised in the United States, but has lived most of her life in Ecuador and written numerous books (in Spanish) about Andean food. This recipe yields a light and fruity chicha de jora.

MAKING YOUR OWN JORA

Start with dry, raw, whole-kernel corn. For *Chicha Fuerte*, page 124, use 2 pounds/1 kilogram of corn; for *Chicha de Jora* you could use much less. The seeds do not remain viable forever; the fresher the dried corn is, the higher your germination rate will be. Use any variety of corn, so long as it is still viable as seed. Soak the corn for two days in hot weather or three days in cooler weather, changing the water each day. This long soak enables the corn to swell fully, absorbing water into the very center of the seed, where germination begins. After the long soak, drain the water off the corn.

Keep the kernels moist—but not waterlogged—with good air circulation and protection from light for roughly five days. I use bamboo steaming baskets lined with moist tea towels, and I mist the corn with a spray bottle twice a day. For a larger amount, use a cardboard box, or otherwise improvise. The corn should be in a layer no deeper than 2 inches/5 centimeters, and it should get gently stirred each day. After the five days, or once the sprouts reach a length of about 1 inch/2.5 centimeters, grind well using a traditional Corona corn masa grinder, if you have one available, or a food processor. The jora is now ready to be added to the chicha.

TIMEFRAME

2 to 5 days

VESSEL

Ceramic crock, plastic bucket, or other vessel with a capacity of about 2 gallons/8 liters

Jars and/or bottles with a total capacity of 1 gallon/4 liters

INGREDIENTS

for 1 gallon/4 liters

1 cup/125 grams jora flour, or twice as much ground fresh jora

½ cup/100 grams panela or another unrefined sugar

2 cinnamon sticks

2 allspice berries, whole

2 cloves, whole

2 or 3 tablespoons lemon verbena, dried

2 or 3 tablespoons chamomile flowers, dried

2 orange leaves (if available)

1 pineapple, with the skin included but cut from the flesh, and the flesh chopped

4 guavas, quartered (if available)

PROCESS

Boil 3 quarts/3 liters of water in a large pot.

Mix the jora flour in 2 cups/500 milliliters of cold water and stir well to make sure all the flour is moist, thus preventing it from clumping when it is added to the hot water.

Add the moist jora flour to the boiling water, whisk to combine well, then return to a gentle simmer for about 10 minutes. Remove from the heat and allow to cool.

Bring 1 more quart/1 liter of water to a boil, then gently simmer the panela, cinnamon, allspice, and cloves for 20 minutes.

Remove from the heat and add the lemon verbena, chamomile flowers, and orange leaves (if using). Experiment with other aromatics as desired.

Combine this small pot of aromatics with the larger pot of jora. Cool to below body temperature, then transfer to the fermentation vessel.

Add the pineapple flesh and skins, along with the guava (if available), to the cooled liquid. Stir well and cover.

Ferment for 2 to 5 days, stirring daily and tasting to evaluate flavor.

Strain the chicha before serving. If desired, sweeten to taste with additional panela or sugar.

Store chicha in jars or bottles in the refrigerator, where fermentation will slowly continue.

Freshly malted (sprouted) corn.

CHICHA FUERTE

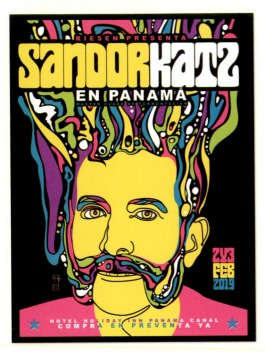

Pico de Pajaro Zurdo's psychedelic
poster for my workshop in Panama.

Fuerte is Spanish for "strong," and this Panamanian chicha is the strongest of the ones featured in this book. This recipe comes from my host in Panama, Chef Hernan Correa of the restaurant Riesen in Panama City. It is very simple, made from just jora, sugar, and water. It uses no starter, relying upon wild yeasts drawn from the air. You can speed it up a lot by backslopping with another active chicha, or adding pineapple skin or even a little yeast.

My host in Panama, Hernan Correa, chef and proprietor of the
restaurant Riesen in Panama City, with his mother and grandmother,
who help him and his fiancée Maria Laura run the restaurant.

TIMEFRAME

2 to 3 weeks, including corn-sprouting time

EQUIPMENT

Corona corn masa grinder or food processor

Fine-mesh sieve

Jar or crock with a capacity of at least 6 quarts/6 liters

Jars and/or bottles with a total capacity of 1 gallon/4 liters

INGREDIENTS

for about 1 gallon/4 liters

2 pounds/1 kilogram dry whole corn kernels

2 pounds/1 kilogram unrefined sugar ✳

PROCESS

Germinate the corn as described in "Making Your Own *Jora*" on page 122.

Rinse the corn thoroughly.

Grind the corn using a traditional Corona corn masa grinder if you have one available; otherwise, use a food processor.

Place the ground corn in a pot and cover with 5 quarts/5 liters of dechlorinated water.

Bring the corn and water to a boil and cook over medium-high heat for 10 minutes, stirring continuously to prevent scorching.

Remove from heat, strain through a fine-mesh sieve, discard the solids (or incorporate them into polenta or corn bread), and combine the strained corn liquid with the sugar. Stir well to dissolve the sugar.

Transfer the chicha to a jar or crock and cover with a cloth.

Allow the chicha to ferment. In Panama, according to Hernan, it can become active within 5 days to a week. In cooler locations, it may take considerably longer. Stir it at least daily. It will become vigorous much more quickly with some pineapple skin, other raw botanical elements, backslopping from a previous batch, or adding yeast.

Once the chicha starts bubbling vigorously, keep stirring daily, and after about 5 days, try it. Once you are happy with the flavor, store it in jars or bottles in the refrigerator. It will keep for up to one month.

Serve very cold.

✳ panela, rapadura, jaggery, or another type

CHICHA BLANCA DE QUINOA

During my chicha research and experimentation, I came across Peruvian recipes for *chicha blanca*—white chicha—that I love. It is made from quinoa in a traditional Cuzco style. This recipe is adapted from a few different Cuzco recipes, which I created in anticipation of an eventual visit there.

TIMEFRAME

1 to 4 days

EQUIPMENT

Blender

Cheesecloth or woven fabric

Ceramic crock, plastic bucket, or other vessel with a capacity of about 2 gallons/8 liters

Jars and/or bottles with a total capacity of 1 gallon/4 liters

INGREDIENTS
for about 1 gallon/4 liters

½ cup/100 grams quinoa

¼ cup/50 grams dried white corn

¼ cup /50 grams dried, peeled fava beans (or other white beans)

3 cinnamon sticks

5 cloves

2 star anise pods

A few teaspoons fresh and/or dried herbs, including any combination of lemon verbena, lemon balm, chamomile, fennel

1 cup/200 grams sugar (to taste)

2 apples, cored

1 pineapple, including peel

PROCESS

Soak the quinoa, corn, and beans in water for at least 8 hours (24 is better).

Drain the soaking water.

Blend the soaked quinoa, corn, and beans in a blender with 2 cups/500 milliliters of fresh water. Blend for a few minutes, until the solids are thoroughly pulverized into the liquid.

Boil 3½ quarts/3½ liters of water with the cinnamon, cloves, and star anise. After the water comes to a boil, add the blended quinoa, corn, and bean mixture. Return the pot to a boil and simmer over low heat about 30 minutes, until the foam subsides. Watch the pot and stir frequently, to prevent foam from overflowing.

Remove the pot from the heat, add the fresh and/or dried herbs, and stir. Cover the pot and leave it to cool slowly, until the chicha is easy to handle for straining.

Strain the chicha through cheesecloth or woven fabric. Discard the solids.

Add the sugar to the chicha and stir until it is completely dissolved.

Blend the chicha in a blender with the apples and half the pineapple flesh (not skins). Enjoy the remainder of the pineapple fresh.

Add the pineapple skins and ferment 1 to 4 days, stirring and tasting daily.

When it tastes ready to you, remove the pineapple skins and strain again before serving. Add more sugar if desired.

Starchy Tubers of South America

Potatoes originated in the Andes Mountains, where people living at high altitudes began cultivating the earliest varieties. These early potatoes were bitter and toxic, and they required extensive processing before eating. The bitter potatoes were fermented and freeze-dried to form a storage food called *chuno*. (See my book *The Art of Fermentation* for a description of the process.) These potatoes are still grown and processed in the traditional way, mostly at high altitudes, but through generations of selection across ever-wider geographic distribution, the bitter tuber has evolved into the multiplicity of delicious nonbitter potato varieties that do not require fermentation (but that certainly can be and are fermented).

Cassava, also known as tapioca, yuca in Spanish, and *mandioca* in Portuguese, originated in the Amazon basin. The original varieties were similarly bitter and toxic, requiring fermentation or other processing to render them safe to eat, though most of the cassava available outside the regions where it grows are varieties that do not require such processing. Sweet potatoes, too, are widely thought to have originated in Central or South America, though due to their early wide distribution, there is much debate about it. South America also spawned many other starchy tubers—storable, hardy, and nutritious—most of which have remained regional foods, without garnering the same worldwide attention as potatoes, cassava, and sweet potatoes. Examples include *arracacha*, *mashua*, *melloco*, *oca*, and *yacón*. These starchy tubers fill bellies, fuel people with slow-release energy, store and travel well, and feature prominently in cuisines throughout South America, in fermented as well as unfermented forms.

In this delicious lunch served at one of my Ecuador workshops, you can see a variety of different tubers.

CHICHA DE YUCA Y CAMOTE

Chicha de Yuca y Camote made with purple sweet potato.

This is a very different chicha, made from cassava with sweet potato. It's really delicious, with an appealing starchy texture. I made this with purple sweet potatoes that I grew, and it was so incredibly gorgeous! Esteban brought to my attention the fact that sweet potatoes contain amylase enzymes that can break down complex carbohydrates, similar to those present in koji, saliva, and germinating grains. Perhaps this was recognized by the Amazonian peoples who since ancient times have made chicha by fermenting mashed cooked yuca with a relatively small proportion of raw sweet potato. The raw sweet potato also provides the yeast and bacteria for the fermentation.

TIMEFRAME

4 to 7 days

EQUIPMENT

Potato masher or wooden pounding tool

Vessel with at least 1-gallon/4-liter capacity

Jars and/or bottles with a total capacity of 3 quarts/3 liters

INGREDIENTS

for about 3 quarts/3 liters

About 2 pounds/1 kilogram (roughly 2 small or 1 large tuber) yuca/cassava

About ½ pound/250 grams (1 small) sweet potato, unpeeled

PROCESS

Peel the cassava and chop it coarsely. I slice it in half lengthwise, then crosswise into 1-inch-/2.5-centimeter-wide half-moons.

Place the cassava pieces in a pot, cover with about 1 quart/1 liter of water, and bring to a boil.

Cook about 30 minutes, until the pieces are easy to pierce with a fork. Remove from the heat.

Mash the cooked cassava in its cooking water while it is still hot. A potato masher, or any blunt wooden pounding tool, is perfect. I like to scrape the buildup along the bottom of the pot by twisting the potato masher so I can re-mash it. Keep breaking up lumps and it will get smoother and smoother. At the end, the chicha will get strained and any remaining clumps will be strained out anyway.

Grate the raw sweet potato, with its skin.

Cover the grated sweet potatoes with 1 quart/1 liter of water.

Once the mashed cassava has cooled to body temperature, mix in the grated sweet potatoes and water.

Transfer to the fermentation vessel and ferment roughly 4 to 7 days. Stir daily and start tasting after fermentation gets bubbly. It will get stronger, then at some point more acidic.

Strain to drink when it reaches a stage that is appealing to you. Enjoy it fresh, or transfer to jars or bottles to refrigerate.

Sweet potato–only variation: Skip the cassava and use only sweet potatoes (2½ pounds/1.25 kilograms). Peel all but one of the sweet potatoes, and save the skins to add raw with the one unpeeled whole raw sweet potato, which will be grated. Then proceed as above, substituting the flesh of the peeled sweet potatoes to cook in place of the cassava.

TORTILLA DE YUCA PODRIDA

Yuca is the Spanish name for cassava. *Podrida* is the Spanish word for rotten. I would not describe yuca podrida as rotten at all, but as is usually the case, the fermentation adds flavor and complexity to what is otherwise among the plainest of foods. *Tortilla de Yuca Podrida* is basically yuca podrida mashed into a dough with fried onions, garlic, salt, and sometimes egg; stuffed with cheese and/or other yummies; then panfried into a hot, crispy, and delicious treat. Javier Carrera, my host in Ecuador, introduced me to yuca podrida and first explained the basics of how to make it.

TIMEFRAME

3 or more days

EQUIPMENT

Bowl, crock, or jar with a 2-quart/2-liter capacity

Potato masher or other blunt pounding tool

INGREDIENTS
for about 6 to 8 tortillas

2 pounds/1 kilogram cassava/yuca tubers

1 tablespoon salt (to taste)

1 onion

A few garlic cloves and/or other vegetables as desired

A few tablespoons of oil, butter, and/or lard

1 egg (optional)

3 ounces/85 grams cheese (optional)

PROCESS

Peel the tubers. (Generally, beyond the tropics where cassava is grown, the tubers are waxed for longevity; peel the wax and the skin.)

Slice the tubers lengthwise and remove the tough fibers that run through the centers.

Cut the tubers into chunks and place in a bowl, crock, or jar.

Cover the cassava chunks with water and weigh down to keep submerged. If the cassava has sustained contact with air, it discolors and becomes inedible.

Ferment for about 3 days, or longer, changing the water every day or two. A longer fermentation will yield a more pronounced flavor.

After fermentation, remove the cassava chunks from the water and boil them in fresh, salted water for at least a half hour, until they are soft and easily crushable.

While the cassava is cooking, mince the onion, garlic, and any other desired vegetables, and sauté them in about 2 tablespoons of oil. Sauté 5–10 minutes, until onions are soft and just beginning to brown. Lightly salt the vegetables.

Once the cassava is cooked, remove from the cooking water into a bowl and mash the chunks into a smooth paste. A potato masher, or any blunt, wooden pounding tool, is perfect. Keep mashing until

My hosts in Ecuador: Javier Carrera of the organization Red Semillas (www.redsemillas.org), his wife Fernanda, and their son Gael.

all the chunks are broken down. Add a little of the cooking water, if necessary, to achieve a smooth texture, like gluey mashed potatoes.

Add salt to taste, the sautéed vegetables, and an egg, if desired. The egg will make the tortillas lighter. Mash everything together until you have a smooth, consistent dough.

Forming the dough into tortillas is much easier with wet hands, so keep a bowl of water at the ready. Form a handful of the dough into a ball. Use your thumb to create an indentation. Fill the indentation with cheese or other tasty filling. Then pull the edges of the dough around the indentation to bury the filling in the center of the ball, and gently flatten the ball into a disk.

Place it on a wet plate or work surface, and then use the same technique to form the rest of the dough into filled disks.

Melt 2 tablespoons of oil, butter, or lard, in a hot skillet. Fry the tortillas on high heat. Leave some space between them. Cook until golden and crispy, then flip and cook the other side. Add more oil as necessary. Press down gently on the tortillas as they cook.

If you don't use all the dough in one serving, you can store formed tortillas or unformed dough in the fridge for up to a week.

An alternative method, easier but not quite as texturally appealing to me, is to grate the fermented yuca chunks, mix in grated cheese if you like, add a little salt, and fry like potato pancakes.

Tucupí

The most distinctive fermented food that I was introduced to in South America—unlike anything else I have ever seen or tasted—is tucupí. I first encountered tucupí in a restaurant in Bogotá, Colombia. The chef, Camilo Ramírez, had already wowed me with his bright orange chontaduro kimchi. Then he brought out a mysterious black, tarry paste, which was deliciously earthy, umami, a little sour, and a little spicy—an exciting condiment to enhance our meal. Camilo explained that this was tucupí, the toxic juice of bitter cassava, fermented to break down the toxic compounds, then cooked down into a tarry paste. He did not make the tucupí himself, but rather sourced it from Amazonian producers.

Tucupí is produced in the Amazon exclusively by women, who also tend the cassava. According to Esteban, "The stewards of this ancestral delicacy say that it is the blood of the mother, the essence of the sacred feminine."

Camilo Ramírez serving his chontaduro kimchi.

Esteban and the El Taller de los Fermentos team traveled to the Amazon to learn about how tucupí is made, and they documented it in a beautiful short film.[8] The first step in making tucupí is preparing a starter from a particular variety of cassava (there are many in the Amazon, where the plant evolved) called *jaiyaju*. Unpeeled tubers are fermented in water, becoming soft enough to mash by hand into a purée. This purée is then added to a much larger batch of peeled tubers in water and fermented for about five to seven days. Then, the softened, fermented cassava is either grated or mashed (it varies by tribal tradition) and is spread out on a woven mat, which is used to wring out the juice.

Tucupí is only one of the products made with this fermented cassava. The starch is used to make a sacred beverage called *caguana*, enjoyed only by women. The fiber is used to make *cassabe*, a cassava pancake. Tucupí is made by simmering the liquid for 12 to 36 hours, stirring constantly to prevent burning as the thin liquid concentrates into a thick black paste. Toward the end of the process, chilies, dried fish, different types of ants, or other Amazonian delicacies are often added.

Tucupí, a delicious Amazonian condiment fermented and cooked down from toxic cassava juice.

Indigenous Practices

So many of the fermentations described in this book are ancient legacies of indigenous wisdom and practices. Glimpses of people living traditional lifestyles have been a highlight of the traveling I've done. I've journeyed far in order to visit remote villages in India and China, and my Latin American hosts have often brought me to Indigenous communities to learn about their fermentation traditions.

Yet indigenous traditions are not all equally well preserved, practiced, or celebrated. In many places, indigenous practices have been lost due to long, shameful histories of genocide, mass relocation, forced assimilation, removal of children from their families, and other forms of cultural destruction. I have met a couple of young Native American people specifically interested in trying to piece together what their peoples' traditional ferments may have been, in the absence of living memories or written documentation.

Certainly, there are many examples of indigenous North American fermentation practices that persist. In southeast Alaska, I had the chance to ferment with a Tlingit elder (see "Stinkheads" on page 287). And in southern Arizona, writer and seed activist Gary Nabhan invited local Indigenous friends of his—a group of Tarahumara people who live on both sides of the border—to a workshop. The Tarahumara have an ancient fermented beverage called tesgüino, or *tiswin*, an alcoholic malted corn beverage something like chicha. I wrote about tesgüino in *Wild Fermentation* and included a recipe. In my recipe, I improvised a starter by saving some of the raw malted corn when I brewed the rest. Then, after the brew had cooled, I added the raw malted corn as a starter. I had read that, traditionally, the fermentation vessels, called *ollas*, were not washed, so they developed a dried corn crust that functioned as a starter.

For our workshop, some of Gary's Tarahumara friends brought ollas that have long been dedicated to tesgüino and had a crusty buildup from previous batches, including dried yeast and bacteria to start the ferment. Gary and a colleague from Native Seed/SEARCH sprouted corn

PLATTI E PAPILLE'S OSPITANO
SEAN SHERMAN & INDIGENOUS
FOOD LAB: LA CUCINA DEI
NATIVI D'AMERICA

MENU – Indigenous Pop Up Dinner:

• ONE: MEXICO
chilaquiles – tortillas messicane
• TWO: MIDWEST
Trout crust of wild rice – Trota in crosta di riso
• THREE: SOUTHWEST
acorn soup – coniglio brasato su crema di
agave, ghiande e semi di zucca
• FOUR: PACIFIC COAST
venison stew– cervo stufato con amaranto e
ristretto di frutti di bosco
• FIVE: NORTHEAST
blue corn pudding – budino con sciroppo
d'acero e bacche fresche

Aperitivo con Deltetto metodo classico brut
2013 e cena con i vini di Franco Maria Marti-
netti (Gavi del comune di Gavi 2017 – Barbera
d'Asti Bric dei Banditi 2015 – Moscato d'Asti
2017), tutti piemontesi

The menu from the
Indigenous Food Lab
meal at Terra Madre, 2018.

from two different traditional Tarahumara varieties. I wish I had photographed those gorgeous, crusty ollas to share here, but unfortunately in those pre-smartphone days, I rarely traveled with a camera.

I have also learned a little bit about Cherokee fermentation from my friend Tyson Sampson, who is Cherokee, from land in western North Carolina. Tyson taught me the Cherokee name for the mortar his grandmother used to grind corn, *kinona*. He told me about different kinds of corn bread she made, some with a small amount of wood ash mixed right into the dough. Tyson learned the Cherokee language from his grandmother and is very involved in carrying on the harvesting of traditional wild plants. He has also brought me buckets full of ramps (*Allium tricoccum*, aka wild leeks) at harvest time in the spring, most of which I fermented—yum!

Other than that, I am quite frankly embarrassed by how little I have learned about indigenous fermentations in North America. I recognize that there are lots of reasons the people who are carrying on their peoples' traditional practices might prefer not to share them with someone like me. Fermentation traditions do not exist in a vacuum; they are manifestations of relationships with the land, with plants, with spirit, and with ancestral tradition. Without a commitment to returning stolen lands and respecting Indigenous people and cultures, outside interest in ancestral practices can be superficial and predatory.

But ancestral practices can also be reclaimed, renewed, supported, and celebrated. I had the great pleasure of attending a dinner organized by Chef Sean Sherman of the Oglala Lakota Sioux tribe, and the organization he started, the Indigenous Food Lab. The meal was a collaborative effort, with each course prepared by an Indigenous chef from a different region of North America. Every course was beautiful and delectable, featuring indigenous ingredients, including corn, acorns, wild rice, trout, and venison. It is ironic that this dinner took place in Torino (Turin), Italy, at Terra Madre, the international Slow Food event; that I traveled to Europe for an experience like this, a celebration of North America's diverse indigenous food heritage.

Indigenous fermentation processes are sometimes portrayed as crude or backward (see "*Kiviaq* and other Greenland Fermentation Traditions" on page 292), and

The team of Indigenous chefs from around North America who collaborated on the Indigenous Food Lab meal: Sean Sherman, Shilo Maples, Vincent Medina, Louis Trevino, Maizie White, Mackee Bancroft, and Brian Yazzie.

sometimes they are invisiblized altogether. In the early years of my interest in fermentation, when I was looking to see if I could find any examples of culinary traditions without fermentation, I was repeatedly told that the Indigenous peoples of Australia had never developed any fermentation processes. Then, when I went there, on a native-foods walk in Queensland (they call that a "bush tucker" in Australia), our guide, a local Aboriginal elder, showed us a tree that produces a nut that is not safe to eat until after it is soaked in water for a few days. Well, one thing that happens when you soak a dry food, such as a nut, in water, is that it awakens microorganisms that were dormant, but that once hydrated can begin to access and digest nutrients in the nut. Sometimes one organism's toxin is another's nutrient, and in the case of this nut, as for a wide range of other botanicals, fermentation breaks down a potentially toxic compound into harmless or even nutritious or beneficial by-products. Since then, I have learned about several traditional fermented alcoholic beverages made with plants that are found in different parts of Australia.

The persistent myth that the Indigenous peoples of Australia had no fermentation traditions is based less on ignorance than on ideology, and a need to dehumanize the people that the colonial settlers killed, displaced, and separated from their families, and delegitimize their cultures. "It's that old tale of the Indigenous population being nomadic, not being able to farm, harvest crops, dam rivers or govern themselves, let alone ferment," reflects Australian writer Jane Ryan. "We now know all this was just propaganda that we (shamefully) swallowed."[9]

Many organizations in Australia and Canada, and increasingly in the United States, have developed a culture of explicitly acknowledging the traditional peoples of the land where any event is held, which is not always straightforward. Outside of the capitalist land ownership paradigm, many lands were not inhabited or controlled by a single group. In *Wild Fermentation*, I wrote that the land where I live was Cherokee land. Friends who later did more in-depth research learned that the story (like most) was actually more complicated than that: "This land was the common hunting grounds of many tribes, including Creeks, Cherokees, Choctaws, Chickasaws, Seminoles, Iroquois, Shawnees, and Euchees,"[10] writes my friend Lynne Purvis and her collaborators in their self-published booklet, *Way Before Daffodil Meadow*. Land acknowledgment is an important gesture, but it can hardly compensate for the stolen lands and the continued marginalization of Indigenous people in our societies, and their cultural practices.

And yet, if we are to find ways to live in greater harmony with our environments, and shrink our ecological footprints, we need the wisdom of Indigenous traditions. As Robin Wall Kimmerer of the Citizen Potawatomi Nation writes in her wonderful book, *Braiding Sweetgrass*, "For all of us, becoming indigenous to a place means living as if your children's future mattered, to take care of the land as if our lives, both material and spiritual, depended on it."[11] Embracing Indigenous values means respecting Indigenous people and their traditions. Much wisdom has been lost, but much remains to be learned, celebrated, and practiced.

FOUR

MOLD CULTURES

This chapter is somewhat a continuation of the last, in that it mostly involves fermentation of grains and starchy tubers. However, whereas the previous chapter focuses on simple, spontaneous fermentation processes, this chapter turns to ferments that involve growing filamentous fungi, more commonly known as molds. There is some inevitable overlap. In chapter 3, I include a recipe for Chinese alcohol made by fermenting sticky rice, which calls for Chinese yeast balls as a starter (*Nuo Mijiu*, page 114). Chinese yeast balls are similar to koji and related fungal cultures explored in this chapter. And here, I explore many different uses of sake lees, which do not involve growing a fungus, but are the by-product of a rice alcohol made using a fungus. Categories are imperfect organizing tools, always overlapping.

Many people are intimidated by the growing requirements of the molds used in these fermentation processes. They thrive in a moderately warm (80–90°F/27–32°C) and humid environment, requiring some air circulation and periodic monitoring. If the substrate gets too wet, the fungus will grow very quickly and generate a lot of heat, as well as invite the development of unwanted bacteria; if it gets too dry, the fungus will not grow; and if it gets too hot, the fungus will die and bacteria will rapidly succeed it. These fungi can grow at slightly cooler temperatures but do so much more slowly.

Start with small batches, improvise, and learn as you experiment. I have used a variety of methods to create these conditions. When I first started growing molds, I did so in an oven with the pilot light on and the door slightly ajar. For years now, I've used an old, nonfunctional refrigerator as an insulated chamber, with a greenhouse temperature sensor and controller into which I plug a simple light fixture with an incandescent lightbulb as the heat source. I've used a heating pad buffered by towels; a dehydrator; and a big plastic storage bin with a hotel pan floating in several inches of water, heated by a tropical fish aquarium heater. I've also grown these molds without incubation in hot, humid summer weather. Do not be intimidated! Once you learn the ideal growing conditions, you can create them with a little ingenuity.

Koji and Related Fungi

The single biggest factor that distinguishes the ferments of Asia from the ferments typically found in the rest of the world is the widespread use of molds, grown primarily on grains and legumes. These molded grains and beans have a rich array of digestive enzymes capable of breaking down a wide range of nutrients, including carbohydrates, proteins, fats, and more. This is why koji (the Japanese name for grains and beans grown with molds of *Aspergillus oryzae* and a few other related strains) and its many cousins, across Asia and beyond, are key ingredients in many fermented foods and beverages, only a few of which we explore here. Koji-derived foods include soy sauce, miso, and a huge variety of related rich, umami seasonings, with quite infinite possibility.

The most widespread use of koji and its relations is in the production of alcohol. Whereas diluted honey, fruit juice, and plant saps contain abundant simple sugars that are readily accessible for yeasts to metabolize into alcohol, grains and starchy tubers are composed of complex carbohydrates, whose long chains must be broken down into simple sugars by one of various enzymatic processes before yeasts can access them. In the Western tradition of beer brewing, this is accomplished by means of malting, which is germination. The germination of the grain activates enzymes that break down the complex carbohydrates into simple sugars. Another way this has been accomplished since ancient times, in many different locales, is through the use of digestive enzymes present in our saliva. Cooked grains and starchy tubers are chewed in order to saturate them with salivary enzymes, and then they are spit out for further processing. The third approach to saccharifying grain carbohydrates, prevalent across contemporary Asia, is to use enzyme-rich filamentous fungi. Koji is becoming known and increasingly widely used around the world.

Barley koji sporulating.

Koji Tradition and Innovation

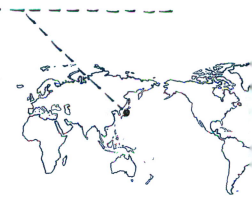

In Japan, I visited a number of sake and miso producers who make koji all the time. Two sake breweries stand out: Terada Honke in Chiba prefecture, where they are making koji and sake in very traditional ways, and Daimon, a sake brewery outside of Kyoto, where I got to witness fully automated robotic koji production.

To me, these two contrasting approaches encapsulate the strong countervailing forces of tradition and innovation in Japan. On the one hand, Japanese culture emphasizes respect for tradition, and specific traditions in the production of foods and beverages are expected to be honored. Yet simultaneously, Japan has been extremely receptive to technological innovation. While most of Asia relies on traditional methods for producing its koji equivalents (as we shall discuss), Japan embraced advances in microbiology as they emerged, and started using pure-culture starters very early.

When Chef Shinobu Namae brought me to visit Terada Honke, Masaru Terada introduced himself as the 24th-generation brewer at the brewery. Rather than buying laboratory-produced pure-strain starters to make his koji, as most contemporary brewers do, he collects spores from the air (not just anywhere, but in the brewery where they have been making sake for 350 years) in the heat of summer, using a special substrate. To favor *Aspergillus oryzae* rather than any of its potentially toxic relations or some other mold, he adds to the cooked rice substrate a very small proportion (less than 0.1 percent) of wood ash from the *tsubaki* tree. The rice, slightly alkalinized by the ash, draws spores from the air, and the koji fungus develops. Rather than harvest the koji after two days, when the grains of rice are covered with chalky white mycelium growth, as he would for making sake, Masaru leaves it for two to three weeks so it will fully sporulate, covering the grains with a yellowish-green growth. The brightly colored spores will be the starter for

Terada Honke
koji-kin in dispenser.

the brewery's koji in the upcoming year. For each batch of koji, rice is steamed in huge wooden steamers, removed, cooled, moved to the koji room, inoculated, and mixed by hand. Throughout the 48-hour process, the rice's temperature is monitored, and it is periodically mixed by hand to release heat that builds in the center.

At Daimon brewery, in stark contrast, koji making is done by a sophisticated machine. Electronic sensors monitor the temperature and humidity of the rice, as well as oxygen and carbon dioxide levels. As heat builds from fungal growth, robotic arms redistribute the rice in order to release heat from the center. Much less human effort is required for the process, and this high-tech approach, too, produces excellent koji.

Steaming rice in a huge
wooden steamer at
Terada Honke.

Mixing koji-kin into rice by hand
at Terada Honke brewery.

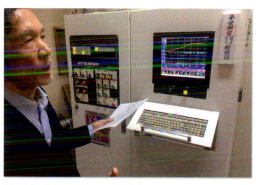

Yasutaka Daimon shows me his
brewery's robotic koji maker.

Chef Shinobu Namae (*left*) and
Terada Honke head brewer
Masaru Terada in the brewery.

Traditional wooden koji trays
inside Daimon brewery's robotic
koji-making machine.

HOW TO MAKE KOJI

This is the basic procedure I use for making koji. The process that I am describing here is specifically for rice or barley. Different varieties of rice or barley can vary in terms of cooking time and moisture content. I typically use short- or medium-grain Japanese white rice or pearled barley. Barley tends to hold more moisture than rice, therefore barley koji grows more quickly and generates more heat. For more about growing koji on other types of substrates, see "Koji on Other Substrates" on page 146.

TIMEFRAME

36 to 48 hours

EQUIPMENT

Steamer or pressure cooker

Incubator to maintain temperature in the range of 80–90°F/27–32°C. Improvise with ideas described in the chapter introduction on page 139.

Wooden tray, or hotel pan or other pan with sides, lined with clean, lint-free cotton cloth big enough to fold over and cover the top of the koji

Spray bottle for misting in case substrate seems dry

INGREDIENTS

for about 3 pounds/ 1.5 kilograms koji

4 cups (2 pounds/1 kilogram) uncooked rice or barley ✴

½ teaspoon or recommended proportion of koji starter

PROCESS

Rinse the rice or barley a few times to remove surface starch. Place the grains in a bowl and cover with plenty of water, then swirl it for a moment; drain, and repeat until the water runs clear. (You can save and use the rice-rinsing water. See "Fermented Rice Starch Water" on page 113.)

Soak the rice or barley for at least 8 hours in twice their volume of water.

Drain the grains well.

Steam the rice or barley, held above the water not in it, as it cooks. I use a bamboo steamer for this, lined with cotton cloth. The bamboo steamer fits tightly over a pot, which I fill with about twice as much water by volume as rice. If the steamer is above a wok, be sure to check the water level as it boils and add additional hot water as necessary. Once you can see steam rising through the grains, cover and steam for an hour or longer until the grains are fully cooked, soft, and supple but still holding the shape of each grain. Or you can steam the grain in a pressure cooker for about a half hour after it reaches pressure.

✴ Typically, white rice is used, or pearled barley. Whole grains can be used, but should generally be lightly milled to scratch up the outer surfaces so the fungus can easily penetrate the grain; alternatively, they can be pressure steamed.

While the grain is steaming, prepare the incubation chamber where the developing koji can be kept between 80 and 90°F/27 and 32°C.

Allow the rice or barley to cool to body temperature. You can speed this by transferring the steamed grain from the steamer into a large bowl, to break it up and release heat.

Add the starter after the grain cools to body temperature. Different formulations of koji starter may have different proportions of spores relative to the rice or other substrates. Follow the suggested guideline for the specific starter you are using.

Stir the starter into the grain. Take care to stir from the bottom and edges in order to distribute starter thoroughly. Stir for a few minutes.

Transfer the inoculated grain to the lined tray, arranging it as a mound in the center. Put a thermometer into the center of the mound and fold the sheet over the mound and around the thermometer, so you have a fabric-wrapped mound with a thermometer sticking out.

Place the tray with the mound into the incubator, and maintain the temperature in the range of 80–90°F/27–32°C.

Check the incubating koji after 12 to 16 hours. Break up the mound, stir the grain around, form a new mound, cover it, and return it to the incubator. If at this stage, or any time moving forward, the grain feels dry, mist it with a few sprays of water and mix the water evenly into the grain.

By 24 hours, the koji should be growing. The temperature will rise as the fungus generates heat. The koji will develop a sweet fragrance, appear to be dusted with a chalky white mold growth, and start to clump together. Once these developments have occurred, your objective switches from keeping it warm enough to preventing it from overheating. Spread the mound out into an even layer between 1 and 2 inches/ 2 and 5 centimeters thick. If the koji mat is too thick, heat can accumulate in the center and kill the mold. If the pan holding your koji is too small, divide it into two baking pans. Improvise as necessary. To further modulate temperature, run your fingers over the koji like a rake and leave it with furrows, which increase surface area for releasing heat. Cover the koji with a cloth and return to the incubator.

Keep checking the koji every few hours. Stick your (clean!) hands right into it, find clumps and break them up, spread out grain from hot spots, relevel, re-furrow, rewrap, and return to the incubator. Enjoy the seductive aroma of the developing koji as you work with it. As koji develops, the white mold growth will increase and cover each grain. You can use your koji once grains appear to be covered with mold growth; definitely stop incubating the koji if you begin to notice yellow-green patches on the surface, indicating that sporulation has begun.

You can use koji fresh and warm, or spread it out in a thin layer to cool to room temperature then wrap and refrigerate for up to a few weeks. For longer storage, dry koji briefly in the sun or a dehydrator, then refrigerate or keep it dry and cool for a few months or longer, though enzymatic potency will diminish over time.

Koji on Other Substrates

The koji fungus is very adaptable to other grains, soybeans, beans and seeds, starchy tubers, and more. Moisture content is key, so with substrates that hold a lot of moisture (soybeans, other beans and seeds, starchy tubers, and the like), moisture levels must be carefully managed. Roasted flour or cracked grains (any kind) are often used to dry out the surfaces and promote healthy mold growth. Alternatively, in the case of substrates that are too dry, a spray bottle for light misting can provide enough moisture to get the fungus growing. Roasted flour can also boost the carbohydrate content of high-protein substrates, from soybeans and fava beans to pork chops. "Koji essentially just wants starch and some protein," write Rich Shih and Jeremy Umansky in their book, *Koji Alchemy*.[1]

I learned how to grow koji from William Shurtleff and Akiko Aoyagi's *The Book of Miso*, informed by their time in Japan. Only slowly did I branch out beyond rice and barley. First, I grew koji on soybeans to make soy sauce and fermented black beans. Later, I grew koji on chestnuts and nixtamalized corn. To make *doubanjiang* (Making *Doubanjiang* I: Growing Fungus on Favas and Wheat, page 170), I grew koji on fava beans.

If you want to dive deeper into growing koji on a vast array of substrates, or if you're interested in using streamlined, restaurant-friendly methods, I strongly recommend *Koji Alchemy*. Jeremy and Rich have developed techniques to grow koji on almost anything, breaking a lot of traditional rules in the process. Inspired by their book, I have tried unlikely koji applications such as growing it on carrots and beets, and adding it to ricotta cheese (Ricotta "Miso," page 272). Each new application has resulted in an explosion of different flavors.

It is a special pleasure when a onetime student becomes my teacher and proceeds to deepen my understanding of a process to which I first introduced them. When I met Jeremy, he was a very enthusiastic student at a workshop I taught at the Culinary Institute of America. In subsequent years I took great pleasure in witnessing his bold experimentation with koji via social

Koji growing
on beetroots.

media. When he teamed up with Rich, who had blown my mind at a fermentation event with his popcorn koji, and they told me they were coauthoring a book on koji, I was thrilled. Their book helped me realize that koji can be grown on almost anything, and that it does not necessarily require all the particulars of the traditional Japanese methods that I learned and have typically used. Other books in English with great koji sections include Kirsten and Christopher Shockey's *Miso, Tempeh, Natto & Other Tasty Ferments*, and René Redzepi and David Zilber's *The Noma Guide to Fermentation*. All the authors concur on this: experiment and improvise.

SAKE BY THE BODAIMOTO METHOD

Sake is the wonderful Japanese alcohol made from rice that has become widely known and available around the world. The day that I visited the Terada Honke sake brewery (see "Koji Tradition and Innovation" on page 141), the head brewer, Masaru Terada, came to understand my interest in simple, streamlined, accessible processes as he answered my many questions about his methods. I had made a few batches of sake while writing *The Art of Fermentation*, and I had made it in the typical contemporary manner, which I found technically demanding. Most difficult, without thermostatic heating or cooling, was maintaining a constant temperature about 60°F/16°C. Also, the schedule of multiple additions of koji and rice turned out to be very challenging.

Masaru Terada sharing tastes of the different styles of sake his Terada Honke brewery makes. I loved them all, especially a fresh bubbly one and a dark one that had been aged 14 years—so smooth, rich, and caramelly.

Masaru told me about an ancient sake method, *bodaimoto*, that sounded deceptively simple. I had just seen his brewery's method for creating a *moto*—the rice-based active yeast and lactic acid bacteria starter to which the koji and fresh rice is added to produce sake. His typical process takes about two months; the first few days involve mixing the moto (and singing to it) three times a day for 15 minutes, and there is daily mixing and warming after that. The bodaimoto method he described to me, by contrast, takes just a few days.

What's distinctive about this faster method is that the starter is derived from a rice and water mix in which only half of the rice is cooked, while the other half is left raw. The raw rice serves as the primary source of yeast and lactic acid bacteria, while the cooked rice serves as the primary source of nutrients to feed these until-now dormant organisms. Once the water is bubbly with yeast and bacterial activity, the raw rice is removed and drained (easiest if in a mesh bag), then cooked. Once cooled, this rice is combined with an equal amount of koji rice. This rice blend is then mixed into the bubbly water with the original cooked rice. After a week to 10 days of fermentation, the liquid is strained and the remaining solids are pressed: easy, do-it-yourself sake.

TIMEFRAME

About 2 weeks

EQUIPMENT

2 small mesh or cloth bags fine enough to hold rice

Wide-mouth vessel with a capacity of at least 6 quarts/ 6 liters

INGREDIENTS

for about 3 quarts/3 liters of sake

2 pounds/1 kilogram uncooked rice (typically but not necessarily white rice)

1 pound/500 grams rice koji

PROCESS

Cook half of the rice (1 pound/500 grams) however you typically would. I measure the rice, then add water at a ratio of 1.25 times the volume of the rice for white rice (1.5 times the volume for brown rice). I use a pot with a tight-fitting lid, bring it a boil, then gently simmer for about 20 minutes for white rice (40 minutes for brown rice). Then I remove the rice from the heat and leave the pot lidded for five or ten minutes before opening.

Fill one mesh bag with the uncooked portion of the rice. Fill the other with the cooked rice, once it is cool enough to handle.

Fill the vessel with 2 quarts/2 liters dechlorinated water.

Add the two mesh bags of rice to the water.

Gently massage the bag of cooked rice a little to help break some of it down into the water and make nutrients easily accessible to yeast and bacteria. Continue to gently massage the bag of cooked rice for a few minutes each day.

It's time for the next step when the water is bubbly and starts to taste a little sour. Depending on the temperature of the environment, this might range between 2 and 5 days.

Remove the bags of rice from the water, retaining the liquid that drains from them in the fermentation vessel.

Remove the soaked raw rice from its bag, then cook (as described in the first step) and cool until still warm but comfortable to the touch.

Mix the warm rice with the rice koji, as well as the original cooked rice (removed from its bag), combining them thoroughly.

Return the rice to the water in the vessel.

Ferment 10 days to 2 weeks, stirring daily and tasting periodically. At first, the rice will absorb nearly all the water and swell. Then it will slowly liquefy, but vigorous bubbles will cause the solids to float above the liquid. As the bubbling slows, solids will sink. When it tastes strongly alcoholic and not so sweet, and bubbling has receded, the sake is ready.

Strain the sake through a mesh bag or cloth-lined colander to remove solid residue. Press the residue to remove as much liquid as you can—the remaining solids are known as sake lees, or kasu. (See the following sections for ideas for using this flavorful by-product.)

The sake will be cloudy at first, and is delicious this way. If you leave it still, the starch will sink to the bottom, and you can gently pour clear sake from above it.

Enjoy!

KOSHU SAKE

Masaru Terada, the brewer at Terada Honke brewery, gave me my first taste of *koshu* (aged) sake. It was so dramatically different from all the other sake I had tried, with a dark color and earthier, even umami flavor. I had the opportunity to try more koshu sake when Melissa Mills, an Australian sake educator, brought a few different bottles to one of my workshops, which ranged in age from 4 to 44 years. The 44-year-old bottle, from Kidoizumi Sake Brewing, was quite amazing. Melissa's tasting notes captured it well: "Raisin, tobacco, shoyu with intense burnt caramel notes and some Christmas spice. Beautifully integrated and smooth." Time changes everything, even sake.

The collection of aged sakes that Melissa Mills shared with us. *From left to right*: Kidoizumi Afruge Ma Cherie 2016 Junmai Koshu; Waketakeya Genrokushu Junmai Koshu blend of 2005 and 2010; Mukai Natsu No Omoide 2000; and Kidoizumi New AFS 1976 Junmai Koshu.

Kasu

Known as kasu in Japanese, and as sake lees in English (after the name given to the residue of winemaking), this solid residue from fermenting rice alcohol is an inevitable by-product of the process and it has considerable flavor, enzymes, and nutritional value. Evidently, most of the kasu produced in Japan goes into skin care products; indeed, ferments are increasingly being used in skin care products as those products are reconceptualized as food for the skin. Fermentation makes nutrients more bio-available, whether they are taken orally or transdermally. However, kasu also has many varied culinary applications.

After we toured the Terada Honke brewery, Masaru's wife, Satomi, prepared an elaborate, beautiful meal featuring many different kasu dishes. There were vegetables prepared au gratin, with a creamy topping that included kasu and tasted cheesy, though there was no cheese in it; a warm, kasu-based *bagna càuda*–like dip for vegetables; little cubes of steamed tofu sprinkled with kasu; white bread baked with kasu; and kasuzuke, which are vegetables pickled in kasu. Satomi's creative use of the sake lees illustrated vividly for me just how versatile this by-product is. Satomi graciously shared the recipes for her kasu dishes, two of which I have adapted here.

The gorgeous lunch that Satomi Terada prepared for us at Terada Honke sake brewery, many of the dishes featuring sake lees, which are a by-product of the sake-making process.

SATOMI TERADA'S SAKE LEES GRATIN

This is a delicious vegan version of the typically cheese-based dish. Satomi made it with kabocha squash and cauliflower, which were perfect, but you can make this flavorful gratin with any vegetables you like.

TIMEFRAME

30-45 minutes

EQUIPMENT

Food processor (optional)

INGREDIENTS

for 4 to 6 servings as a side dish

6 ounces/100 grams sake lees

½ cup/100 grams rice flour

4 tablespoons + 2 teaspoons vegetable oil, divided

About a tablespoon salt

1 cup/100 grams onion, finely sliced

2 ounces/60 grams mushrooms, finely sliced

1 cup/250 milliliters soy milk

Dash of pepper

½ pound/250 grams lightly cooked mixed vegetables ✳

3 tablespoons/15 grams panko or other breadcrumbs

1 teaspoon finely chopped fresh parsley

PROCESS

Preheat oven to 350°F/175°C.

Combine the sake lees, rice flour, 3 tablespoons of the vegetable oil, and 1 teaspoon of the salt in a food processor and run until the mixture is crumbly, or stir the ingredients together by hand, if you prefer. (If your sake lees are hand-pressed, and therefore have a higher water content than machine-pressed lees, they may produce more of a paste than a crumble; that's okay.)

In a medium pot, heat a tablespoon of the oil over medium heat. Sauté the onions until soft, then add the mushrooms and stir to coat with oil.

Turn the heat to low, add the sake lees mixture, and stir to combine. Cook the mixture for 5 minutes.

Slowly add ½ cup/125 milliliters water. Bring the mixture to a boil, then gently simmer until it thickens to a creamy consistency. Stir in the soy milk and season with salt and pepper, to taste.

Arrange the vegetables in a baking dish. Pour the hot, creamy mixture over the vegetables.

Combine the breadcrumbs, 2 teaspoons of the oil, and parsley, and sprinkle on top.

Bake for 10 to 15 minutes, cool for a few minutes, then serve.

✳ such as cauliflower florets, kabocha or other squash, turnips, and/or potatoes, cut into large pieces and steamed or parboiled until just soft enough to eat

SATOMI TERADA'S SAKE LEES BAGNA CÀUDA

Bagna càuda, which translates as "hot bath," is a hot dip from Piedmont, Italy, typically made from garlic and anchovies. Satomi's tasty version is vegan, replacing the anchovies with sake lees and mushrooms.

TIMEFRAME

About 15 minutes

EQUIPMENT

Food processor (optional)

INGREDIENTS

for about 1 cup/250 milliliters

4½ tablespoons/70 grams sake lees, divided into a 2½-tablespoon/40-grams portion and a 2-tablespoon/30-grams portion

6 cloves garlic, minced

2 teaspoons salt, divided

3 tablespoons vegetable oil, divided

3.5 ounces/100 grams maitake or other mushrooms, sliced

3 tablespoons olive oil

PROCESS

In a small pot, combine 2½ tablespoons/40 grams sake lees, garlic, 1 teaspoon of the salt, and ½ cup/125 milliliters water. Stir over medium heat for 5–10 minutes, until the mixture thickens. Remove from the heat once a wooden spatula drawn through the mixture reveals the pot's bottom.

Heat 2 tablespoons of the vegetable oil in a frying pan and stir-fry the remaining 2 tablespoons/30 grams sake lees over medium heat. When the lees start to brown slightly, add the mushrooms. Add 1 teaspoon of salt and reduce heat to low. Fry over low heat until the entire mixture becomes fragrant.

In a food processor or using a whisk, combine 3 tablespoons of olive oil, another tablespoon of vegetable oil, and the two different cooked sake lees mixtures. Mix until a paste forms.

Transfer the paste into a bowl and use as a dip for seasonal vegetables.

SAKE LEES CRACKERS

Crackers are a delicious and easy way to
enjoy sake lees.

TIMEFRAME

30-45 minutes

EQUIPMENT

Rolling pin

Cookie sheet

INGREDIENTS

for about 20 crackers

½ cup/120 grams sake lees

2 to 3 tablespoons olive or
other oil

½ teaspoon salt

Other seasonings such as
garlic, parsley, caraway, cumin,
or anything, as desired

About ½ cup/85 grams cooked
rice, oatmeal, millet, or other
grains (optional)

½ cup/70 grams sesame or
other small seeds (optional)

½ cup/80 grams sauerkraut,
onion, and/or other vegetables,
finely minced

1 to 2 cups/150–300 grams flour,
whole wheat and/or others

PROCESS

Preheat oven to 350°F/175°C.

Mix the sake lees with the oil, salt, and other seasonings, if using.
Add about ½ cup each of leftover cooked grains, if you have some,
and seeds, if you like. Add the sauerkraut, onion, and/or other vegetables. If the mixture feels very dry, then add a few tablespoons of
sauerkraut juice or water.

Add the flour, a little at a time, until it forms a ball of dough that is
easy to handle.

Divide the dough into two balls.

On a floured surface, roll each of the balls into a thin (less than
¼ inch/7 millimeters) layer.

Cut into complementary geometric shapes and use a spatula, knife,
or other support to transfer to an oiled cookie sheet.

Use a fork to poke little holes in each cracker. This helps make
them crisp.

Bake 15 to 20 minutes, until the crackers are dry and toasted but
not burned.

Cool on a rack.

Enjoy fresh or store for a few days.

MORE IDEAS FOR USING SAKE LEES

There is no end to the ways that sake lees—so rich in flavor, nutrients, enzymes, and organisms—can be used in the kitchen. Here are a few more examples of how I have used them myself or have seen them used:

- As a flavorful pickling medium for kasuzuke (see "*Kasuzuke*" on page 80).
- In kimchi, as an element of the spice mix.
- As an element in breads, cookies, cakes, and pancakes. Sake lees add leavening power and flavor.
- Scrambled with eggs. Yum!
- In marinades and dressings. The enzymes in sake lees can bring out flavors in almost anything.
- As a flavoring, sweetener, and thickener in soups and stews.

SHIO-KOJI

Misa Ono with shio-koji eggs and tofu that she shared with me.

Shio-koji, or salt koji, is a mixture of koji, salt, and water, fermented into a starchy liquid used as a marinade and seasoning. It has become increasingly well known internationally, thanks to publications such as *The Noma Guide to Fermentation* and *Koji Alchemy* and other works outside of Japan. My first exposure to it was in Japan, when I met Misa Ono, a Japanese shio-koji enthusiast who has written eight books on it and related topics! Shio-koji is an ingredient I have come to use constantly in my kitchen. It is best in marinades, where koji's enzymes have time to work their

transformative magic, breaking macronutrients down into an array of smaller, more flavorful molecules. But shio-koji is also a seasoning that can build flavor in stir-fries, salad dressings, sauces, soups, and beyond. Misa introduced me to shio-koji via her delicious shio-koji–cured eggs and tofu. The tofu reminded me of feta cheese.

As I have met more people working with shio-koji, I have seen how varied it can be, both in terms of substrate—since koji can be made from anything carbohydrate-rich—and in terms of texture and proportions. I usually blend my shio-koji in a blender following the initial fermentation, to make a smoothy, starchy liquid. I also make my shio-koji with about half as much salt as Misa does, and I have met other people who use half as much again. Due to the lower salt content, I store it in the refrigerator after the initial room temperature fermentation. As with so many ferments, you have wide latitude. My all-time favorite shio-koji is made with chestnut koji. Experiment with whatever carbohydrate sources are abundant or significant to you.

Here is Misa's recipe for shio-koji, shio-koji–cured egg and tofu, and a couple of her other shio-koji ideas.

Misa Ono's illustrated "How to make shio-koji."

SHIO-KOJI

TIMEFRAME

1 to 2 weeks

VESSEL

Jar or other vessel with a capacity of 1 quart/1 liter, with lid

INGREDIENTS
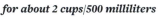

for about 2 cups/500 milliliters

1½ cups/200 grams koji

¼ cup/60 grams salt

PROCESS

Break up the koji by hand if it is lumpy, put it in a bowl, and mix with the salt.

Place the salted koji in a jar or other vessel. Cover with 1 cup/250 milliliters of dechlorinated water. Mix lightly, and loosely cover with a lid.

Ferment at room temperature, mixing once a day, for 1 to 2 weeks (shorter in summer, longer in winter).

When it smells good and the rice is soft, it is ready.

Store at room temperature; refrigerate in summer heat.

Mix occasionally when it separates.

SHIO-KOJI-CURED EGGS

Peel the boiled eggs, then coat each egg with about ½ tablespoon of shio-koji. Seal in a zip-locked bag and place in the refrigerator for a week.

SHIO-KOJI TOFU

Cut a block of tofu in half and drain under a heavy weight. Coat the drained tofu with about 2 tablespoons of shio-koji and wrap in plastic wrap. Place in the refrigerator for a week.

MARINATE MEAT OR FISH WITH SHIO-KOJI

Spread shio-koji over the surfaces of the meat or fish (roughly 10 percent of the weight of the meat or fish) and wrap in plastic wrap. Place in the refrigerator for 1 to 3 days. Grill or sauté, taking care not to burn.

PICKLED VEGETABLES WITH SHIO-KOJI

Finely chop vegetables, then mix with shio-koji (about 10 percent of the vegetables' weight). Seal in a zip-locked bag and store in the refrigerator. Enjoy pickles after a week, or age longer.

MIRIN

Mirin is a sweet, syrupy form of rice alcohol that I love to use in cooking. It is made from koji and rice fermented for a year or longer with liquor. It gets super sweet, as the koji enzymes break down rice carbohydrates into sugars, but the high alcohol content of the liquor prevents the sugars from fermenting. When I stir-fry, I add mirin and soy sauce at the very end and cover for a brief, fragrant steaming. I also use it to lightly sweeten sauces. I've been using mirin for decades, having learned about it during my study of macrobiotics in the late 1980s. But only when I was in Japan did I learn—from Hiromi Yamagami, who teaches classes on traditional Japanese foods (including ferments) in Kyoto at Kitchen-Minori—how simple and straightforward it is to make.

TIMEFRAME

1 year or longer

EQUIPMENT

Cloth-lined steamer

Wide-mouth vessel of 2-quart/2-liter capacity

Bottles with lids for storing

INGREDIENTS

for about 1½ quarts/1½ liters

1 pound/500 grams uncooked sticky rice ✳

1 pound/500 grams rice koji

1 quart/1 liter shochu †
or other neutral grain alcohol under 100-proof

PROCESS

Rinse the rice and soak it overnight in twice its volume of water.

Drain the rice well.

Steam the rice for about 30 minutes, until it is soft and sticky. Use a cloth-lined steamer, and steam the rice above the water, not in it.

Cool the rice until it is comfortable to touch.

Mix well with the koji.

Transfer the rice and koji mixture to the fermentation vessel.

Pour the shochu over the mixture.

Press so the solids are fully submerged.

Cover to protect from flies and dust.

Stir every few weeks.

✳ also called sweet rice or glutinous rice

† Japanese distilled alcohol

MIRIN CONTINUED

Ferment for a year, or longer. It should be very sweet and syrupy when finished.

Strain the mixture through a fine mesh bag into a measuring cup or mixing bowl. Press the bag with the solids to remove as much liquid as possible. (Solids can be used like kasu. See "*Kasu*" on page 151.)

Let the strained mirin sit for a few hours so the milky starch settles at the bottom. Gently pour the clarified mirin off the starch into bottles.

Mirin is shelf-stable and does not require refrigeration.

Vegetable *Garum*

Garum is a classical Roman name for fermented fish sauce. Many chefs around the world have been using this term to describe mostly animal-protein based seasonings fermented with koji (see "Experimental Animal Garums" on page 163). Vegetable garum is similar, except that it uses plant substrates. The fermentation produces a dark, rich, salty, umami broth, something like soy sauce, but made from other plant-based materials, typically food scraps. You can make it from a random mix of whatever your kitchen happens to generate (including coffee grounds), or you can make it out of one or two scraps of which you have a lot; for instance, celery ends, onion ends, potato peels, apple cores, or tomato skins and seeds.

I was introduced to vegetable garum by Patrick Marxer in Switzerland. Based in Zurich, Patrick is a onetime laboratory technician who turned his attention to smoking and curing fish and meat, and he built a successful business doing just that. Influenced by his climate activist daughter, he has come to believe that our society cannot survive without moving away from our heavy dependence on meat and fish. And so he is engaged in a long-term process of developing new plant-based products that can gradually replace the meat and fish that he processes and sells. Among his plant-based products are vegetable garums. Zurich restaurants and food producers save vegetable scraps for Patrick to turn into unique house seasonings for them. Patrick generously shared details of his process with me at a workshop in Basel.

The koji can be made with anything. For our demo, Patrick had made beautiful koji from horse beans and buckwheat. He ran the vegetable scraps through a hand-cranked meat grinder. Patrick's generic proportions are 3 pounds/1.5 kilograms of veggie scraps to 2 pounds/1 kilogram koji. He then covers the mixture with an equal weight of water (2½ quarts/2½ liters), and adds salt at 4 percent of the total weight, including the water (7 ounces/200 grams). Patrick suggests that miso can be substituted for some of the koji, but that a lower amount of salt should be used, since miso is already so salty.

Patrick Marxer using a meat grinder to grind up a variety of vegetable scraps.

The hard part for me to follow was Patrick's guidance to incubate it at 140°F/60°C for a month, due to the constraints of my off-the-electrical-grid situation. The significance of this temperature is that it optimizes many of the enzymes in koji, thereby speeding the process. Traditional soy sauces and fish sauces are fermented for much longer periods, though at lower ambient temperatures. The lower temperature process allows for bacterial development, which I view as an enhancement but that Patrick views with concern. To compensate for lower temperature, increase the salt content 50 percent, from 4 percent to 6 percent. The lower temperature also allows for abundant mold growth at the surface. The best way to avoid this is to stir it daily, or to make it in some vessel that effectively protects it from oxygen.

All the vegetable scrap garum ingredients except water: veggie scraps (he included coffee grounds), koji, and salt.

With water added, ingredients are ready to ferment into veggie scrap garum.

EXPERIMENTAL ANIMAL GARUMS

I first saw the word *garum* used to describe fermented sauces from animals other than fish when I was invited into the kitchens at Noma, in Copenhagen, and its semiautonomous research and development arm, the Nordic Food Lab, located on a houseboat moored outside the restaurant. The lab was conducting experiments with an eye toward creations that could eventually become part of the Noma menu, but they functioned apart from the restaurant's day-to-day operations.

On the boat, lead researcher-chef Ben Reade showed us some of their experimental fermentation projects, among them several different garums made from an array of animal sources—including pheasant, rabbit, and grasshopper—and enhanced by the enzymatic power of koji. Each one had its own funky essence. Some years later, in *The Noma Guide to Fermentation*, René Redzepi and David Zilber reflected on their use in the restaurant's menu: "They don't play a starring role, but they're there under the surface, imbuing dishes with an intangible magic, focusing and enlivening natural flavors. . . . In a way, garums have allowed us to reverse the role of animals and vegetables at Noma, so meat becomes the seasoning and vegetables are the stars."[2]

A few years later, at a class in Margaret River in Western Australia, one of my co-presenters, chef Paul Iskov (a onetime Noma chef), shared some of the garums he had fermented from different Australian land and sea creatures, including crocodile, emu, eel, and stingray. They all were extremely delicious and dense with salty umami flavor, but each had its own very distinctive character.

For meat- and fish-based garums, *The Noma Guide to Fermentation* uses the ratio 1 kilogram of meat to 225 grams of koji (22.5 percent) in 800 milliliters of water. To this total weight of just over 2 kilograms, they add 240 grams salt (12 percent). This ratio assumes that you will elevate the temperature to 140°F/60°C. They add a note about making garums at room temperature: Increase salt proportion to 18 percent, and ferment at least 8 to 9 months.

In their book *Koji Alchemy*, Rich Shih and Jeremy Umansky coin the generic terms *amino sauces* and *amino pastes* to describe the infinity of possible substrates and products. "These more generalized styles can be

transformed into wildly amazing and captivating variations," they write. "The possibilities are limited only by your imagination."

Paul Iskov's garums fermented from different Australian animals and fish.

Miso Culture and Experimentation

Having learned how to make miso, the Japanese style of soybeans fermented into a paste with koji and salt, from a book (William Shurtleff and Akiko Aoyagi's *The Book of Miso*), and then having done so for decades before I ever went to Japan or saw how anyone from Japan made it, I felt humbled while learning certain nuances of miso making from Japanese people.

For instance, I learned that many miso producers make it much drier than I typically have, and that they often form the relatively dry, solid miso mix into balls. One person I've seen do this is Hiroshi Sugihara, whom I met at a workshop in Australia. Hiroshi moved to Australia from Japan with his family when he was a kid. He was familiar with all the Japanese ferments, but after he learned how to make sauerkraut, he became interested in studying Japanese fermentation, and he spent time in Japan learning how to make koji and miso. In his home kitchen in Fremantle, Western Australia, Hiroshi now hosts small miso-making workshops.

Hiroshi grinds his miso ingredients together using an old hand-powered meat grinder. Then he forms the mix into balls before packing it into the fermentation vessel. "I have two reasons for forming miso balls," Hiroshi explained to me. "The first is to squeeze the air out of the mixture before packing into the fermentation vessel. The second is to check the consistency of the mixture and if the miso ball crumbles easily, it indicates that it needs more moisture added." Hiroshi says he learned that the texture of the miso mixture should be the "same softness as your ear lobe."

Hiroshi Sugihara talking about making miso at a workshop in Margaret River, Western Australia.

In Canada, I met another Japanese transplant teaching classes on miso and other traditional foods—primarily to Japanese-Canadian youth—in an effort to transmit culture. Shiori Kajiwara came to Canada from Fukuoka 10 years ago with her family, and she lives in Toronto. She says she is "keen to embrace Japanese culture, and hand down this important and beautiful knowledge correctly to the next generation."

Miso can be a path to cultural roots, and it can also be a path to innovation and experimentation. I've experimented since my second batch, both with different legumes and different koji substrates. But it wasn't until after *The Art of Fermentation* was published that I saw miso made with a protein other than beans. I first saw nut misos at the Momofuku restaurant test kitchen, run at the time by Dan Felder. The *New York Times* culture writer Jeff Gordinier interviewed me over lunch at Momofuku, where we talked about the many ferments they served us. Afterward, we went around the corner to the test kitchen, which he had arranged for us to visit, as well. As Gordinier documented in his subsequent *New York Times* article: "There, in the Momofuku test kitchen, Mr. Felder gave Mr. Katz a glimpse of a brilliantly demented-fermented future: Erlenmeyer flasks full of new iterations of soy sauce, jars of vinegar conjured up from ingredients like strawberries and cherries, little mounds of paste that represented the next wave in miso. There were vials of explosively flavored tamari, a mere droplet of which might garnish an oyster."[3]

A pyramid of miso balls.

Experimental misos at the Momofuku test kitchen: mung bean, sesame, lentil, pine nut, and pistachio.

The pine nut and pistachio misos really rocked my world. It had never occurred to me to look beyond beans for miso. I was thrilled and excited by the ways they were using koji to cure lardo and meat. Though such ideas have become increasingly widespread, at the time I had never heard of such a thing. "Mr. Katz reacted to the lardo and everything else like a kid in a kimchi shop, even going into a brief reverie when a jar of Basmati koji was opened and his nasal passages got to bask in the fragrance. 'Oh, my God, what a beautiful aroma,' he said. 'It's a gorgeous mold. I am so in love with koji.'"[4] Since then, others have pushed the envelope even further, as more people experiment beyond beans, with misos from bacon, cheese, bread, and other unlikely substrates.

TAPÈ

Koji-like fungal starters are used across Asia. *Tapè* is an Indonesian dessert, fermented from rice or cassava, using *ragi tapè*, the Indonesian name for fungal starters. I was introduced to tapè in Bali, where I taught in 2012. Bali is a beautiful, friendly place, and I was lucky enough to be there during a season of temple festivals, and everywhere—on the streets, in front of and inside people's homes and businesses—were colorful decorative shrines.

You can make tapè from rice or cassava (or potentially other carbohydrate-rich substrates). Either way, it requires a fungal starter. You can find *ragi* on the internet, generally from Indonesia or Malaysia. You can also substitute Chinese yeast balls, which are widely available in Asian markets and on the internet, or koji.

Shrines in Bali.

Sprinkling powdered ragi starter on cassava and rice for tapè

TIMEFRAME

2 to 4 days

EQUIPMENT

Steamer

Banana leaves, plastic bag, or a crock or jar with a capacity about 1 quart/1 liter

INGREDIENTS

for 1 pound/500 grams

1 pound/500 grams uncooked sticky rice ✳ or cassava tuber

1 small cake or ball of ragi or Chinese yeast ball

PROCESS

If using sticky rice, rinse and then soak for about 12 hours. Drain the rice well, then steam it for about 30 minutes, until soft. Use a cloth-lined steamer, and steam above the water, not in it.

If using cassava, peel, cut into serving-size pieces, and steam for about 20 minutes, until soft.

Cool the rice or cassava until comfortable to touch.

Crush the ragi cake or Chinese yeast ball into a powdery crumble, and mix it with the steamed substrate.

The Indonesian method is to wrap tapè in a banana leaf. Do that if you can; otherwise, loosely pack the warm rice or cassava into a jar, crock, or plastic bag.

Cover the vessel loosely and ferment in a warm place for 2 to 4 days, until there is liquid in the vessel, and the smell is sweet.

Enjoy! The sweetened solid portions are the tapè. The liquid is called *brem*, and it is sweet and very lightly alcoholic after this short fermentation.

✳ also called sweet rice or glutinous rice

Doubanjiang

One ferment that I learned about for the first time in China, and use in my kitchen frequently, is doubanjiang, a Sichuanese seasoning fermented from fava beans and chilies. Doubanjiang's bright red color and bold, earthy, spicy flavor infuse into everything with which it is cooked. I use it mostly in stir-frying, adding it to the hot oil at the beginning, along with onions and garlic.

In Pixian, an hour's drive from Chengdu, we visited a factory where doubanjiang is made on an incredible scale. The main fermentation space was by far the largest greenhouse I have ever been in, and the doubanjiang was fermenting in row after row of huge built-in vats, each containing 10,000 kilograms (about 11 tons) of doubanjiang, mixed daily using massive augers. On the roof of another building were 100-liter ceramic vats fermenting higher-quality, "artisanal" doubanjiang, mixed by hand. (You can see a video from the factory in *People's Republic of Fermentation*, episode 3.)

The process of making doubanjiang has four distinct steps: (1) grow fungus on favas; (2) brine fungus-covered favas; (3) ferment salted chilies; then (4) mix everything together to ferment, exposing it to direct sunlight as often as possible to facilitate evaporation and thus concentrate flavor. The fermentation time can range from one year to many years. In Pixian, we tried 7-year-old doubanjiang. The aged doubanjiang was earthier and had more depth, while the younger ones were brighter red in color and had more heat from the chilies. In my home version, the longest I've aged it is about two years.

The quantities in the recipes that follow will produce about 1 quart/1 liter of doubanjiang.

Doubanjiang aged several years, *top*, next to a one-year-old batch, *bottom*.

The scale of the doubanjiang factory we visited was immense. A vast greenhouse structure contained huge vats, mixed daily with industrial augers.

Ode to doubanjiang: Theses figurines adorned our table at a restaurant in Pixian where doubanjiang is made.

MAKING DOUBANJIANG I: GROWING FUNGUS ON FAVAS AND WHEAT

Koji fungus growing on fava beans.

The first step in the process for making doubanjiang is growing the fungus. At the doubanjiang factory, although they were very welcoming and eager to show us their operation, the one space we were not invited to see is where they actually grow the fungus on the beans. I imagine they didn't bring us to the fungus-growing room because they wish to minimize the number of people carrying random, extraneous microorganisms into the space where they cultivate the fungus their process relies upon. We were led to understand that the room has been dedicated to this use for many years, and that for their large-batch factory production they use a starter, but for small-batch artisanal-quality production they do not. In my version, I use a koji starter. If your koji starter source offers a choice of types, choose the koji for soybeans. The process for making koji is explained in How to Make Koji, page 144, and at greater length in my book *The Art of Fermentation*. It requires a warm space, roughly 80–90°F/27–32°C.

Fava beans have a very heavy outer layer, which the koji fungus cannot penetrate. Therefore, you need to peel each bean after their brief cooking—doable, but slow—or else purchase peeled fava beans, which are widely available.

TIMEFRAME

3 days, including presoaking

EQUIPMENT

Heavy skillet

Incubator to maintain temperature in the range of 80° to 90°F/27° to 32°C. Improvise with ideas described in the chapter introduction on page 139.

Wooden tray, or hotel pan or other pan with sides, lined with clean lint-free cotton cloth big enough to fold over and cover the top of the inoculated fava beans

INGREDIENTS

for 1 quart/1 liter doubanjiang

1 pound/500 grams fava beans

¾ cup/100 grams whole wheat flour

¼ teaspoon koji starter, or as otherwise directed by the producer of the starter

PROCESS

Soak the fava beans in cold water for at least 8 hours.

Toast the whole wheat flour in a dry heavy skillet over moderate heat, stirring constantly to prevent burning, for about 10 minutes, until the flour gets warm and fragrant.

Flash-cook the soaked fava beans in boiling water for about 2 minutes.

Drain the favas in a colander. (If your favas are not pre-peeled, peel off the skins at this point.)

Mix the favas with the toasted flour.

Once the flour-coated favas cool to body temperature, add the koji starter and mix well to distribute it.

Lay the cloth over the tray and transfer the inoculated fava beans into the center in a mound. Cover them with the cloth and keep in a warm (80–90°F/27–32°C) and humid space. Mix beans around every 12 hours or so, and once they start to generate heat, spread beans out into a layer no thicker than 2 inches/5 centimeters. Incubate for about 48 hours, until beans are covered in a chalky white growth or beginning to develop yellow patches.

MAKING DOUBANJIANG II: BRINING FUNGUS-COVERED FAVAS

Molded fava beans fermenting in a brine solution.

Once the fava beans are covered with fungus, they will need to be fermented in a saltwater brine solution for a few months.

TIMEFRAME

Roughly 3 months

EQUIPMENT

Large jar or small crock with a capacity of at least 2 quarts/ 2 liters

Light weight that fits inside the vessel

INGREDIENTS

for 1 quart/1 liter doubanjiang

6 tablespoons/100 grams sea salt

Fungus-covered fava beans (Making *Doubanjiang* I: Growing Fungus on Favas and Wheat, page 170)

PROCESS

Mix brine by dissolving the salt in 1 quart/1 liter of dechlorinated water.

Place the fungus-covered fava beans in the vessel.

Pour the brine over the fava beans to cover.

Place a light weight on top of the beans to keep them submerged under the brine.

Loosely cover the vessel (so carbon dioxide can escape) and ferment at room temperature for about 3 months, gently stirring occasionally.

MAKING DOUBANJIANG III: FERMENTING CHILI PEPPERS

Salted chilies fermenting for doubanjiang.

This roughly three-month process is simultaneous with the fava fermentation described in Making *Doubanjiang* II. At the end of the three months, the favas and chilies will be mixed together and fermented further. Traditionally, this step includes just chili peppers and salt. I've been adding garlic to mine, which I think makes the doubanjiang even more delicious.

TIMEFRAME

Roughly 3 months

EQUIPMENT

Food processor (optional)

Jar or crock about 1-quart/1-liter capacity, or a little smaller

Light weight that fits inside the vessel

INGREDIENTS

for 1 quart/1 liter doubanjiang

1 pound/500 grams red chili peppers (any variety)

¼ pound/125 grams garlic (optional)

1 generous tablespoon/ 18 grams salt (about 3 percent weight of other ingredients)

PROCESS

In a food processor or by hand, purée or coarsely chop the chilies with seeds, along with garlic, if using.

Add the salt and mix to evenly distribute.

Pack into a jar or crock and weigh down to keep the chilies submerged under their juices, which the salt will draw out of them.

Cover loosely and leave to ferment for about 3 months.

Mixing fermented fava beans and
fermented chilies together for doubanjiang.
At the factory we visited, this looked like
the confluence of two rivers.

MAKING DOUBANJIANG IV: COMBINING AND FERMENTING

Finally, after the favas and chilies have each fermented for about three months, they are mixed together for the duration of the fermentation. The most unusual part of the process is that the mix is exposed to the sun as often as possible, and it is also stirred frequently.

TIMEFRAME

At least 9 months, up to several years

EQUIPMENT

Wide-mouth crock or jar at least 2 quarts/2 liter capacity, big enough to stir the doubanjiang

Light weight that fits inside the vessel

INGREDIENTS

for 1 quart/1 liter doubanjiang

Fermented fava beans from Making Doubanjiang II

Fermented chili peppers from Making Doubanjiang III

PROCESS

Combine the fermenting fava beans with the fermenting chilies. Stir together well.

Place the mix in a wide-mouth crock or jar to ferment, weighted and loosely covered.

Expose the surface to direct sunlight as often as you can, and stir well after you do. This is most important to do frequently in the early stages of fermentation, to reduce water content; as fermentation continues, expose it to sun as you can.

Ferment anywhere from 9 months to several years, tasting periodically to evaluate the evolving flavor.

Faf and Koji's Many Other Cousins

Koji is the most widely known example, but all across Asia, people grow fungi on grains and legumes as part of their fermentation processes. Every region has its own variants. In contrast to koji, which is typically made using laboratory-propagated pure cultures of *Aspergillus oryzae* or a few other related strains, most other molds used for fermenting are mixed cultures. They are made with traditional methods, generally relying upon the repeated use of a specific, dedicated spore-rich space and/ or container, and/or botanical ingredients, and/or back-slopping (adding some from a previous generation) as the sources of the fungal spores. Most of them incorporate yeasts as well as filamentous fungi, so that in addition to accomplishing the enzymatic carbohydrate breakdown, the starter contains its own yeasts—which initiate the alcohol fermentation—as well as bacteria, inevitably.

Anand Sankar, who arranged our trip to Kalap and brought us there.

Examples of these molded grain starters can be found everywhere across the vast Asian continent. Most such starters that I have encountered in my travels, and in Asian markets in the US, have been mass-produced. But thanks to the work of various obsessed documentarians, I know that traditional techniques for making these starters vary widely. So I was not exactly surprised, but still very excited, to find a homemade molded starter in the most remote place I've ever visited: the village of Kalap in the Tons Valley of Uttarakhand, in the north of India.

Departing from Dehradun, where I was teaching at seed-saving activist Vandana Shiva's educational farm, Navdanya, we drove north for a full day, along sometimes-harrowing windy mountain roads. After a night as the only guests at a small hotel, we were dropped off at a trailhead in the town of Naitwar for the 11-kilometer trek to Kalap. I was traveling with my old friend Margot Cohen, who was working in Bangalore in the south of India and agreed to meet me in the north. I wanted to go trekking in the mountains; she was more interested

Leaving the town of Naitwar, climbing into the mountains.

On the trail to Kalap.

An incredible view from the trail.

in cultural experience than in wilderness. We each independently found Anand Sankar, who organizes small trekking tours bringing travelers to Kalap. Margot and I turned out to be the first foreign visitors there.

The 11-kilometer hike into the mountains was quite challenging. For those of us who take for granted being able to drive right to our front door, or even take the bus, living like this is quite inconceivable. I don't want to romanticize it; on our way in we passed a family walking out carrying their very sick child, seeking medical care. People in the village mostly eat what they grow themselves; anything beyond that they must haul the 11 kilometers.

Of course, the people who live there are generally in excellent shape as a result of their way of life. Anand had hired a couple of local young men to haul our bags, and it was humbling to see how seemingly effortless the hike was for them, even hauling our luggage and other supplies, as we struggled and required frequent rests. But as we climbed higher, the breathtaking panoramas were a powerful incentive to go on.

Anand's local friend Rajmohan, who spoke English, hosted us in the village and functioned as our primary

Rajmohan and Anand at Rajmohan's house.

Kalap village sights.

guide and interpreter into the local Bihari language. Like many of the houses in Kalap, Rajmohan's house was built on a slope, with two main levels plus a half-size lower level where livestock was kept. There were wires and some hanging lightbulbs from when the government had brought electricity to Kalap. But after a short time, a transformer along the way blew. Still, years later, it hadn't been replaced, so the fixtures were a vestige of a brief technological moment.

Rajmohan's wife, Guddu, cooked for us over a fire in an indoor kitchen space with limited ventilation and no running water. None of the houses had toilets. They had created an improvised outhouse for us and the other periodic visitors that Anand brought, but to relieve themselves, the residents of Kalap wandered into the surrounding woods.

There were lots of small terraced garden plots, where people grew grains, beans, and vegetables. When we were there, in early autumn, many houses had hay spread to dry on porches for use as winter fodder for the cows and goats. Most families had a separate structure, in most cases padlocked (unlike the houses), for food storage. When I asked about this, it was explained to me that this stored food was people's most valuable possession; and this way, if a house burned down, at least the family would still have food so they wouldn't starve. The village had a small house with a water-powered grain mill, open and available for everyone to use. I don't know who built it or maintained it, but in exchange for using it, each person would leave a small share of the grain that they had milled.

We were served dahi, India's yogurt-like fermented milk, made from skimmed milk. The cream floating atop the milk is always skimmed for butter. The butter making we observed involved an ingenious foot-powered churn. One thing we ate that I had never encountered before was a delicious, savory, homemade seasoning made from the dried, ground root of an Angelica family plant called *chora*, sprinkled on fresh cucumbers. I asked if anyone in the village made alcohol, and the following day we hiked a few kilometers farther, to a satellite village at a higher altitude, where some villagers grazed their animals in summer. It was here that we met Lalbahadour, the local brewer.

Lalbahadour was very friendly, and he was happy to answer my questions, translated by Rajmohan. The

Lalbahadour, the Kalap brewer, with a jerrican of fermenting alcohol wrapped in blankets on his bed.

beverage he made was from amaranth and millet, both grown in the village, fortified with jaggery, the Indian style of dried, unrefined sugarcane juice. His latest batch had just started fermenting, in a weathered plastic jerrican wrapped in blankets on his bed. He told me that in the cold weather he sleeps with the ferment to keep it warm. After fermentation, he distills it in a homemade still. The beverage Lalbahadour makes, which Rajmohan said had no particular name, just "country alcohol," must be popular, because there was none on hand for me to sample.

But what he did have on hand, even more exciting to me than the alcohol would have been, was the starter he produces himself to make it. I wrote down *faf* as a phonetic interpretation of the sound I heard used to describe the starter. Jyoti Prakash Tamang's book *Himalayan Fermented Foods* makes reference to *phab*, while Dr. S. Sekar of Bharathidasan University in Tamil Nadu, in his online "Database on Microbial Traditional Knowledge of India," uses the word *pham*. In the realm of indigenous fermentation practices, nothing is standardized. Lalbahadour said it was made from amaranth, although upon inspection there were clearly other botanical

Close-up of faf starter. Note stalks and other botanical elements visible at the surface.

Lalbahadour with faf he makes and uses as a starter for the alcohol he brews.

ingredients besides grains embedded within the amaranth cake, as stalks and other elements were visible at the surface. As Drs. Tamang and Sekar have both documented, people from diverse traditions incorporate a wide range of botanicals with grains to create these mixed-culture starters for grain-based beverages across Asia.

Unfortunately, I did not have the time to stay long enough in Kalap to witness how Lalbahadour makes his faf starter cake. I am deeply grateful for the documentarians who have explored this fascinating realm of ethnobotany. Some of the sources I have enjoyed are listed in "Traditional Mixed-Culture Fungal Starters Resources." There is much documentation of indigenous traditions like this yet to be done.

TRADITIONAL MIXED-CULTURE FUNGAL STARTERS RESOURCES

Science and Civilisation in China, Volume 6, *Biology and Biological Technology,* Part V: Fermentations and Food Science by H. T. Huang. This book provides a comprehensive historical review of the history of fermentation in China, including detailed descriptions of ancient methods of growing fungal starters.

"Grandiose Survey of Chinese Alcoholic Drinks and Beverages" by Xu Gan Rong and Bao Tong Fa. Available online at www.spiritsoftheharvest.com /2014/03/grandiose-survey-of-chinese-alcoholic.html. Created by two Chinese scholars, this document has lots of information on different Chinese fermented beverages and how they are prepared. Chapter subsection 2.3 titled "Jiuqu-making Technology" has detailed flowcharts for producing fungal starters.

"Database on Microbial Traditional Knowledge of India" by Dr. S. Sekar is available online at www.bdu.ac.in/schools/biotechnology-and-genetic -engineering/biotechnology/sekardb.htm. This document, prepared by an Indian scholar, is a broad survey of Indian ferments. One downloadable subsection, "Prepared Starter for fermented country beverage production," contains detailed descriptions of fungal starters in a range of locales.

Himalayan Fermented Foods: Microbiology, Nutrition, and Ethnic Values by Jyoti Prakash Tamang. A survey of Himalayan fermentation, with a section on fungal starters.

Bribri *Chicha*

Though lesser known, there do exist traditions of growing molds on grains outside of Asia. I encountered one such tradition in Costa Rica, where I visited at the invitation of Fabian Pacheco, an environmental activist, gardener, seed saver, and organic agriculture educator. Fabian had seen my Himalayan faf, and he told me that an Indigenous Bribri community he had worked with make a similar moldy mass, called *oko*, with corn, and used it as a starter for their traditional chicha (see "Chicha" on page 116). In Spanish, oko is known as *mohoso*, which translates as "moldy."

Fabian took me on a road trip to the Caribbean coast so we could visit Finca Loroco, a diversified organic farm and educational center run by his Bribri friends. They served us a couple of different chichas as we helped them make oko. We had delicious (and strong) chicha, made from corn that was neither malted nor molded, but simply ground and cooked into a paste, then mixed with sugar and water to ferment. We were also served a chicha made by adding steamed bananas to the corn paste,

A platter of steamed wraps ready to ferment, alongside their component parts, a stack of bijawa leaves and bowl of the raw corn dough.

Mauricia Vargas wrapping corn dough in bijawa leaves.

Wrapped corn masses in a pot cooking over an open fire.

allowing the mixture to ferment in a solid state, then mixing it with water immediately prior to serving. They also described chicha made with cacao and corn. The chichas prepared without the moldy oko require sugar or bananas as a source of fermentable simple sugars; the oko is only necessary for chicha made from just corn and water so that the amylase enzymes from the molds can break down the starchy corn into fermentable sugars.

In keeping with the vast majority of indigenous traditions around the world in which women are the brewers, the oko in progress was being made by Mauricia Vargas, the mother of the family. As Mauricia explained it to me, dried kernels of (starchy) corn had been soaked in water for three days. Just before our arrival, the soaked (and thus already fermenting) corn was ground into a thick paste, like a masa dough for tortillas or tamales (except not nixtamalized). We participated in the next step, placing handfuls of this dough into the large leaves of a plant they

Mauricia Vargas and her family with Fabian Pacheco, my Costa Rican host, who brought me to meet them.

Oko at four days.

called *bijawa* (genus *Calathea*). Each mass of dough was wrapped like a tamale, except in two leaves. The technique was to fold the stacked leaves in half, in order to break their spines in the middle, then form the mass of dough into a rectangular shape on the stacked leaves, roughly 6 inches/15 centimeters high by 3 inches/7.5 centimeters wide and ½ inch/1.5 centimeters deep. (I did not measure; these are my estimates, and the masses varied quite a bit in size.) The important thing is that the mass be small enough for the leaves to fold around and completely enclose it.

The corn-dough wraps were then cooked in a big pot, most of them covered with water, but the ones at the top steamed rather than boiled. They were cooked for about an hour, then they were removed from the pot and left to spontaneously ferment and mold. We did not stay for the entire fermentation period, but as Mauricia explained it to us, the wrapped corn is left undisturbed for four days. On the fifth day, the leaves are opened and the corn masses are removed. Then the leaves are turned over and the corn masses are rewrapped, with what had been the outer surfaces of the leaves now in contact with the corn mass. This brings different leaf surfaces into contact with

Oko at eight days.

the corn mass, exposes everything to air (molds need oxygen), and helps evenly distribute mold formation. After four more days, the mass is partially dried in the sun, then rewrapped; again, flipping the leaves to vary surface contact. Finally, after four more days, the moldy masses are dried in the sun and ready to use or store.

I participated in the initial wrapping stage only, and I was sent off with a couple of the wrapped corn masses to age as they described. When I first examined the corn masses after four days, mold growth was patchy. By color and by smell, I could recognize some of the mold as *Aspergillus*, like that I have grown many times on rice and barley to make koji. But there was green mold as well, indicating more than a single type of mold. Four days later, mold covered most, but still not all, of the surface. Some of the molds were long and hairy and clearly sporulating. I did not remain in Costa Rica long enough to complete the process or make chicha with the oko, nor did I dare try to bring it home with me to complete the process.

Since I was not there long enough to see the process in its entirety, and due to the limitations of our communications and translation, this is certainly not a comprehensive or definitive account of oko making. But because nothing (that I have come across in the English-language literature) has been written about it, I thought it was important to share this information, incomplete as it may be. Was this practice the result of an accidental discovery, as so many fermentation processes are, with similar molds developing on grains both here and across Asia? Or was there perhaps some past Asian influence here, long since forgotten? The origins of fermentation practices are always shrouded in mystery. But over and over we see repeated patterns, with microbial phenomena manifesting similarly (and at the same time uniquely) in disparate locations.

After I wrote this section and had moved on to later sections of the book, I received an email from Alessandro Barghini, an anthropologist at the University of São Paulo in Brazil, sharing with me his research showing that mold use in fermentations of cassava "was widespread throughout the Amazon basin." Perhaps the use of molds in fermentation was once much more widespread in the Western hemisphere? With so much cultural destruction and assimilation, traditions can quickly be lost. Perhaps they can also be revived, or rebirthed into new forms.

Village Tempeh Making

Tempeh is an Indonesian style of fermenting soybeans and other substrates, in which filamentous fungi are grown on cooked beans wrapped in leaves or contained in perforated plastic, binding them into blocks that are then sliced and cooked. The process is similar to koji making in its environmental requirements: It needs a warm (80–90°F/27–32°C), humid space with some air circulation. Home tempeh making is covered extensively in my earlier books. Here I want to share photographs of one family's small-scale commercial tempeh production in a village called Gianyar in Bali, Indonesia. This family produces tempeh from 110 pounds/50 kilograms of soybeans each morning. We were invited there by a daughter of the family who sells the tempeh at a market where Mary Jane Edleson, my Bali host, shops.

First, the soybeans are soaked in water for about 24 hours. In the tropical heat, this initiates a first lactic acid fermentation that lightly acidifies the beans. Then the soaked beans are split in half using a small electric mill, enabling the hulls to be rinsed off.

The beans are cooked, then drained and spread out to cool and dry on a table, with a fan blowing on them. A family member uses a small wooden rake to move the cooling, drying beans, releasing heat, exposing different surfaces, and creating furrows that increase surface area.

The tempeh starter they used was in a very different form than I've seen before. Instead of the typical commercially available starter—a powder ground from rice grown with a single strain of *Rhizopus* fungus under very controlled conditions—it was a leaf, to which pieces of soybeans had adhered, along with more than one strain of sporulating fungi, as indicated by the black (*Rhizopus*) and yellow (*Aspergillus*) coloration. Traditional fermentation processes never involve single pure strains!

The method for inoculating the soybeans with the spores on the leaf is very simple. The tempeh maker held the moldy leaf in the palm of one hand, spore side out, held in place with his pinky and thumb. Then he used both hands to pick up beans and rub them between his hands, letting them fall back onto the table. He walked around the table doing that for perhaps 10 minutes, stirring the beans as he went.

The inoculated beans are scooped into perforated plastic bags. The filled bags are heat sealed and placed into a wooden form. At markets there, I saw tempeh wrapped in leaves, the traditional way, but most of what was commercially available was in perforated plastic.

To make sure the blocks of tempeh are fairly square and uniform, they are patted and gently pressed using a flat wooden board with a handle. The form is flipped over onto a board, then removed, allowing air to circulate and freeing the form to make more blocks of tempeh.

The boards are
stacked on a shelf.

Some of the inoculated soybeans are placed on *waru*
leaves to make more starter. Inoculated soybeans are
sandwiched between two waru leaves, then left to
develop for several days, until they sporulate.

The leaves come from a tree, in the hibiscus family, growing right outside the tempeh production room.

Here you can see a mature block of tempeh alongside a bag of beans that has been inoculated and prepared, but not yet fermented.

Tempeh Bowls

I encountered a wonderfully creative application of tempeh during a lunch at the Mediamatic Café in Amsterdam—an attractive, hip, multiuse space where I was participating in a fermentation event called Rotzooi. I was surprised and delighted when our soup arrived at the table in edible bowls made of tempeh. The tempeh bowls were beautiful and elegant, and they were also a delicious end to the meal, having soaked up the flavor of the soup. At the café, they are referred to as Tempeh Ware. The inspiration to make the bowls came to Mediamatic's founder, Willem Velthoven. Sasker Scheerder, who runs Manenwolfs foodlab in Rotterdam (see "Dehydrated Brine Salts" on page 92), consulted on the project, and Mediamatic kitchen interns Corinne Mulder and Iris van Hulst experimented with and refined the process. The bowls are effective at holding hot soup; the live mycelium are naturally water repellent, and the bowls are baked at 350°F/180°C for a short time before serving.

Tempeh is typically fermented in perforated bags or, traditionally, in banana leaves. The Mediamatic team used existing plasticware for the base shapes, then molded plastic inserts for them, which they perforated to create an environment where the fungus could thrive. The inserts provide enough protection to retain most of the moisture, and enough airflow for the fungus to get the oxygen it needs. With a little ingenuity, tempeh can be made into any shape. "The most challenging part was finding the right substrate," explained Sasker. "We wanted the bowl walls not too thick, for both culinary and aesthetic reasons." Their experiments led them to use Puy lentils and crushed toasted lupine "bits." According to Willem, "These two base materials are small enough to grow bowls with a weight between 55 and 70 grams (2 to 2.5 ounces). A nice serving size."

Tempeh bowls.

A toasted tempeh bowl.

A divided tempeh bowl,
for serving soup and salad.

POTATO TEMPEH

My conception of tempeh and its versatility has expanded very gradually. First, I tried using different beans. Then, I tried mixing in some grains, which has become my typical method. Then, encouraged by my friend Spiky, grains alone. Somehow it never occurred to me to try making tempeh with potatoes or other starchy tubers, but it did occur to Matteo Leoni, an Italian chef living in Switzerland. Fried potato tempeh is extremely delicious. Matteo describes the flavor as "really nutty," and says it reminds him of chestnuts.

Together with his Swiss partner, Petra, Matteo runs a food business in Basel called pureTaste. Their motto: "We give veggies a second chance." According to Matteo, potatoes, sweet potatoes, and tropical yams work best for this process, but beets, cassava, corn, taro, and parsnips also work well. You can try other root vegetables, too. I describe his process for making pieces of potato or other roots into blocks of tempeh, but the tempeh fungus can be grown on whole roots and ears of corn. These processes are all extremely versatile.

Whole ears of
corn tempeh.

Different styles of
potato tempeh.

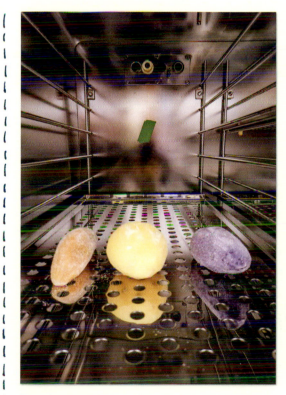

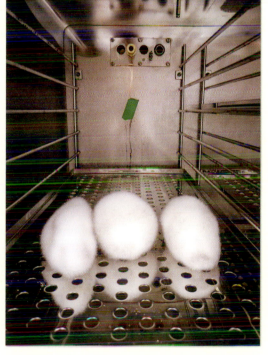

Tempeh grown on
whole potatoes.

POTATO TEMPEH

TIMEFRAME

24 to 36 hours

EQUIPMENT

Dehydrator (optional)

Incubation chamber to maintain a temperature of 80–90°F/27–32°C (see chapter introduction on page 139 for ideas)

INGREDIENTS

for two blocks of tempeh

2 pounds/1 kilogram potatoes

A few tablespoons of vinegar

½ teaspoon tempeh starter ✳

PROCESS

Boil the potatoes (with their peels) in water, with a few table-spoons of vinegar to mildly acidify them. Cook them only partially, as the fermentation will break them down further. Specific cooking time will vary with different-sized potatoes. You do *not* want them to get fully cooked and soft. Cook them al dente.

Peel the potatoes and cut them into cubes. Experiment with the size of the pieces; smaller pieces with more surface area will generally bind better. Or leave the potatoes whole, if you like (but still peel them), for a different kind of tempeh experience.

Dry the potatoes, ideally in a dehydrator at about 104°F/40°C for about an hour. You can also dry them in an oven on its lowest setting for 10 minutes, or with a fan. If the roots are too wet, bacteria will grow instead of the desired fungus, and the tempeh will get slimy in the incubator.

Inoculate the potatoes with the tempeh spores. Sprinkle spores lightly to distribute them over the surfaces of the potato. If you are working with small pieces, stir well to make sure all the edges come into contact with spores, then place inoculated pieces into a perforated bag as you would do for other styles of tempeh (see *Wild Fermentation* or *The Art of Fermentation* for more details). If you left the roots whole, try to distribute spores lightly over the entire surface. You will not need the bag.

Incubate at about 86°F/30°C. Fermentation time will vary. Pieces of potatoes bound together by the fungus can take as long as 36 hours. They should be tightly bound in the shape of the bag, covered with white growth and maybe a little gray or black growth where the perforations are in the bags. Whole potatoes will ferment a bit faster, about 28 hours. Yams even faster, about 24 hours. "With the potato tempeh, it is quite important to open the incubation chamber for a few seconds from time to time to get rid of excess moisture," advises Matteo.

✳ or manufacturer's recommended amount

Enjoy, however you like to eat tempeh. I agree with Matteo, who says: "I highly recommend deep-frying it, like classic fries."

If you won't be eating the potato tempeh right away, Matteo says it's really important to get rid of excess moisture and stop the fungus from continuing to grow. He does this by placing the tempeh in his dehydrator again, this time at 158°F/70°C for 3 to 4 hours. Alternatively, you can dry the tempeh in an oven on low heat for a shorter time, or freeze it. Matteo cautions that "if you don't stop the growing and get them get dry, they will quickly turn really soft and acidic."

Cooked, dried, and inoculated potato pieces in a plastic bag ready to ferment into tempeh.

Potato tempeh close-up.

Using Tempeh Enzymes for Umami Flavor

Like koji's *Aspergillus* mold, tempeh's *Rhizopus* mold possesses enzymes that can break down nutrients and build flavor. In fact, most traditional koji and tempeh made without pure culture starters involve mixed cultures that include *Rhizopus* as well as *Aspergillus* fungi (and more). When I was teaching in Barcelona, one of my students was Bernat Guixer, a PhD chemist who works as a research chef at a renowned Spanish restaurant, El Celler de Can Roca, in Girona. He told me about his experiments using tempeh enzymes in longer-term applications. I was very curious, so he sent me papers he had published in scientific journals about these experiments.

Bernat and his team took fresh tempeh, vacuum-sealed it, and kept it in the range of 115–130°F/45–55°C for various lengths of time. These moderately high temperatures encourage frenetic enzyme activity. Bernat and his colleagues report that:

> The combined actions of enzymes and Maillard reactions lead to the substantial changes in appearance, texture and flavour of the tempe. The proteolytic enzymes liberate free amino acids and peptides, while the battery of enzymes that break down complex carbohydrates release simple sugars. The two classes of compounds react with each other in the Maillard reactions and following Strecker degradations. The orange-brownish product colour derives from the Maillard reaction products, in the form of different melanins. The complex malty, roasted and caramel notes also derive from the cascade of Maillard reactions that occur in a food matrix. The changes in texture derive from the macro-component breakdown of proteins and complex carbohydrates that are responsible for the texture and structure of the cooked legumes.[5]

They named the enzyme-transformed tempeh *tempeto*, and made different styles of it aged for different lengths of time—up to four weeks—sometimes with grains added. Longer aging led to more flavor: It "develops intense malty and toasted flavours as well as caramellike, umami, and some bitterness, while the colour became dark and the texture more dry," with flavor notes of aged delicacies such as miso, sherry, or balsamic vinegar.[6] As chefs everywhere are experimenting with new uses for koji enzymes, this research into tempeh enzymes suggests that they too could have many fruitful, innovative applications.

Bernat Guixer and his team's experiments. *Top row,* tempeh; viewed from above (*left*) and cross section (*right*). *Middle row,* tempeto after six days at 125°F/52°C. *Bottom row,* tempeto after four weeks at 125°F/52°C.

MAO DOFU

Mao dofu is widely available in China at markets and from mobile vendors.

Mara Jane King and Pao Liu in my kitchen with the mao dofu we made with the *Actinomucor elegans* starter Pao brought us from Taiwan.

Another food that is widely grown with mold in China is tofu. This moldy tofu, known in China as *mao dofu*, is generally dominated by *Actinomucor*, *Mucor*, or *Rhizopus* genera. I saw mao dofu for sale at markets everywhere I went in China. The mold gives the tofu a beautiful, creamy texture. The mao dofu can be fried as is, or it can be further fermented. Many households we visited in China ferment tofu at home, but all of them buy mao dofu for this purpose rather than trying to grow it themselves.

The traditional methods of making mao dofu, of course, do not involve pure-culture starters. They rely upon botanical ingredients, such as rice straw or pumpkin leaves, as the source of the fungus. I have tried using pumpkin leaves and straw (from wheat, not rice), but instead of white molds like the ones I saw everywhere in China, the resulting molds were bright red and yellow—another failed experiment destined for the compost. A onetime student of mine, Pao Liu, who lives in London but was born and raised in Taiwan, brought me some Taiwanese mao dofu starter, spores of *Actinomucor elegans*, which works beautifully. Unfortunately, I have not been able to find this starter in English-language internet searches. But one of the other common molds found on mao dofu, the genus *Rhizopus*, happens to be the same genus as tempeh starter, which is easily available online and can be used to make mao dofu.

TIMEFRAME

30 to 40 hours

EQUIPMENT

Bamboo steamer or a wooden or cardboard box, and a light cloth to cover the tofu

INGREDIENTS

for 1 pound/500 grams

1 pound/500 grams tofu

1 tablespoon rice (or any other) flour

¼ teaspoon (about .75 grams) spores (ideally *Actinomucor elegans*; alternatively, tempeh starter [*Rhizopus*]) per 1 pound/500 grams of tofu

PROCESS

Clean the tofu by pouring boiled water over its surfaces.

Remove the hard skins (if there are any), then cut the tofu into roughly 1-inch/2.5-centimeter cubes.

Dry the cubes by placing them on a clean kitchen towel and gently swabbing moisture from the edges of the tofu.

Dry-roast the rice (or other) flour in a cast-iron or other heavy pan over medium heat. Stir frequently to prevent burning, and roast for 5-10 minutes, until flour is fragrant and hot to the touch. The idea is to use heat to sanitize the flour so that it is a medium with relatively few surviving microbial inhabitants that might compete with the spores. Allow the flour to cool.

Mix the spores with the cooled, toasted flour, and stir or agitate to thoroughly combine. Place the spore–flour mixture on a small tray or plate.

Using chopsticks or small tongs, dip each cube of tofu in the spore mixture, making sure each of the six sides of each cube comes into contact with it.

Place the spore-inoculated tofu cubes in the bamboo steamer or alternative vessel.

Cover the basket and ferment in a warm (ideally 80–90°F/27–32°C), humid spot for 30 to 40 hours, until it is covered in a cloud of white, hairy mold.

Dust the finished cubes of mao dofu with cornstarch or another starch to fry fresh, or use for *furu* (see "*Furu* or *Dofuru* Fermented Tofu" on page 228) or other styles of fermented tofu.

Molds in Unexpected Places

At a fermentation symposium at the Basque Culinary Center in San Sebastian, Spain, I met Ramón Perisé Moré, who made a wonderful presentation of some of the surprising projects he and his team were working on in the test kitchen of the restaurant Mugaritz, outside of town. What they were doing was conceptually different from anything else I have seen. I did not get to eat at the restaurant, but it seems their intention is to deliberately subvert people's expectations of food.

One way they were doing this was by serving food with *Penicillium* molds intentionally grown on it. Two examples Ramón showed me were a *Penicillium* brioche and various fruits grown with the mold. The dessert pictured here features a pear grown with *Penicillium* mold, hollowed out and filled with pear liqueur foam, served alongside a pickled wild pear fermented in a far more traditional way.

Ramón was also interested in creating different kinds of surface growth and membranes to incorporate into dishes. For instance, he was growing kefir in big trays

Brioche grown with *Penicillium* molds and served at Mugaritz.

A pear grown with *Penicillium* mold, hollowed out, and filled with pear liqueur foam, served at Mugaritz alongside a pickled wild pear.

in order to maximize surface area and encourage the growth of a luxuriant velvety textured skin, dominated by the fungus *Geotrichum candidum*, more commonly associated with soft, bloomy rind cheeses. Most kefir makers minimize surface area and stir the kefir to prevent it from developing a skin. At Mugaritz, these skins were dried, then used as layers and toppings in the restaurant's unexpected concoctions. The Mugaritz team was also experimenting with different, extra-starchy nutritive substrates—such as Jerusalem artichokes and sweet potatoes—to grow kombucha, with an interest not in the liquid product but rather the surface biofilm pellicle that forms, usually called the mother or the SCOBY.

Ramön Perisé Moré, who runs the research kitchen of the restaurant Mugaritz in the Basque countryside, shows the skin formed by the fungus *Geotrichum candidum* on a tray of kefir.

LEAFCUTTER ANTS

Humans are not the only cultivators of fungi. In Costa Rica, I had the opportunity to witness a phenomenon that contradicts the notion that humans alone practice fermentation in an intentional way: the strange life of leafcutter ants.

Leafcutter ants live in underground chambers, to which they transport fragments of leaves, which, true to their name, they have trimmed with their jaws. The ants cannot eat the leaves, but they use them to cultivate a fungus that they do eat, and which even develops swollen tips that the ants use to feed their young. The arrangement is fully mutualistic, in that the ants can't live without the fungus and the fungus isn't found except where cultivated by the ants. Future queens of new colonies store mycelium in dedicated chambers in their mouths to use as "starters." And because the ants are engaged in monoculture, which is such an inherently vulnerable state, the fungus they grow is susceptible to a particular parasitic fungus. But the ants are equipped to protect against it by harboring and feeding bacteria in dedicated chambers in their cuticles that produce compounds that inhibit the parasite. Isn't evolution elegant and bizarre?

FIVE

BEANS AND SEEDS

Beans and seeds are nutritionally rich, containing proteins that break down into amino acids with strong umami flavors when fermented. Just as chapter 3 had some overlap with chapter 4, so too does this one. In some of the recipes and processes featured in the previous chapter, beans and seeds are used as substrates for growing molds and subsequently fermented using those molds. However, beans and seeds can be fermented in many other, simpler ways. These are frequently spontaneous, wild fermentations, and it is these methods that we explore here.

One big focus of this chapter is natto, Japanese fermented whole soybeans—how to make it, how to learn to love it, how to eat it, and how to dehydrate it to incorporate it into seasoning mixes. I share what I have seen and learned about cousins of natto—some that I encountered inadvertently in China and Burma (Myanmar), others that I learned about from American immigrants from West Africa, from an Australian immigrant from the Himalayas, and others from research and kitchen experimentation.

This chapter also includes what I have learned about methods for fermenting tofu, mostly from my travels in China. In addition, it explores the role of fermentation in the processing of coffee and cacao. Finally, I'll show how I've learned to ferment two preparations that are not always fermented, but are greatly enhanced by the process: Afro-Brazilian *acarajé* and Mediterranean *farinata*.

Natto and Its Many Cousins

Natto is a Japanese fermentation of whole soybeans, less well known internationally than many other soy ferments, such as soy sauce, miso, and tempeh. The bacterium that transforms soybeans into natto is *Bacillus subtilis*, which is common in soil. These bacteria are generally present on all beans and seeds, and their spores can survive boiling temperatures, which kill most bacteria that could compete with them, so it is very easy to instigate spontaneous fermentations of cooked beans and seeds. Natto is a much-sensationalized food. The fermentation creates a slimy, mucilaginous coating on the beans, which forms strands when the beans are stirred or pulled apart. The alkaline by-products of *Bacillus* fermentation give natto its characteristic smell and flavor, with notes of ammonia. In Japan, natto is typically eaten wet and stringy, while in most other places that produce *Bacillus* ferments, they are dried for stability, which eliminates the sliminess.

I ate lots of natto when I visited Japan. I tried it in its traditional presentation, packaged in rice straw, called *wara natto*. I ate mochi (sticky rice pounded into a smooth paste and formed into balls) with natto. In Tokyo, I ate natto for breakfast one morning from a vending machine.

To be honest, I did not like natto at all the first time I tried it. But long before I visited Japan, I came to love it, encouraged by two different people to give it another try. William Shurtleff, coauthor (with his Japanese wife Akiko Aoyagi) of several books that have been important to my fermentation education (including *The Book of Miso* and *The Book of Tempeh*), emailed me to tell me he had read *Wild Fermentation*. He was extremely positive, but then he pointed out several omissions that he felt diminished the book, including natto. "You left out one of my favorite bean ferments, natto," Shurtleff wrote. "They are a whole food with a Camembert flavor, ready in 24 hours." I love Camembert, and I greatly admire Bill Shurtleff, so I determined to give natto another try.

Shortly after, I spent some time with Betty Stechmeyer, the cofounder of GEM Cultures, the first business in the United States to provide starters and cultures for home fermentation. Betty had long been importing Japanese *natto-moto*, the bacterial spores to start natto, to distribute in the US. She was a natto afficionado, but her husband Gordon did not share this appreciation. Betty developed techniques to hide natto in creamy salads such as potato salad. She was determined to feed it to her husband because of research suggesting that natto was a beneficial food for the heart problems Gordon was having. Betty came to participate in one of my workshops with some hidden-natto salads to share, and she proceeded to teach us how easy it is to make natto. I've been making natto ever since (How to Make Natto, page 208).

The more I developed a taste for the flavor and texture of natto, the less I wanted to hide it. I learned of a simple Japanese way to eat natto from another non-Japanese person, Lawrence Diggs, who founded and runs the International Vinegar Museum in Roslyn, South Dakota, and participated in one of the earliest fermentation

Natto on rice the way I typically enjoy it, dressed with soy sauce, rice vinegar, mustard, and scallions.

residency programs that I hosted. I was served natto this way when I finally got to eat natto in Japan, and it remains my favorite way to eat it: Place a scoop of natto atop a bowl of warm rice. Add some mustard, rice vinegar, and soy sauce, and if you really want to enhance the sliminess, some raw egg. Use chopsticks to swirl the natto and all the juicy condiments together into a stringy, slimy mass. Top with some chopped scallions or chives, and add some little strips of nori if you have it, and enjoy it all with the rice.

When I traveled in Asia, I was surprised by the number of foods similar to natto that were made and used elsewhere on the continent. Actually, I was not looking for natto outside of Japan, mostly because I did not realize it was there. But while we were in the small village of Qinfen in Guizhou in southwestern China, we encountered a household ferment with a smell and texture that was unmistakably natto-like.

We had seen the small, dry, brown cookies with red flakes used in the village to create a flavorful dipping sauce. When we asked about them, we were told they were called *douchi*, a name we recognized as describing the fermented black, whole soybeans commonly found in Chinese markets and restaurants around the world, made by growing *Aspergillus* molds, like koji, on the soybeans (these are known in English as Chinese fermented or salted black beans). So it was only natural for us to assume that these

Douchi "cookies" that we encountered in Qinfen.

The fermented soybeans to make douchi in Qinfen that looked, smelled, and felt like natto.

As we mashed it and added spices, it got stringy . . .

. . . and the more we mashed, the stringier and gluier the douchi got.

douchi cookies involved first growing *Aspergillus* molds, and we were excited to learn the rest of the process.

As soon as we entered the house where the soybeans were fermenting, I recognized the smell of natto. Then, when I was handed a wooden tool to start mashing them, the gluey texture and mucilaginous strands that formed confirmed without a doubt that what the people of Qinfen called douchi was much more closely related to natto than to koji. Fermentation practices are never standardized. Whether the variations are minor or major, they always exist.

This is how the people of Qinfen made what they call douchi: The soybeans were soaked overnight, steamed until soft, then spontaneously fermented in a warm spot for about four days. Then the beans were mashed, and lots of dried crushed chili pepper and some salt were added, and this was all mashed some more until the ingredients were well blended. The sticky paste was formed into large patties and dried on a high shelf in a room with a woodstove for about four days. Then, we were told, the dried patties would be steamed until soft, pounded again, and formed into cookies to dry once more. These douchi cookies would then be shelf-stable and stored. To use them, people pulverized them into a powder, and then mixed them with some water, soy sauce, and vinegar to make a delicious and complex dipping sauce.

It was not only in the small village that we heard the word douchi used to describe what we recognized as a natto ferment. At a big market in Yunnan's capital, Kunming, we saw other cookies similar to the ones we'd eaten in Qinfen: a sticky, wet, spiced version of the cookies and also some natto-style fermented soybeans, all called douchi. I've also encountered natto-like seasonings in Burma, and I had one gifted to me from Nagaland, which is a state in northeastern India that borders Burma. In addition, I've long been interested in the many different fermented seasonings used in cuisines throughout West Africa. These seasonings are traditionally made from African locust beans and other leguminous seeds, and they are also fermented by *Bacillus subtilis*.

In the sections that follow, I explain how to make natto and a shelf-stable, natto-based seasoning that has become a staple in my kitchen. I then explore some of the natto-like *B. subtilis* fermentation traditions elsewhere in the world.

HOW TO MAKE NATTO

Natto is easy to ferment. The main challenges are cooking the soybeans until they are good and soft, which can take up to eight hours, and figuring out how to keep the developing natto warm. The bacteria grow fastest (in about 24 hours) above body temperature, about 104°F/40°C. I use an oven with the pilot lit and the door held ajar (if closed it gets too hot) to incubate the soybeans. I've seen people use insulated coolers warmed with hot water or heating pads, or a dorm fridge with an incandescent lightbulb and digital thermostat. It is also possible to make natto in a cooler environment, though the process is much slower. Like koji or tempeh, natto needs oxygen, but also humidity. If you use plastic to hold moisture in, be sure to poke some small holes in it so there will be some airflow.

This recipe describes the process of making natto with soybeans. In Japan, natto is typically made with special soybeans that are bred to be small, likely to increase surface area and, thereby, sliminess. In the US, I have found a source of these small soybeans (Signature Soy), but I have also had fine results with typical, larger soybeans. I have made natto with various beans and seeds, from lentils to jackfruit seeds. Other beans have less protein and less fat than soybeans, so while the bacteria develop reliably and produce the typical natto aroma, the sticky surface growth is generally not as luxuriantly slimy (which some might prefer).

If you are experimenting with certain seeds or beans with tough skins, the outer protective layer of the seeds must be removed so that the bacteria can access the germ, which is where the nutrients are concentrated. Generally, the seeds are boiled until the outer skins are soft enough to peel. After they are peeled, they are boiled again, if necessary, until the interiors of the seeds are soft.

Bacillus subtilis, the bacterium that produces natto, is generally present on soybeans and other seeds, so natto can be made without a starter; however, expect it to take a little longer, and to have an even funkier taste than natto made with a starter. All the commercial starters that I know of come from Japan, but increasingly they are becoming available in different parts of the world. Mature natto can also be used as a starter for another batch. Just mince it finely and mix it with cooked soybeans.

TIMEFRAME

2 days

EQUIPMENT

Glass or metal baking dish, big enough to spread natto in a layer no deeper than about 2 inches/5 centimeters

INGREDIENTS

for about 2 pounds/1 kilogram

1 pound/500 grams soybeans

A tiny amount (about 0.05 gram) natto-moto (starter, optional)

1 teaspoon rice or any other flour (only if using starter)

PROCESS

Soak the soybeans for at least 8 hours. Cover with lots of water, as the soybeans will more than double in size.

Drain the soaking water, transfer the soybeans to a pot, and cover with fresh water. Use at least 3 quarts/3 liters of water, as the beans will need to cook for a long time.

Bring the water to a boil, then cook the soybeans until they are soft, generally at least 6 to 8 hours. Some people speed this process by pressure cooking or pressure steaming the soybeans. (If you are planning to rely on the bacteria on the beans rather than a starter, do not pressure cook, as the higher temperatures will kill *Bacillus subtilis*.) I like the beans to be soft enough that I can easily crush them between two fingers. If your soybeans are not soft, your natto will not be good.

Drain the cooked soybeans in a colander. Shake well to remove as much surface water as possible.

Mix the tiniest amount of natto-moto, if using (it comes with a tiny measuring spoon), with the flour. Mix well so the spores are thoroughly distributed.

Transfer the soybeans to a bowl and add the flour-starter mixture, if using, stirring well to distribute. With most ferments, you want to cool down the cooked substrates to body temperature; with natto, add the starter immediately, as the spores not only survive boiling temperatures but also appear to benefit from the shock of the heat. (If you are not using a starter, don't worry; the bacteria is present on the beans.)

Transfer the soybeans to the fermentation vessel. I use rectangular, glass baking dishes. Be sure to keep the beans in a pretty shallow layer, no thicker than about 2 inches/5 centimeters. The natto needs to breathe. Distribute into more than one dish if necessary. I've also made natto in a cooking pot, with the lid on.

Cover the vessel. The natto needs to maintain its high level of moisture, but it also needs some oxygen. My best results have been with plastic wrap pulled taut over the surface of the dish, with a few holes poked in it so the beans can breathe. I've also used wax paper held down by chopsticks around the edges, which works all right, but the edges end up drying out.

HOW TO MAKE NATTO *CONTINUED*

Incubate the natto near or above body temperature for about 24 hours. The temperature 104°F/40°C is optimal. Stir it around once or twice during the latter part of the fermentation. If you love the flavor and texture of natto, you can let it ferment longer. If full-force natto scares you, try some after 16 hours and see what you think. As with all ferments, the fermentation by-products accumulate over time.

Refrigerate the natto after fermenting. Generally, people like to let it sit for a day or two in the refrigerator before eating. The flavor slowly strengthens in the fridge. If it sits in the refrigerator for a while and becomes too strong for me to enjoy fresh, I dehydrate it and use it as described in the following recipe.

SPECIAL SAUCE

When Mara Jane King, my travel companion in China, visited me in Tennessee to assist with my residency program a couple of years ago, we made a big batch of natto. Mara suggested that we dehydrate some of it, and then use it to make a table condiment loosely inspired by the douchi we saw and enjoyed in Qinfen. We toasted some sesame seeds and ground them along with the dehydrated natto and some chili peppers, Sichuan peppercorns, and salt. We called it Special Sauce (even though it is a powder), and it has become a favorite condiment in my kitchen.

Since then, I've tried lots of different variations, all of them delicious. In one batch, we made natto from the big seeds of tropical jackfruits rather than soybeans, and that worked great; it retained the same characteristic natto-ness. We boiled the seeds until soft, peeled the outer skins, added natto starter, and incubated as I typically do for natto. I imagine this process, with beans whole or mashed, could work with many different seeds.

My partner Shoppingspree3d/Daniel loves Special Sauce, too. We eat it every day and have experimented with different seasonings: plain (just natto, toasted sesame, and salt), super-funk (a higher proportion of natto), caraway, coriander, and original (with chili peppers and Sichuan peppercorns). For the latest batch, we dehydrated some douchi, or Chinese fermented black soybeans, and added that to the mix. "Next level," Shoppingspree pronounced. I put Special Sauce on almost everything, as a table condiment, and I often incorporate it in cooked or raw dishes, as well. I love natto on its own, but what I've learned—and had reaffirmed again and again by people who are put off by its texture and strong flavor—is that natto, along with its cousins in other culinary traditions, adds incredible and frequently inscrutable depth to almost anything savory when used as a seasoning.

As with all recipes, but even more so for a seasoning mix, please take these proportions as a rough guideline. Taste and add more of any element to find the balance that suits you. Note that the suggested amount of natto refers to its wet form; it will dry to a bit less than half its original weight. I have used Korean *gochugaru*, ground from chilies that are relatively mild. If you use a very hot chili instead, adjust accordingly. And consider this a point of departure. Experiment with other combinations, and unleash the power of natto in your own seasoning blends.

SPECIAL SAUCE

TIMEFRAME

About 8 hours

EQUIPMENT

Dehydrator (optional)

Jar

INGREDIENTS

for about 3 cups/375 grams

½ pound/250 grams wet natto

6 ounces/170 grams
sesame seeds

3 ounces/85 grams powdered
gochugaru or other powdered
chili pepper

1 tablespoon salt

1 teaspoon Sichuan
peppercorns

PROCESS

Dehydrate the natto in the sun or in a dehydrator. If you use a dehydrator, keep the temperature below about 115°F/46°C to maintain live bacteria. Length of time will vary with the intensity of the sun, the temperature of the dehydrator, and the exposed surface area. Because natto is so sticky, it clumps together when wet. As it dries, break up clumps to increase surface area and facilitate drying. Make sure the natto is fully dried.

Toast the sesame seeds over moderate heat in a cast-iron or other heavy pan. Stir frequently to prevent burning. Toast until fragrant and slightly darkened.

Allow the sesame seeds to cool.

Combine all the ingredients, then grind. I use a Corona-style hand grinder for this.

Store in a jar at room temperature and enjoy sprinkled on food. The seasoning blend will be stable, though the flavor will slowly fade if you leave it for too many months.

Jars of different flavors of
Special Sauce in my kitchen.

TUA NAO

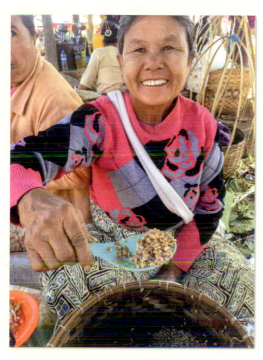

A vendor at a market in Burma shows me the natto-like beans she is selling.

Burma's largest ethnic minority, the Shan people, use a natto-like seasoning called *tua nao* in their traditional cuisine. Non-Shan people sometimes call tua nao "Shan *ngapi*," ngapi being fermented shrimp paste used as a seasoning there. Tua nao is used either fresh, as a paste, or dried into disks. I enjoyed food seasoned with tua nao, and I bought some disks to bring home. I learned how they are made from Naomi Duguid's gorgeous book *Burma: Rivers of Flavor*. She has allowed me to share the process she describes, which I have adapted slightly. Naomi writes of tua nao:

> *The disks can be used as a flavor base for curries and soups (pounded to a powder and combined with aromatics to make a flavor paste that is cooked in oil), or they can be lightly toasted (over a flame or in a dry heavy skillet), then pounded into a powder. Tua nao powder is an essential flavoring in a number of salads . . . and vegetable dishes . . . it gives a nutty toasted undernote. The moist soybean paste can be fried in oil as part of a flavor base in curries and stir-fries. It can also be wrapped in a banana leaf or in foil, grilled or steamed, then used as a condiment for rice.*[1]

TUA NAO

TIMEFRAME

About 3 days to make the paste; a few more days to dry into disks

EQUIPMENT

for drying

Wax or parchment paper or heavy plastic

Metal drying rack, bamboo mat, or woven basket

INGREDIENTS

for about 3 cups/750 milliliters of paste or 40 small disks

½ pound/250 grams soybeans

Salt

Other seasonings, such as ground chilies, sesame seeds, minced ginger, galangal, and/or lime leaves (optional)

PROCESS

Soak the soybeans for at least 8 hours.

Boil the soybeans in water until soft (about 6 to 8 hours). Do not pressure cook, as that will destroy the bacteria that will ferment the soybeans.

Drain the soybeans.

Ferment 2 to 3 days in a warm spot, until fragrant. In Burma, the cooked soybeans are typically fermented in a rice sack. Naomi places them in a basket and covers them with a cotton cloth, though she says she has had fine results leaving them in the pot they were cooked in, as did I.

Grind the fermented soybeans into a smooth, thick paste, adding a little water if necessary.

Add salt to taste. Start with about ½ teaspoon per cup of paste, then add more if desired.

Add other seasonings if you like. You can use a combination of the suggested seasonings, or experiment with others. If you want to try a few different seasoning options, just divide the paste.

You can use the paste fresh as a seasoning in cooking, and store it for about a week in the refrigerator. Naomi does not recommend eating it raw, but rather using it in cooking "as a flavoring in place of shrimp paste." Alternatively, you can form it into disks for longer storage, drying them in the sun, a dehydrator, or an oven, as follows.

Forming the disks is something like forming masa dough into tortillas. It's easiest to flatten the disks between two layers of heavy plastic, or wax or parchment paper. I had my best success with wax paper. Have a bowl of water on hand, and a piece of wax paper (or parchment or plastic) at least 6-by-12 inches/15-by-30 centimeters, folded in half (or two smaller pieces). Keep the disks small until you develop your technique, about a tablespoon of paste each. Dip a spoonful of paste into the water, flatten it with wet hands into a round on half of the wax paper, then fold the other half of the wax paper onto the round, and use your palm to flatten the disk into an even layer roughly ⅛ inch/3 millimeters thick; not too thin.

Gently peel the top layer of wax paper off the disk. Don't panic if it sticks; use your wet hands to peel it off and repair as necessary. Then flip the exposed side of the disk onto a drying rack, bamboo mat, or basket, and peel the wax off the disk, again using your wet hands to peel it off and repair as necessary. Clean the pressing paper or plastic with water if any paste sticks to it, and keep it wet to minimize sticking.

Dry the disks in the sun for a couple of days, flipping a few times, and taking inside at night. If you have a dehydrator, dehydrate at a low temperature, 95–105°F/35–40°C, for about 6 hours, flipping a few times until they feel dry enough to be shelf-stable. Alternatively, dry in an oven at its lowest setting (150–200°F/65–95°C) for about 4 hours, flipping a few times until they feel dry.

"Store stacked in a cool, dry place; a cookie tin is a good option," suggests Naomi. "They should keep indefinitely."

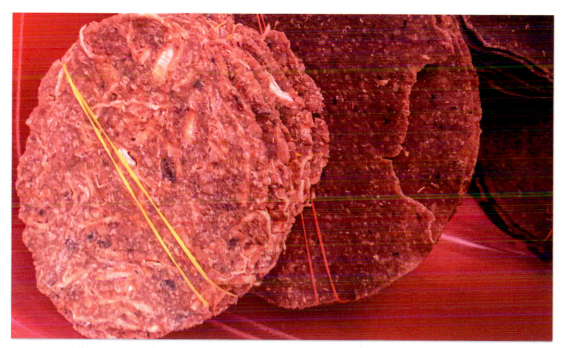

Dried disks of natto-like fermented soybeans, tua nao, that I bought at a market in Burma.

Akhuni

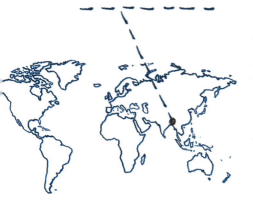

The organizers of my 2020 Australian tour did an amazing job of creating collaborative events with teachers from different places and varied perspectives. The most epic event, held at the gorgeous Daylesford Longhouse near Daylesford, Victoria, featured a few different Asian chefs, including Harry Mangat. Harry grew up in a family that moved around his home country of India, and this exposed him to India's very diverse cultures and regional cuisines. He told me that after reading my book, he became interested in exploring his homeland's many fermentation traditions. I am so gratified that my work can be such a catalyst! During a workshop, Harry demonstrated how to make and use *akhuni* (sometimes transliterated as *axone*). Akhuni is a natto-like fermented soybean seasoning traditionally prepared in the northeastern Indian state of Nagaland.

A few days after I met Harry and he first introduced me to akhuni, a woman born and raised in Nagaland

Harry Mangat with the akhuni he made for our workshop.

The Daylesford Longhouse, a bright, beautiful setting for a memorable workshop day.

introduced herself after one of my talks, and she gave me a few fermented gifts from her homeland, including dried akhuni. She was Dolly Kikon, an anthropologist who teaches at the University of Melbourne. In addition to the akhuni, she sent me off with fermented bamboo shoots, shredded and dried. Yum! Echoing Harry, Dolly told me that reading my book had helped her recognize that the traditional ferments of her homeland were topics worthy of scholarly attention. Her recent works—academic papers, films, and a book in progress—document how akhuni and other Nagaland ferments are made.

Akhuni is made without a starter, relying on the inevitable presence of *Bacillus subtilis* on soybeans, and the bacteria's ability to survive boiling temperatures. This is the process as Dolly documented it in the kitchen of a woman named Anoli Sumi in Nagaland: "First, the soya beans were soaked overnight, and then boiled. The cooked beans were placed in a bamboo basket lined with banana leaves, teak leaves or those of *Phrynium placentarium*. After that, a hole was made at the bottom of the basket to drain away the fermentation juice."[2] Fermentation time ranges from two or three days in warm places to more than a week in cool places.

Anoli Sumi making akhuni in Nagaland.

After the fermentation, the soybeans are generally mashed, wrapped in leaves, and smoked above the fireplace. After smoking, akhuni is ready to use, and because it is somewhat dried by the smoking, it is stable for a while. Dolly told me that she prefers to freeze akhuni. "That way I can use it for a longer time," she says. "I have to cut a piece, soak it in hot water for a few minutes, and it is fragrant and ready to be used."

Beyond documenting the methods used to make akhuni and other traditional Naga ferments, Dolly's work investigates the shifting meanings of these foods. "On the one hand, making and consuming akhuni are important parts of tribal identities like Naga and shared identities between Himalayan communities—a kind of sensory imagined community," she writes, noting that akhuni-like foods are enjoyed throughout the eastern Himalayan region. "On the other hand, akhuni is part of a larger culture of food preparation and consumption that casts these same communities as less sophisticated in

Finished akhuni, ready to use.

the culinary order of India, and South Asia more broadly. To consume and produce akhuni is to be traditional and occasionally cast as backward and simple—a construction that circulates among akhuni consumers as well as non-consumers."[3]

Dolly writes a lot about the smell of akhuni. In fact, she told me that the word itself means strong or deep smell in the Sumi Naga language:

> *Capturing the smell and taste of akhuni is a challenge. A metabolic process that transforms the chemical balance of soya beans—texture, taste and smell—it also alters the relationship of the food to its consumers forever. Some become lifelong connoisseurs, while others detest it and develop a long-lasting repulsion to it. Anthropological literature informs us how dietary habits and taste are never neutral grounds. Moralities, transgressions and boundaries can be traced to everyday practices of production and consumption within and across human societies. Unlike categories of food that fall into the dominant classificatory list of clean and unclean food, fermented food or smelly food is something else entirely. While smell is local, it is also invisible. It crosses borders. There is something unnerving and subversive about the way it manages to pollute and infringe the most intimate and sacred spaces. It enters the nostrils and, in some, produces feelings of revulsion. For others, the same smell invokes feelings of comfort or remembrance of home.*[4]

The power of akhuni's smell, as well as its fundamental similarity to natto, is illustrated by a story Dolly recounts, told by her grandmother. During World War II, when Japanese soldiers searched her grandmother's house for food, they found the akhuni and wept for joy as they devoured a food whose familiar flavor recalled home. The smell of akhuni has also been the cause of conflict in Delhi and other Indian cities, where migrants from Nagaland have faced conflict with neighbors and officials. "It is in the intimate spaces of the kitchen, the blurred boundaries of a geographical region, and the routine negotiations between masala eaters and akhuni consumers in New Delhi," Dolly writes, "that everyday notions of citizenship, belonging and democratic spaces are constantly challenged and redefined in powerful ways."[5]

DOLLY KIKON'S AKHUNI AND GINGER CHUTNEY

This is a simple chutney, to enjoy as
a seasoning to embellish rice or soup,
showcasing akhuni with ginger and chilies.

TIMEFRAME

About 10 minutes

EQUIPMENT

Mortar and pestle, or
food processor

INGREDIENTS

for a small amount of
chutney for 4 to 6 servings
as a seasoning

A few whole green chilies
(to taste)

Salt (to taste)

½ teaspoon crushed ginger
(to taste)

About 3 tablespoons akhuni,
or substitute natto, mashed
(to taste)

PROCESS

Roast the green chilies in a hot pan for about 5 minutes. Stir
frequently as chilies become fragrant and their edges darken.

Grind the roasted chilies with salt. For best results, use a mortar
and pestle; or use a food processor.

Add the crushed ginger and akhuni, and lightly mash together. Use
a spoon to mix the ingredients well.

DOLLY KIKON'S AKHUNI AND TOMATO CHUTNEY

Another simple akhuni chutney, this one with tomato. Enjoy it with rice or soup.

TIMEFRAME

About 10 minutes

EQUIPMENT

Mortar and pestle, or food processor

INGREDIENTS

for a small amount of chutney for 4 to 6 servings as a seasoning

A few whole green chilies (to taste)

1 whole tomato (ripe and red)

2 garlic cloves, crushed (to taste)

½ teaspoon crushed ginger (to taste)

Salt (to taste)

About 3 tablespoons akhuni, or substitute natto, mashed (to taste)

PROCESS

Roast the chilies and tomato in a hot pan for about 5 minutes. Stir frequently as they become fragrant and their edges darken.

Grind the roasted chilies and tomato. For best results, use a mortar and pestle. Add the crushed garlic, ginger, and salt, and mash them in.

Add the akhuni, and lightly mash it.

Use a spoon to mix the ingredients well.

DOLLY KIKON'S AKHUNI AND YAM STEW

Me with Dolly Kikon and the fermented akhuni and bamboo shoots she gave me.

This recipe uses akhuni's wonderful flavor to accent the mild starchiness of taro, called *yams* in Nagaland. It's something Dolly grew up eating. "I still love it," she says. Me, too, especially the sticky, starchy texture of this stew.

TIMEFRAME

About 45 minutes

INGREDIENTS

for 4 to 6 servings

About 1 pound/500 grams small taro corms

Salt (to taste)

About 4 tablespoons of akhuni, or substitute natto, mashed (to taste)

About 4 garlic cloves, crushed (to taste)

A bunch of mustard greens, washed and chopped (optional)

PROCESS

Wash the unpeeled taro corms and boil them for 25 to 30 minutes, until tender. Do not peel the taro before boiling, as the sap may cause skin irritation before it is cooked.

Drain the water, peel the taro, and mash it well.

In a pot, combine the mashed taro with enough water to make a soupy consistency.

Bring this mix to a boil, then reduce the heat.

Add the salt, akhuni, and garlic to taste, as well as the mustard greens, if using.

Mix well and gently simmer for another 5 minutes or so.

Enjoy!

✳ called *yams* in Nagaland

Fermented African Locust Beans

Cuisines across West Africa incorporate seasonings prepared by fermenting African locust beans (*Parkia biglobosa*) and other legumes. Although these beans are very different from soybeans, and they require much more elaborate processing, the bacteria that dominates the fermentation is the ubiquitous *Bacillus subtilis*, producing the characteristic ammonia notes of alkaline fermentation. In a region of the world with many languages and indigenous traditions, these ferments have many different names: *soumbala, dawadawa, iru, ogiri, afiti, sounbareh,* and *netetou,* among numerous others. My friend and fellow food writer Michael Twitty—who is doing incredible work weaving together history, identity, and food—shared photos of afiti making in Benin, and he tells me that there the ferment is also known as *moutarde* (mustard).

In addition to having a plethora of regional names, the processes for making these fermented seasonings vary quite a bit in their particulars. What unites them is *Bacillus subtilis,* and the characteristic smell and flavor that it produces. In a Slow Food report, I found a detailed description of the process for making sounbareh, a style of fermented African locust beans eaten in Sierra Leone:

> *The harvested pods are shelled by hand and the pulp is washed off to leave clean seeds. The seeds are then fermented together with wood ash for at least three to four days to enable the thick mesocarp to decompose, leaving only the brown cotyledon. These are boiled for a whole day over a hot fire, then the boiled seeds are refermented for three more days. The seeds are dried in the sun for several days until they turn a thick black color. They contain very little moisture, which means the product can be kept for months or even years without decomposing. At this stage, the product can be sold, kept or prepared for final consumption as needed. Apart from the harvesting, which is done by men and boys, all of*

Freshly harvested
African locust beans
in Benin.

Straining cooked
African locust beans.

the other activities are carried out by women, generally during the dry season. During the final processing, the dried black seeds are further roasted in a small pot until they make a cracking sound, then pounded in a mortar together with other ingredients like pepper, fish or salt, and sprinkled on the top of cooked rice. The powder can also be added to green vegetables like spinach and potato or cassava leaves. It can also replace fish or meat in the sauce. The powder can also be used on its own in soup, especially when preparing food like poultry, bush meat or fish for important guests.[6]

The report notes that "the urban or semi-urban populations tend to replace [sounbareh] with Maggi cubes," a brand of bouillon, and that the traditional sounbareh has a vastly superior nutrient profile, "particularly when compared with the ubiquitous industrial stock cubes."

A ball of African locust beans fermented into afiti.

Much commentary about these fermented condiments invokes critiques of bouillon cubes. Cheap, flavorful, and widely available, these factory-produced, artificially flavored seasonings have displaced the traditional fermented seasonings in many kitchens. Nigerian-born chef and food writer Tunde Wey, who produces iru and sells it at www.disappearingcondiments.com, elaborates the comparison on his website:

> For centuries Nigerians have used indigenously fermented seasonings and condiments to imbue their foods with rich complex flavor. Different ethnic groups developed myriad techniques to turn seeds and stems into pungent and powerful pastes and pellets, transforming innocuous ingredients into delicious meals.
>
> In 1969, Nestle entered the Nigerian market, and the ensuing period has seen artisanal fermented condiments, like iru, replaced with factory produced soy-based bouillon cubes.

Twice in my travels, I have been gifted West African fermented seasonings. At a sustainable agriculture conference in North Carolina some years back, I met a man who had immigrated to the United States from West Africa. He was pleased that I knew about this group of fermented seasonings, and the next day he brought me some soumbala that he had brought back from a visit to his family. It was in powder form, with the characteristic ammonia-tinged smell. Another ferment, netetou, given to me by the New York City–based Senegalese chef Pierre Thiam, was a dried ball of mostly intact beans mashed together. Once I cooked with these seasonings, I realized that the flavor they produced was familiar because it had been an underlying presence in stews I ate when I'd traveled in West Africa decades ago. These seasonings have a strong flavor, especially when used in large quantities, but (like so many very flavorful seasonings) when used sparingly, they impart an elusive sense of complexity instead.

Outside of the range where African locust trees grow, these beans are not available fresh; however, they are widely available (via the internet) in fermented, dried form. So, rather than offer step-by-step instructions for fermenting them, I'll instead provide the following recipe for cooking with the already fermented condiment.

EFO RIRO

I learned to make this delicious Yoruba spinach stew from a great food blog called Chef Lola's Kitchen, written by Lola Osinkolu, who was born and raised in Nigeria and now lives in the US. This is my adaptation of her recipe, included with her kind permission.

The iru (fermented African locust beans), along with dried crayfish, stockfish, and palm oil, give this stew a really wonderful and distinctive funky flavor. Although all these ingredients are available in African markets and via the internet, Chef Lola's recipe encourages flexibility and substitutions. For a vegan version, she recommends replacing the meat and fish with tofu and/or mushrooms. She even suggests that you can skip the iru, but its flavor is really at the heart of this stew; if you can't find iru but can make or find natto, use natto for a similar flavor. Like all the *efo riro* recipes I find online, Chef Lola's recipe calls for bouillon cubes, which I think are redundant and unnecessary with iru. Similarly, although most cooks I met in China use monosodium glutamate (MSG) quite liberally, to me, adding it to dishes full of soy sauce, doubanjiang, vinegar, and other umami seasonings also seems redundant. I'm not concerned about eating food with bouillon cubes or MSG, but it can be satisfying to enjoy the traditional seasonings without further enhancing them with their industrial substitutions.

Most of the steps in this recipe involve preparing the ingredients, which can be done in advance. Once they are prepared, the stew itself takes only about 20 minutes to make. Serve the efo riro over rice, or with West African "swallows" (thick starchy paste from tubers) such as *fufu*.

TIMEFRAME

A few hours, including soaking time

EQUIPMENT

Food processor or mortar and pestle

INGREDIENTS

for 4 to 6 servings

¼ pound/125 grams stockfish (**dried fish**), or substitute fresh fish or none

1 pound/500 grams beef, or substitute another meat, fish, tofu, or mushrooms ✱

2 tablespoons dried crayfish, or substitute smoked fish or turkey

2 onions

3 large red bell peppers

2 scotch bonnet peppers, or substitute 1 habanero

1½ pounds/750 grams spinach or other leafy greens

¼ cup/60 milliliters palm oil, or substitute another oil

2 tablespoons iru, fermented African locust beans, or substitute natto (to taste)

Salt

PROCESS

Soak the stockfish in fresh water for a few hours to hydrate it. Once hydrated, drain and separate the flesh from the bones and break it into small, flaky pieces.

Cut the beef into bite-size pieces, just barely cover with water, simmer for about 10 minutes, and remove from the heat. Remove the meat from the cooking water, and reserve the water.

Grind the crayfish into a powder using a food processor or a mortar and pestle, then reserve to add to the stew later.

Grind ½ onion, bell peppers, and scotch bonnet peppers into a coarse paste using a food processor or a mortar and pestle. Dice the remaining 1½ onions.

Blanch the spinach. Bring a pot of water to a boil. Add the spinach and stir it into the water. As soon as the water returns to a boil, remove the pot from the heat and pour the water and spinach into a colander. Rinse the spinach with cold water to completely stop its cooking. Squeeze the spinach to remove as much water from it as possible.

In a pot with a heavy bottom, heat the palm oil and stir-fry the diced onion until it is golden brown.

Add the blended pepper and onion mixture and fry, stirring frequently, until the sauce thickens.

Add the crayfish powder, iru, and a big pinch of salt, and stir the seasonings into the sauce. Add the meat and stockfish and some of the water the meat was cooked in to reach the consistency of a stew with plenty of sauce. Stir everything together and simmer a few minutes.

Finally, add the spinach and simmer a few minutes longer. Taste and adjust seasonings as desired.

✱ Chef Lola recommends using a mix of beef, tripe, and cow skin; I used just stew beef

Furu or *Dofuru* Fermented Tofu

Fermented tofu deserves its own book. From my very limited experience, having spent two weeks in China, I would say that there probably exists as much variation in fermented tofu as in cheese. Like cheese, fermented tofu runs the gamut from mild to extreme, with varying fermentation methods and durations and a huge variety of seasonings.

Before addressing how tofu is fermented, I think it is important to contextualize this widely known but little-understood food and discuss how it is made. Beyond the regions of Asia where it is traditionally eaten, tofu is widely associated with vegetarianism. In China, and indeed in much of Asia, it is a food that is eaten by most everyone. While tofu can serve as a meat substitute, in the Chinese context it is often cooked and served with meat. Tofu is not the only example, in China and elsewhere in Asia, of a food turned into a curd. In culinary cultures that celebrate contrasting textures, soft gelatinous masses are made from many different ingredients. The most surprising to me was what is called blood tofu, or coagulated blood from pigs. In the markets, I saw stalls selling variously colored blocks made from mung beans, chickpeas, rice and other grains, and starchy tubers such as taro. The ones I tried had sweet, mild flavors. They also have remarkable absorptive capacities. Tofu's many cousins are eaten hot or cold, in slices or chunks, or as noodles.

Blood tofu.

A few different types of curds at a market in China.

During my visit to the village of Qinfen in Guizhou, we woke up before dawn one morning to visit a neighboring village called Xi Mi Cun, to visit a woman named Wu Tai Xiang and learn from her about making tofu. She and her family grow their own soybeans, and for 30 years she has made two batches of tofu a day, each with 2 kilograms (about 4½ pounds) of beans, which she sells to other villagers from a small storefront in her home. She actually begins each day's tofu the night before, by soaking the

Burmese tofu made from yellow split peas.

Wu Tai Xiang's pigs excited for the tofu-making by-products they are fed twice each day.

soybeans in fresh water. Sitting in water overnight, they swell and soften.

The first order of business in the morning was grinding the soybeans. In some places I visited in China, I saw (and got to try) hand-turned wet mills, but Wu Tai Xiang has a small electric mill. It grinds the beans and separates the bean juice liquid, soy milk, from the pulp. In order to extract the maximum amount of nutrients from the beans, she adds more water to the pulp, and then runs it through the mill a second time. Then, the soy milk is heated over a wood fire in a huge wok. Meanwhile, the pulp is taken out back to the family's side business: six pigs they are raising, who devour it. In China, the soy pulp by-product from tofu making feeds a lot of pigs.

As the soy milk came to a boil, Wu Tai Xiang skimmed off the foam that formed. This was the indicator that it was time to coagulate the soy milk. For a coagulant, Wu Tai Xiang uses gypsum, or calcium sulfate dihydrate, which is a chalky mineral. Any number of coagulants can be used to make tofu, including magnesium chloride (nigari), magnesium sulfate (Epsom salt), and glucono delta lactone (GDL), as well as acids such as citrus juice,

Soy milk heating in a wok. Here, Wu Tai Xiang removes foam, which she feeds, along with the soy solids, to her pigs.

Bowls of fresh, warm, soft curds of dofu hua, tofu flower.

vinegar, and lactic acid. Wu Tai Xiang dissolved the gypsum in some water, then poured the hot soy milk into a bucket with the gypsum solution and left it to coagulate.

After about 10 minutes, the soy milk had formed soft curds with the consistency of yogurt. Wu Tai Xiang scooped some of the warm, jiggly, unpressed curds into bowls for us to eat. The warm, unpressed curds are called *dofu hua*, tofu flower. In the chill of the early morning, the warm, soft curds, served with a little sugar sprinkled on top, were the ultimate comfort food.

After our delicious snack, we returned to the coagulating curds, now a bit firmer, though still quite soft. Wu Tai Xiang scooped the curd into two cheesecloth-lined wooden forms. She then placed buckets with water atop the forms to force more liquid out of the tofu and make it firmer. She left the weight on for a couple of hours, after which she unwrapped gorgeous blocks of tofu, firmer though still soft, which she cut into smaller pieces.

Pressed, unwrapped, and cut, the tofu blocks are ready to sell. In the small village context, the tofu is sold fresh the day it is made, without refrigeration or formal packaging. Today, in China and around the world, mass-produced tofu is made more or less like this, but then the tofu is heat-processed and vacuum-sealed for refrigerated distribution and storage. To state the obvious: until the last century, there was no way for anyone to keep tofu fresh. Like milk, the only way it could be preserved was by fermenting it (or drying it).

There is no single way to ferment tofu. During my brief visit to China, I tasted many different versions: some mild, and some strong; some red, and some white; some spicy, others not at all. Most of what we ate and learned about was called furu or *dofuru*. Typically, the starting point for making furu is mao dofu (*Mao Dofu*, page 198). This is the biggest challenge of the process, but it is imperative. This initial fungal ferment is what keeps the rest of the process safe and prevents harmful bacteria from developing. In the United States, there have been cases of botulism from home-fermented furu. From what I have been able to glean from the reports, the starting point in each case was fresh tofu rather than mao dofu, which is not widely available here. Additionally, the tofu was spontaneously fermented under tight plastic wrap, exactly the anaerobic environment in which *Clostridium*

Wu Tai Xiang scoops
fresh curds into
cloth-lined forms.

Here, the form is full of soft curds
and Wu Tai Xiang places a top on it,
in preparation for pressing.

A bucket partially filled with
water functions as a weight to
force water out of the curds
and make the tofu firmer.

After pressing, the tofu is
smaller and firmer.

Wu Tai Xiang with the finished tofu,
ready to cut into blocks and sell.

Mrs. Ding shows us her furu.

The Zhang family's furu had a much stronger flavor.

botulinum can thrive. Do not attempt to make furu without mao dofu.

The hairy mao dofu cubes are generally dipped into distilled alcohol, and then rolled in a mixture of salt, spice, and sometimes sugar. "Red yeast rice," or rice grown with the fungus *Monascus purpureus*, can also be added. This is what produces the bright red pigment in some fermented tofu. The seasoned tofu cubes are then packed into a crock or other vessel; covered with oil, brine, or fermented alcohol; and left to ferment for varying lengths of time.

Mrs. Ding, the woman who served us lunch and gave us tastes of all her ferments on our first day in Chengdu, fed us delicious furu that was relatively mild—a very accessible introduction, especially compared with some of the furu we tried later. Her method was a variant of what is described previously: Dip cubes of mao dofu in baijiu liquor; coat each cube with a mix of salt, sugar, star anise, chili pepper, Sichuan peppercorns, and some other, unfamiliar spices; place coated tofu cubes into a crock; cover with cooked and cooled rapeseed oil; and ferment. It seemed that she kept the furu fermenting in the crock as she and her family ate it, never refrigerating it. Based on how full the crock was when we arrived, and how mild the furu was, I would guess that what she served us was just a few weeks old.

A few days later, we visited the Zhang family at their farm in the mountains outside Chengdu and tried their year-old furu. They placed a single cube onto a serving plate and recommended using chopsticks to take just a small portion, break it up, and mix it into our food as a condiment, as the flavor was strong. The interior of the tofu cube was no longer white, but rather a caramel-like light brown. The furu had a sharp, acrid flavor that was too strong for me to enjoy it on its own, but it provided a delicious accent when mixed into the food. As with natto-like seasonings, fish sauce, and some other foods with extremely funky flavors, a stronger furu can be over-powering on its own, yet it contributes a wonderful layer of complexity when mixed sparingly with other flavors.

A few years later, when Pao Liu showed up at my place with mao dofu starter (*Mao Dofu*, page 198), Pao, Mara, other students, and I made two variations of unconventional furu using ingredients we had on hand.

My alcohol- and spice-dipped cubes of mao dofu in a jar prior to fermentation into furu.

For the first, we dipped the cubes in salt; mixed them with cooked, unfermented soybeans, red yeast rice, and shio-koji; then packed it all into a jar and covered it with a mixture of moonshine and *doburoku* (unstrained sake with its lees). For the second, we dipped the cubes in moonshine, then in Special Sauce (page 211) mixed with extra salt, and covered the mix with moonshine. I left them both to ferment for about four months. They both were very tasty, not especially extreme, but with completely different flavors. The tofu eventually decomposed in both, I'd guess because of the addition of enzyme-rich koji in the first, and natto in the second.

As I was writing this section, I made another batch of furu. First, I made mao dofu using tempeh starter, and it turned out wonderfully well. Then, I dipped each cube in bourbon, followed by Special Sauce mixed with a little sugar and additional salt. I packed the spice-covered cubes into a jar, and then covered them with some shio-koji and the brine left over from garlic-dill pickles. After a few weeks, this furu smelled and tasted fantastic, with a creamy texture and mildly tart and spicy flavor, that slowly got tarter and funkier as it fermented for months.

My furu when I tried it five months later. Delicious!

I hope you can see, from these improvisational homemade examples, how flexible the process for furu is, once you have the mao dofu. Many Chinese families make it themselves, the way they like it. For the experimentalist, there are many possible variations.

There are other approaches to fermenting tofu that do not require starting with mao dofu. They generally involve using other fermented products as protective fermentation mediums. In Japan, I encountered tofu fermented in shio-koji (*Shio-koji*, page 156), miso (*Tofu Misozuke*, page 240), and soy sauce. In China, tofu is sometimes fermented in brine from fermenting vegetables or other ingredients.

One notable style is what is called stinky tofu, or *chou dofu*. The brine for stinky tofu is called a *lu*. There are many regional variations on what is used to prepare the lu, and how long it is left to ferment. I have made stinky tofu based on an account by Fuchsia Dunlop, who writes about Chinese cuisine in English. Stalks of mature amaranth are fermented in brine until they develop a "special fragrance." The brine is used as a medium in which to ferment tofu, while the fermented stalks are steamed and eaten, with a flavor that Dunlop describes as "putrescent and wildly exciting at the same time."[7] According to Dunlop, hydrogen sulfide produced by the breakdown of amino acids is the source of stinky tofu's stinkiness. The wide variation in how stinky the tofu becomes reflects varying ingredients and lengths of fermentation of the lu itself, and of the tofu in the lu.

SENSATIONALIZING THE FLAVORS OF FERMENTATION

Stinky tofu is one of those fermented foods that have been widely sensationalized. I first heard about it when someone pointed me toward an episode of a television show called *Bizarre Foods with Andrew Zimmern*, in which Zimmern goes to Taiwan to try its legendary stinky tofu, but cannot bring himself to swallow it, and spits it out. "There's a sour spoiled flavor in my mouth that is absolutely singular," he says, declaring the stinky tofu "too putrid and foul for me."

I do not love everything that I taste, but I find that show's underlying premise of adventuring in order to try "bizarre" foods to be completely offensive. Given the incredible adaptability and flexibility of our human palates, and how different the available food resources are in different environments, to label someone's food as "bizarre" or "putrid and foul" on the basis that it violates your sensibilities is to needlessly project otherness upon them for a laugh, for ratings, for fame, for personal enrichment. Let's celebrate the incredible diversity of food traditions, not sensationalize it.

I have eaten stinky tofu in Hong Kong and in Flushing, New York. After all the buildup, I was expecting to be challenged, but in both cases the stinkiness was surprisingly mild. I look forward to visiting Taiwan at some point, and to trying some of its legendary stinkier tofu.

Stinky tofu I bought on the street in Hong Kong.

Village Feast

The day we visited Xi Mi Cun to learn about tofu making, we would walk outside the tiny tofu shop during intervals in the tofu making to explore the nearby village streets. We were a spectacle ourselves, but the streets were abuzz with activity in preparation for a community feast. Women were washing vast quantities of greens. A group of men along with a couple of women were butchering and chopping small mountains of meat.

The most interesting sight was a group of women making egg sausages, *dan chang*. They had a big bowl of scrambled eggs, mixed with chives and other seasonings, that they were making into sausages (*Dan Chang* Egg Sausages, page 238.)

We were told that all the food preparation underway was for a village feast to celebrate the construction of a new home. As we started watching, photographing, and videotaping the preparations, we were invited to the party. Our presence in the village on this occasion was seen as auspicious, and the organizers eagerly invited us to stay and celebrate with them. There was so much wonderful food, and so much baijiu! We ate and drank our fill, and then some.

The Xi Mi Cun village feast.

Preparing greens for the Xi Mi Cun
village feast.

Butchering a pig for the Xi Mi Cun
village feast, with egg sausage
making in the foreground.

DAN CHANG EGG SAUSAGES

Filling sausage casings with scrambled egg mixture.

Thanks to Mara Jane King for talking to the women we saw making these sausages, taking good notes, and then writing this recipe. The egg sausages we ate were served in a beautiful, rich pork stock with mushrooms, but they are so striking and delicious that they could enliven any kind of brothy vegetable- and/or animal-based soup. Have the rest of your soup ready before you make the egg sausages. Making these is definitely a two-person job. One person should hold the funnel with the casing, gently release the casing, and catch the fragile sausages as they form; the other can slowly pour or ladle the egg mix into the funnel.

Slicing partially cooked egg sausages.

Egg sausages puffed up after further cooking, ready to eat.

TIMEFRAME

About 1 hour (not including soup preparation)

EQUIPMENT

Funnel

INGREDIENTS

for about 24 egg sausages

2 quarts/2 liters pork or other animal- and/or vegetable-based soup, seasoned (to taste)

Sausage casing, 2-foot/60-centimeters length of 1-inch/2.5-centimeter diameter

1 dozen eggs

2 heaping tablespoons chopped chives

1 teaspoon soy sauce

1 teaspoon salt

A few pinches white pepper

PROCESS

Have the soup ready and hot for the egg sausages to go into for the last 10 minutes of cooking.

Boil a pot of water for the initial, brief cooking of the sausages.

Rinse the casings, run water through them, and soak them in lukewarm water.

Beat the eggs, then add the remaining ingredients and beat them in.

Gently gather the casing over the outside of the moistened neck of the funnel.

Tie off the end of the casing with a knot.

Hold the funnel over a big bowl. Use one hand to support the funnel, the other to slowly and gently release more of the casing as it fills with egg mixture.

Ask a helper to slowly ladle or pour the egg mix into the casing through the funnel.

Use your hands to gently guide the filled sausages into the bowl and release more of the casing to make room for more egg mixture. Give feedback to the helper to pour slower or faster, as needed.

Gently slide the last of the unfilled casing off the funnel, leaving enough to tie off the casing, with as little air space as possible.

Place the egg sausage in boiling water and gently simmer about 10 minutes, until the sausage is firm.

Cool for a few minutes, then cut into 1-inch/2.5-centimeter chunks, cutting both sealed ends off so all chunks are open on both sides.

Add the cut sausage to the hot soup and simmer for about 10 minutes more, until the egg sausages puff up, expanding out from the casing on both sides, looking something like a two-headed mushrooms.

Watch carefully and pull off the heat when the ends puff up. Excessive cooking will cause further puffing and the eggs will become what Mara describes as a giant "brain fluff."

TOFU MISOZUKE

Compared to the styles of fermenting tofu detailed previously, *misozuke*—tofu fermented with miso—is easy and fast. The enzymes in the miso work their magic, digesting the tofu's proteins into more flavorful umami amino acids, and making the tofu creamier. At its simplest, tofu misozuke is tofu coated with miso and cured that way for a few days. But my onetime student Holly Davis, author of the wonderful book *Ferment*, raised the bar for me with her delectable tofu misozuke, which blends salty, long-fermented miso with a more enzyme-rich, shorter-fermented sweet miso, as well as sweeteners and lemon zest. This is my adaptation of her recipe in *Ferment*.

TIMEFRAME

3 to 5 days

EQUIPMENT

2 cutting boards or flat platters

Cheesecloth or muslin

INGREDIENTS

for 12 ounces/350 grams

12 ounces/350 grams firm tofu

1 cup/320 grams salty long-fermented miso

½ cup/160 grams sweet short-fermented miso

2 tablespoons mirin

1 teaspoon rice syrup (or barley malt syrup or honey)

1 teaspoon lemon zest

¾-inch/2-centimeter piece of dried kombu, ground to a fine powder (optional)

PROCESS

Using the cutting boards or platters, press the tofu to remove excess moisture. Place one of the boards at the edge of the sink and prop up the opposite side so water will run into the sink. Place the tofu on the drain board and the second board atop the tofu to gently press it. Leave for an hour to drain.

Cover a plate with a piece of cheesecloth or muslin more than large enough to wrap the tofu.

In a bowl, combine all the other ingredients and mix thoroughly.

Remove the tofu from the draining board and smear the miso mixture over the entire surface of it, leaving no gaps.

Place the miso-covered tofu on the cloth on the plate. Loosely wrap the tofu with the cloth and leave to cure at room temperature for 3 to 5 days; 3 days in a warm environment, 5 days in a cooler environment.

After curing, remove the block of tofu from the cloth and carefully scrape off the miso layer with a knife. You can use the miso mixture to cure a second block of tofu, or use it in other dishes. Since it is watered down from the tofu, the miso mixture residue is not as stable as miso, so should be used soon.

The misozuke is creamy and wonderfully funky, delicious as a spread or dip. Holly writes: "*Misozuke* tofu is great in celery stalks or blended with a robust *dashi* [a Japanese soup stock] into a 'cheesy' sauce that is excellent poured over cooked vegetables and baked until just set."[8]

Cacao

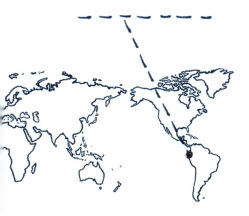

My first encounter with cacao trees—harvesting their ripe pods, tasting their sweet, juicy fruit, seeing that fruit fermented, dried, and then processed into chocolate right on the farm—was in Ecuador, at a beautiful forest restoration project called Mashpi. Mashpi is located in a lush valley not far from the equator, a few hours' drive west from the capital, Quito. One of Mashpi's founders, Agustina Arcos, had been at my Quito workshop and invited me to visit and see what they were doing.

The land that Mashpi is reforesting was once a rainforest, until it was clear-cut to make way for a palm plantation. On our way there, we passed many palm plantations, vast monocultures to supply the global demand for palm oil. Palms yield much more oil per unit of land than any other oil crop, and their oil not only features prominently in traditional cuisines of Africa and some other tropical locales, but it is frequently used in processed foods, cosmetics, animal feeds, and (more than all of these combined) biofuels.

When rainforests are burned in order to clear land for palm plantations, it causes many problems. The burning itself creates pollution and releases into the atmosphere carbon that had been sequestered in trees, thus exacerbating climate change. The lush rainforest provides habitat for Indigenous peoples, as well as plants, animals, and other life forms; deforestation displaces people and disrupts ecological balances, further intensifying the stress on cultures and species that are already endangered.

Like oil palms, cacao, too, is typically grown in vast monocultures. Large-scale crop specialization is capitalism's mode of food production. Unfortunately, it is never sustainable. The Earth sustains itself with interlocking complementarity, not singularity. In West Africa, where most of the world's cacao is grown today on primarily monoculture farms in cleared rainforests, cacao is in crisis, with many trees being damaged by a blight that is yet to be well understood. Like most plants, cacao evolved in the context of diversified forests. It doesn't require monoculture; in fact the trees and the soil are generally healthier, and the producer less beholden to a single crop, in diversified, managed forests such as they are creating at Mashpi.

Mashpi's strategy for restoring the forest is to build biodiversity with a focus on edibles, including different varieties of cacao trees, as well as bananas, sapotes, chicle, cola nuts, and many other species I had never

Cacao fruits. Different varieties of cacao produce fruits of different colors and sizes.

Marco, who works at Mashpi, opening a cacao fruit and removing the pulp.

heard of—some natives, some from other tropical regions around the world. For instance, they are growing salak, a palm native to Indonesia; it is sometimes called snakefruit in English, due to the snakeskin-like feel of its skin.

Agustina's husband and partner in the project, Alejandro Solano, is an ornithologist and all-around naturalist who publishes ornithological studies in journals and leads bird-watching tours all around South America. The afternoon we arrived, he took me for a brisk walk up the mountainside in search of a bird he had been visiting daily. It was a rufous-crowned antpitta, and Mashpi's location was considered beyond this bird's typical range.

I was a little skeptical of our endeavor, and when the bird did not reveal itself to us within a couple of minutes, I was ready to move on. But Alejandro was confident. This was the spot. The bird had come at this time several days in a row, and it would come again. He had worms to reward the bird for showing up. It was actually lovely to be forced to be still and wait after nonstop travel and teaching and introductions to new people. Lo and behold, after a short while the small, colorful bird appeared. Alejandro named the bird Shungito and visited it for three years. He told me that he recently encountered a smaller rufous-crowned antpitta, which he thinks is the offspring of Shungito.

My primary interest at Mashpi was to learn about the growing and processing of cacao. The cacao trees there are interplanted among a variety of other fruit and nut trees, as well as some trees that do not produce edible fruits or nuts. There were several different varieties of cacao, producing fruits with distinctly different shapes and colors. Cacao fruits are harvested every couple of weeks. The harvested fruits are split on the spot to remove the sweet pulp, which contains the seeds. The seeds and pulp are collected, while the shells are discarded around the trees to provide mulch for the trees and habitat for small creatures. The people at Mashpi are striving to organize every aspect of the farm's operations around regeneration rather than extraction.

Fresh cacao pulp is so delicious! It is juicy, sweet, and the fresh juice is wonderful. It becomes even more flavorful after a day or two of fermentation. At Mashpi, the pulp is hung in mesh bags for the juice to drain, then fermented for about four days. The initial

Cacao pulp. The seeds are embedded in the pulp.

Fermentation breaks down the cacao pulp and transforms the seeds, as well.

fermentation is primarily anaerobic, but as the pulp breaks down and there is more airflow, it shifts toward aerobic organisms. The fermentation produces acids, heat, and enzymes, which alter the biochemistry of the beans, darkening their color and developing their unique flavor. After the fermentation, the pulp has almost completely broken down, and the beans are dried in the sun for about a week.

At this point the beans are stable and can be transported. But Mashpi is the rare chocolatier that produces chocolate right on the farm. The beans are roasted, which further develops their flavor and loosens the outer hull on each bean. Then the beans are coarsely ground and winnowed to remove the hulls from the nibs. Finally, the nibs are ground slowly for many hours, becoming finer and finer until they form a smooth, creamy, cocoa liquor, which is then blended with other ingredients, tempered, and molded into chocolate bars.

The most unique chocolate bar they produce at Mashpi incorporates dried cacao fruit pulp. This is the only place where I have ever seen chocolate with bits of cacao pulp mixed in, and it is so scrumptious! The fact that this is so rare highlights how divorced chocolate production is from cacao growing. Cacao is grown in the tropics, but chocolate is generally processed where the affluent markets are. Switzerland may be famous for its chocolate, but it's far from any cacao trees.

Cacao juice fermenting.

Chucula

By Esteban Yepes Montoya

Chucula is a Colombian hot chocolate beverage, a campesino recipe from the plateau between Cundinamarca and Boyacá. The traditional breakfast of the region's Mhuysqa land stewards and farmers, this hot chocolate is an entire meal, substantial, thick, and nourishing, to fuel long days of hard work. Making chucula involves two distinct steps. First, ingredients are combined and formed into dried balls, which I call *tsampas*, that are shelf-stable and easily stored. Then these tsampas can be used as needed to prepare the chucula beverage.

The following recipe is my interpretation of the traditional campesino recipe, incorporating herbal enhancers to make it a nootropic, metashamanic elixir. It is an homage to all who walked before us: stewards of the land, Indigenous people, caretakers of biodiversity, and the grandmothers who keep these traditions alive. Within it are hidden prayers for the care of the territory, and for the preservation of its ethnobotanical treasures. May the variety of reciprocal and restorative practices between the fire of the kitchen and the fertile land evolve and adapt to the new paradigms being born right now as we witness the slow decay of obsolete ones.

Chocolate is one of the world's favorite foods, yet most people ignore its Indigenous and sacred roots and the tree it comes from: *Theobroma cacao*. In the Western world, we have transformed our relationship with this precious plant, traditionally used as medicine and nourishment, into one of indulgence and commodity. In indigenous traditions, cacao has a long history of ceremonial use. Through direct experience and fieldwork with Indigenous communities all around South and Central America, I have come to understand chocolate as a sort of ice-breaking regenerative balm, a counseling medicine, a catalyzer of unconditional love, a daily communion to consecrate with family and enhance motivation.

This is actually what inspired me to share this history when Sandor invited me to share a chocolate recipe

in this book. Chucula is a drinkable manifesto that redignifies our human condition and helps us understand the profound link from the cacao fruit to a gourd of hot chocolate, through the alchemy of fermentation. When we share chocolate with our loved ones with this intention, we keep fermenting within us the memories of the lands where it came from, and we become recipients of the intergenerational living legacy embedded in the ethnobotanical, pharmacological, archetypal, mythological, ceremonial, and social context of this ancient and compassionate Spirit: Xocolatl, Ix-Kakaw, Yeté, Yelá, Muzeyu, Oreba, Sibu, Ix-Balam, Bacau, Ologeliginyabbilele . . .

May you enjoy this with your loved ones while finding ease in the bittersweet nature of the always welcoming and pumping heart. Long life to the mighty monkey and all of those who walk before us!

MAKING CHUCULA

PREPARING THE TSAMPAS

TIMEFRAME

About 1 hour

EQUIPMENT

Bain-marie
(a small pot floating in a
larger pot of water)

Whisk

Sifter or strainer

INGREDIENTS

for 10 to 15 tsampas

½ pound/250 grams cacao paste
or 100% cacao chocolate bar or
baker's chocolate

⅓ cup/100 grams syrup-like
sweetener any kind: honey,
maple syrup, yacón syrup, date
syrup, or panela, piloncillo,
muscovado or coconut sugar
molasses, to desired sweetness

Herbal enhancers

1 teaspoon powdered cinnamon

¼ teaspoon ground cloves

½ teaspoon ground cardamom

½ teaspoon powdered ginger

2 tablespoons real vanilla
extract, or the scraped out
interior of 4 vanilla pods

PROCESS

Melt the cacao paste or unsweetened chocolate in a bain-marie.
Melting the chocolate directly on a heat source can easily burn it.

Gently heat the chosen sweet syrup, without boiling, in a
separate pan.

When the cacao is fully melted, leave it in the hot water bath and
slowly add the pre-warmed sweet syrup, while whisking. Taste to
evaluate sweetness and add more warmed syrup, if desired.

Add the herbal enhancers to the melted paste slowly, using a sifter
or strainer while continuing to whisk.

Add the spices to the melted paste slowly, using a sifter or strainer
while continuing to whisk.

Remove the mix from the water bath.

Mix the roasted grain and legume flours together in a bowl.

While it is still hot, slowly add the melted cacao and spice paste to
the bowl of roasted dry flours and stir well to mix evenly.

Let the chucula dough sit for a couple of minutes at room temperature to partially cool and thicken.

Form chucula dough into balls of 2–3 tablespoons/30–50 grams.

* small amounts of dried, powdered adaptogens and tonic medicinal herbs and
fungi, such as *tulsi*, reishi, chaga, lion's mane, ashwagandha, astragalus, osha,
shilajit, fo-ti, rhodiola, damiana, cat's claw, schisandra berry, bee pollen; use all,
some, none, or others

Pinch of chili powder

Pinch of sea salt

About ¾ cup/100 grams
cereals and legumes,
roasted and ground together ✳

Place the balls on a tray, cover them with a clean cloth, and let
them dry for a few days.

Once the balls are dry, store them in a jar and use them to make
chucula anytime.

✳ as much variety as possible, including any or all of the following: corn, chickpea,
broad beans, peas, lentils, wheat, barley; or other local beans, peas, grains

PREPARING THE CHUCULA BEVERAGE

TIMEFRAME

About 10 minutes

EQUIPMENT

A traditional molinillo (a
wooden whisk for chocolate),
or a whisk or electric beater

INGREDIENTS
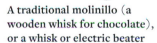
*for 1 cup/250 milliliters
of chucula*

1 chucula tsampa

1 tablespoon ghee or butter
(optional)

Chili powder
(to taste, optional)

Rose water or edible flower
hydrosol (to taste, optional)

PROCESS

For each cup of chucula, heat about ¾ cup/180 milliliters of water
to a gentle simmer (do not boil).

Add the chucula, tsampa, and ghee, if using.

Mix evenly using a traditional molinillo if you have one, or a whisk
or electric beater, until multi-colored rainbow-like bubbles rise to
the surface.

Bring to a gentle simmer again.

Add the chili powder and rose water, if desired.

Serve warm. Enjoy with loved ones, as this chucula elixir invigo-
rates and eases your heart, body, and mind.

Coffee

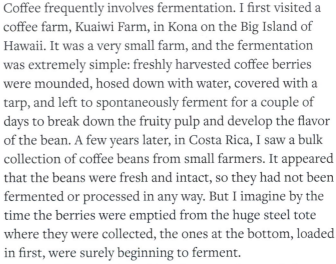

Coffee frequently involves fermentation. I first visited a coffee farm, Kuaiwi Farm, in Kona on the Big Island of Hawaii. It was a very small farm, and the fermentation was extremely simple: freshly harvested coffee berries were mounded, hosed down with water, covered with a tarp, and left to spontaneously ferment for a couple of days to break down the fruity pulp and develop the flavor of the bean. A few years later, in Costa Rica, I saw a bulk collection of coffee beans from small farmers. It appeared that the beans were fresh and intact, so they had not been fermented or processed in any way. But I imagine by the time the berries were emptied from the huge steel tote where they were collected, the ones at the bottom, loaded in first, were surely beginning to ferment.

In Brazil, I participated in a fermentation workshop at Fazenda Ambiental Fortaleza (Environmental Fortress Farm), a coffee farm in Mococa, which is about three hours north of São Paulo. Like the cacao at Mashpi, the coffee there was grown in shaded, wooded areas. The most interesting project at the farm was their experimental research into coffee fermentation. For this research, they control variables and test how different lengths of fermentation, temperature, humidity, and other factors impact the flavor of the resulting coffee. I asked Felipe Croce, part of the family that owns and runs the farm, to share some of what they are learning.

Bulk collection point for freshly harvested coffee berries from small farmers in Costa Rica.

Forest coffee farm at Fazenda Ambiental Fortaleza in Mococa, Brazil.

REFLECTIONS ON COFFEE FERMENTATION

By Felipe Croce

Fermentation used to be considered a defect in coffee production. In traditional farming communities, coffee farmers don't have the skills to properly roast, brew, and taste coffee, so they take their beans, after harvest, to local brokers for evaluation and sale. In traditional commodity coffee language, for a coffee to be fermented would mean off-flavors. The industry trained tasters to positively evaluate clean and sweet flavors. This orientation drastically diminished the role of fermentation in coffee for decades. What ensued was a widespread standardization of coffee flavor. Fermentation was used as a simple way of removing the pulp from the coffee seed, but fermentation beyond that was considered defective.

New ideas emerging in the coffee industry, in pursuit of delicious aromas and flavors, are bringing a new focus onto the flavor precursors in the coffee bean. The principal flavor precursors in coffee come from the genetic phenotype and the environment in which the coffee is grown. The environment varies with climate conditions. The dry harvest season of the Mogiana region, with its cold nights and hot days, produces more sugar and dense body on the coffee cherry, whereas the humid cold nights and cold days of the Espirito Santo region produces crisp acidity and a silkier, light body. Another aspect of terroir is the human element—factors influenced by the farmer, such as composting to enrich soil—and it is here that we must consider fermentation to begin. We also use above-ground foliar sprays, made by fermentation, which new research is showing creates more flavor in the coffee.

The most common use of fermentation in coffee comes at the stage where the cherries are picked. When the coffee fruit is plucked from the tree, a hole is formed where it was attached, and this opening enables microbes to access the sugary pulp of the fruit, and so it inevitably begins to ferment. As farmers, we pick the cherries throughout the day, and we leave them in clean sacks under shade as they fill up. At the end of the day, tractors come around the fields and bring to the patios the day's picking. Once the coffee arrives at the patio, a farmer has a few options, which will ultimately influence the flavor in the cup.

There are two common drying styles. When the coffee is picked, it has a moisture content of roughly 60 percent. It is industry standard to dry the beans to 11 percent moisture, which is a stable point for enzymatic activity, allowing the seed to stay alive and keeping it from suffering dramatic changes. The industry, particularly in Brazil, where commodity coffee and volume has reigned, has established that faster demucilagination (pulp removal) and drying is best. This can be done with the outer skin still intact during drying (called natural) or with the skin removed (called pulped).

For natural-style drying, a farmer simply lays the fruit, skin intact, on the coffee patio to dry. This is a slower process, varying greatly due to the humidity and temperature of the farm, ranging from 7 to 21 days. For pulped drying, a farmer will send the cherries through a de-pulper using water, and then either ferment the beans in a tank with water (called washed) or dry them directly on the patio without the outer skin (called honey). The honey process ferments the beans in about half the time of the natural method, and the washed process is fastest, with the beans submerged under water for 12 to 36 hours.

As yeast and bacteria consume the simple sugars in the mucilage, they create a range of flavorful by-products. One result of this fermentation is the creation of longer chains of polysaccharides, which transform in the roasting process into a sensation in the cup that we call mouthfeel or viscosity. So, making a great generalization: Washed process flavors are crisp and delicate; natural process flavors are heavy, dense, and aromatic; and honeys are in between.

What I've found is that 60 percent humidity is the threshold for making natural-process coffees. Above 60 percent humidity, the bacterial activity produces strong acetic flavors. Above 65 percent humidity, there is a risk of mold developing on the fermenting fruit skin. From 50–60 percent humidity, extreme care and hygiene is needed but there is potential for intense yet positive fruit flavors. Below 50 percent humidity, it is safe to produce a natural-process coffee with clean flavors of red fruits to dried fruits.

When I first arrived on the farm to begin working here, the elder workers would dry on the hottest days, on a black pavement patio, which would heat up immensely and dry the coffees quickly, or even bake them. Today, we have changed our patios to clean cement, and have installed partial shade nets to control the temperature of the drying beans so it never exceeds 28°C/82°F. We have changed the water source for the washing and pulping process to come directly from the natural springs. We constantly clean and sanitize equipment to avoid creating clusters of bacteria or yeast. I believe the coffee industry will evolve immensely in the field of fermentation and flavor development. But for this to happen, first we must develop a market that will support farmers and the investments that will be asked of them.

BICYCLE-POWERED COFFEE GRINDER

Another memorable coffee experience was my visit to a lovely coffee cooperative in Oaxaca. I always feel inspired by collective enterprises, just for showing that there exist alternatives to private ownership, and it turned out that Oaxaca is home to many collectives. I wrote in chapter 1 of my visit to Mujeres Milenarias, a cooperative of women producing pulque there (see "Mujeres Milenarias" on page 10). The coffee cooperative in Oaxaca was part of a network of local cooperative enterprises, and in addition to coffee, they sold chocolate processed by another cooperative, small books published by another, and more.

My favorite sight there was a bicycle-powered coffee grinder. What a great concept for a small enterprise: inexpensive, easy to operate and maintain, powered by people, and invulnerable to power outages or price spikes. More medium-scale food processing like this, and more worker-owned cooperatives, please!

Bicycle-powered coffee grinder at a coffee roasting cooperative in Oaxaca.

ACARAJÉ

Acarajé frying in palm oil.

Acarajé served with shrimp vatapá.

Acarajé served with a vegetarian sauce and cashews.

Acarajé are delicious Afro-Brazilian fried fritters made from a batter of black-eyed peas and onions. I was told about them many years ago by Selma Miriam of Bloodroot, a collective restaurant in Bridgeport, Connecticut. At Bloodroot, they let the puréed peas sit at room temperature for an hour or a few hours. By contrast, over the years I have fermented them for days, one or several. Up to a point, they just keep getting tastier. The fermentation takes something with a rather plain flavor and makes it more interesting, complex, and deep; it makes nutrients more bioavailable; and it also produces bubbles of carbon dioxide, which lift the purée and lighten the acarajé.

I loved the acarajé I ate when I was teaching in Brazil. It's served hot and crispy, typically with a shrimp, coconut, and peanut paste called *vatapá*. Acarajé is always delicious, and there is a beautiful culture around it. On my first day in São Paulo, my host, Leticia Janicsek, took me to Acarajé do Cacá, an open storefront with a counter and a few tables. We had some acarajé with the traditional shrimp vatapá, and a vegetarian version made from whole roasted cashews and a rich, nutty sauce.

The São Paulo acarajé maker was a man with a small beard, wearing a *turbante*, a traditional head wrap worn by Afro-Brazilian women that has become the customary outfit of the street acarajé makers in Salvador, a Brazilian city in the state of Bahia. Leticia explained to me that customarily acarajé makers are women, or sometimes queer men or gender nonconformists. When we briefly visited Salvador, all the acarajé makers we saw were women. But on Boipeba, an island off the coast of Brazil not far from Salvador, we ate delicious acarajé at a restaurant owned and run by Danny, a wonderful cook and gracious host, who was queer and gender nonconforming, and wore a muumuu and beads.

None of the acarajé makers I encountered in Brazil were deliberately fermenting their batter, and all of the acarajé I ate there was absolutely delicious. Perhaps this is because in the tropical heat, especially for street vendors without the option of refrigeration, the batter inevitably starts to ferment within a few hours. That's what happens in the Tennessee summertime, too. I stand by the notion that acarajé is even better fermented. Here is how I do it.

TIMEFRAME

1 or more days

EQUIPMENT

Crock, wide-mouth jar, or other vessel with a capacity of at least 2 quarts/2 liters

Blender or food processor

Whisk, a mechanical or electric mixer, or a food processor with a paddle

INGREDIENTS

for 4 to 6 servings

1 cup/250 grams uncooked black-eyed peas

1 onion, coarsely chopped

2 teaspoons/10 grams salt (to taste)

Black pepper (to taste)

Oil (any kind) or butter

PROCESS

Soak the black-eyed peas overnight.

Remove the hulls (if desired). In Brazil, it is typical to remove the hulls. (It's a lot of work, and I'm content to eat the fiber of the hulls, so I often skip it.) While the beans are still submerged, stick your hands in the water and rub the peas between the palms of your hands, pressing and moving your hands in alternating circles to remove the skins from the beans. You may need to reach in and squeeze individual beans between your thumbs and index fingers, or pound the peas with a heavy blunt tool. Periodically swirl the water so the detached skins will float to the top. Remove them and discard. Add more water if necessary and repeat a few times. The more skins you remove, the smoother the batter will be, but you probably will not get them all. At least I never have.

Blend the peas with the onion, salt, and pepper in a blender or food processor. Blend well into a smooth paste. Add just a little water, if necessary, to moisten and bind.

ACARAJÉ CONTINUED

Leave the paste in a crock, jar, or bowl to ferment, loosely covered to protect from flies but allow gas to release. Make sure the vessel is large enough to accommodate at least a doubling of volume.

Ferment for 1 day or several, until the volume has increased by at least 50 percent. If you let it go for a few days, the flavor will get stronger. After some number of days—fewer if it's hot, more if it's cool—it may begin to putrefy. Before that happens, move fermented batter to the refrigerator until you are ready to make acarajé.

Before cooking the acarajé, beat it for a good long while to make it smooth and stiff, adding water, just a little at a time, as necessary. Use whatever tool you would use for beating cream or egg whites, such as a whisk. This beating changes the batter dramatically, making it much creamier, developing its capacity to hold air, and whipping air bubbles into it.

The typical Brazilian way to cook acarajé is to deep-fry fritters from the batter in palm oil. The way I usually do it is to panfry the fritters in just a little oil (whatever kind you like) or butter, for a couple of minutes on each side, until crisp and golden.

Enjoy the traditional way, with shrimp and vatapá, or experiment with different toppings: kimchi, avocado, pesto, chutney, or a savory yogurt sauce.

FARINATA

Farinata is an Italian fried cake made from chickpea flour. Variations of it are eaten in different regions of Italy, as well as France, and beyond. It is known by a variety of names, among them *socca*, *fainá*, *cecina*, and *torta di ceci*. I was curious about these chickpea cakes, because I have often been asked what bean fermentation traditions exist outside of Asia, where the practice is so widespread. I have not encountered farinata in my travels, but I have done some investigating and experimenting.

None of the recipes I have found for farinata call explicitly for fermenting it. They all mention letting the batter sit for a period, with suggestions ranging from 20 minutes to hours. According to Enrica Monzani, who studies, teaches, and blogs about the cuisine of her native province of Liguria in Italy, the proper amount of time is "at least four hours, better eight." Her blog, *A Small Kitchen in Genoa*, guided me as to proportions and technique for making farinata.

According to Enrica, the reason for the long soak is because "the flour must absorb the water very well." No doubt this is true, and when the ingredients need time to sit together, what happens if you give them more time, measured in days rather than hours? In my experiments, fermenting the farinata batter for a day or two or three, until the batter gets frothy and foamy, makes for a luscious, light, and creamy treat that is almost like a fluffy omelet or soufflé.

Farinata.

FARINATA

TIMEFRAME

2 to 3 days

EQUIPMENT

Whisk

Copper or cast-iron crepe pan with a 10-inch/25-centimeter diameter (If you use a bigger pan, scale up the recipe so that the layer of fresh batter in the pan maintains a depth of about ¼ to ⅓ inch/7 to 9 millimeters)

INGREDIENTS

for one 10-inch/ 25-centimeter cake

¾ cup/100 grams chickpea flour

1 teaspoon/5 grams salt

3½ tablespoons/50 grams olive oil (or other vegetable oil)

A small amount of finely sliced vegetables (onion, sweet pepper, artichoke hearts, mushrooms, anything) and/or grated or crumbled cheese, to sprinkle onto the surface of the farinata (optional)

PROCESS

Combine the chickpea flour with 10 ounces/300 milliliters water, using a whisk to work it well and eliminate any lumps of flour. (Do not add salt until later.)

Ferment this batter, loosely covered, for a few days (shorter in warmer places, longer in cooler places).

Whisk at least once each day, until you notice that it is getting frothy. Then, it is ready to use.

Preheat the oven at its highest setting.

Preheat the pan in the oven. I use a cast-iron pan. A lot of the recipes specify a copper pan, which, alas, I do not have.

While the pan is heating, add the salt to the batter and give it its final whisking.

Carefully remove the hot pan from the oven.

Add the oil and make sure it spreads evenly over the entire surface of the hot pan.

See "An Important Detail of *Farinata* Technique" for Enrica's most helpful advice about how to pour the batter into the hot oil gently, so it floats above the oil rather than mixing with it. Slowly pour the batter down the length of a wooden spoon, held at a 45-degree angle just above the center of the pan, onto the hot oil.

If desired, sprinkle some small pieces of vegetables or cheese or whatever else you can imagine onto the surface of the batter.

Place the pan on the bottom rack of the oven and bake for 10 to 15 minutes, until it has set and it is golden in color.

Broil for a few more minutes to brown the surface.

Cool for a minute, then cut into pieces.

Enjoy farinata fresh and still warm.

AN IMPORTANT DETAIL OF FARINATA TECHNIQUE

By Enrica Monzani, from her blog, *A Small Kitchen in Genoa*

The oil . . . must only form a protective film inside the pan and cover over and under the batter. For this fundamental step some precautions are necessary: the pan must be already hot before pouring the oil, and then the farinata, inside; the farinata batter must be poured very slowly making it slide along a spoon placed in the center of the pan. In this way it will float over the oil without breaking its surface or mixing with it. The oil will then rise along the edges and cover the batter even on the surface. This will create a sort of "pajama" of oil that wraps the batter.

Slowly pouring farinata batter onto hot oil via a wooden spoon held at a 45-degree angle just above the hot oil.

FERMENTING DIVERSITY AND JUSTICE

This chapter, like all the others in this book, spans the globe, with recipes and stories from Africa, the Americas, Asia, and Europe. Unfortunately, in this big, culturally diverse world we inhabit, all people do not have equal access to resources, by which I mean not only money, but also land, space, time, education, information, the opportunity to travel, and so much more. Although fermentation traditions everywhere developed as practical strategies for making effective use of food resources, increasingly, fermented foods and beverages are viewed as niche products for affluent consumers, who are predominantly white. As my friend and fellow fermenter Miin Chan observed in an essay published on the website Eater, "The fermentation industry, like any other, has a whiteness problem." She continues:

> Wherever you look, you'll see that the fermentation industry in the West (meaning North America, the U.K., Europe, and Australasia) is dominated by mostly white fermenters, who often sell whitewashed BIPOC [Black, Indigenous, and people of color] ferments and associated white-gaze narratives about these foods to mainly white consumers. This dearth of diversity is problematic in and of itself, but it's worsened by the fact that white fermenters are commoditizing ferments that are ingrained in the cultural identities of BIPOC, whose centuries-long labor developed and refined the microbial relationships required to produce them. . . .
>
> At almost every level, success is determined by white gatekeepers, from which companies gain access to capital, to who organizes festivals and teaches workshops, to who gets spotlighted by the food media or given book contracts or space on grocery store shelves.[9]

Miin's words sparked controversy online, but to me they ring true. This whiteness problem is not just the result of particular individuals' racist intentions; rather, it's a manifestation of bias that is systemic. Reflecting upon structural racism forces me to acknowledge the degree to which I am a personal beneficiary of many kinds of privilege: I am white and male, bred for success with an elite education. I have learned what I have learned, and I have written what I have written, but I was able to do so thanks to the privilege with which I pass through this world. Once I decided to write about fermentation, I was able to figure how to get a book published thanks to my privilege, and I was able to promote it, too.

Food can be a wonderful way to learn about, enjoy, and appreciate other cultures, but it exists in the context of complex and often very harsh broader historical forces and social structures. I do not have any easy solutions to offer, nor do I believe that easy solutions exist, because the dynamics Miin is calling out are enduring legacies of much larger systems of oppression, such as colonialism and chattel slavery. But when I read through all the hostile social media commentary on her article, calling her racist, projecting their own prejudices upon her words, and somehow imagining that food exists outside these larger social dynamics, I see denial. It is incumbent upon people who benefit from any type of privilege to listen to and try to understand the perspectives of people who do not have such privilege, not deny them or ridicule them. We cannot overcome these overarching social problems without acknowledging that they exist.

We must challenge the misconception that fermentation is primarily for affluent, mostly white consumers. The diverse processes of fermentation highlighted in this book come from diverse cultural traditions. The real experts are the people living these traditions, and we must recognize and celebrate the people and their cultures as we enjoy their foods and beverages. May the next wave of fermentation educators and entrepreneurs consist of fewer people like me, who became interested in fermentation midlife, and may more people from everywhere find opportunities to share the traditions they grew up with and know intimately.

SIX

MILK

Until our age of refrigeration and ultrahigh-temperature processing, milk could only be enjoyed fresh by people in proximity to lactating animals. Other people who drank milk mostly drank it fermented. Raw milk is always host to lactic acid bacteria, and they rapidly proliferate in the milk and acidify it. Raw milk will ferment spontaneously into something quite pleasant—what has traditionally been called *clabber* in English. Or it can be fermented into specific forms such as yogurt, dahi, kefir, or *viili* (to name but a few) by means of various starters that include laboratory-derived pure-culture starters; symbiotic communities of bacteria and yeast (SCOBYs), such as kefir grains; a small quantity of ferment from a previous batch; and a plethora of botanical or other materials. Fermenting milk also can be made to curdle such that water (in the form of whey) can be removed. The result is a firmer, drier cheese that can be aged—in other words, it can be fermented further. Generally, the drier the cheese, the longer it can be aged and stored.

I am a lover of fermented milks of every description, and I have a special weakness for cheese. Although I have enjoyed eating an incredible variety of cheeses in my travels, I have not learned as much about how to make them as I have about other ferments. In recent years, since leaving the community where I shared the responsibilities of raising goats, I have also lacked a regular source of abundant raw milk. When I do have raw goat milk, I generally make chèvre, as I describe in the revised edition of *Wild Fermentation*. The homemade cheeses I get to enjoy most frequently are made by my partner, Shoppingspree3d/Daniel, who lives at the community where I used to live. He milks the goats frequently, and he likes to make cheese when there is extra milk. I also get to enjoy occasional cheeses from my friend and onetime student, Soirée-Leone, who lives about two hours away. She shows up at my place every couple of months bearing culinary gifts that frequently include her amazing aged cheeses. She and Shoppingspree shared their methods with me to share with you in this chapter. I also convey details of cheesemaking I witnessed in China, as well as instructions for making ricotta "miso," a wonderful application of koji to cheesemaking.

This chapter also explores a few different aspects of yogurt, the dairy ferment I do make on an ongoing basis. Remote villages throughout the Balkans traditionally relied upon a wide variety of plants and other traditional starters for yogurt. We'll delve into fascinating ethnobotanical research documenting starters that are no longer in common use but remain in living memory. Finally, I share a recipe for a Turkish preserve of yogurt, wheat, and vegetables—*tarhana*—which can be used as an instant soup, flavoring, or thickener.

Bruce Kemp in his cheese aging room.

Passion Cheesemaking

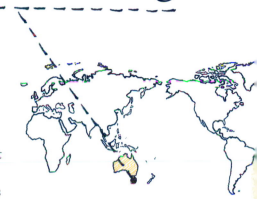

I have visited many dedicated cheesemaking facilities at different scales, and it is always fascinating to see how people design spaces and systems that help them achieve consistent results efficiently. But, as an amateur who makes cheese from time to time when excess milk comes my way, I relate much more easily to people who are passionate about cheesemaking, not as a business venture, but as a source of fun and adventure in their home kitchens.

One especially passionate fermenter I met in my travels was Bruce Kemp, a retiree in rural Tasmania whose home is permeated with the aromas of curing cheeses and meats. Bruce greeted us with an overflowing tray of his home-made delicacies. He doesn't raise animals himself, but with skills like his, it's easy for him to trade with local farmers. "I have been building friendships and community through exploring and sharing my passion for fermentation," he explained. In exchange for milk and meat from neighbors who raise livestock, Bruce shares cheeses and cured meats he makes, as well as knowledge and occasional assistance.

"I aim to have a Tasmanian twist on traditional cheeses," Bruce says. His Romano is flavored with the local pepper berry, his Valençay is dusted with salt bush ash, and his Camembert is made from milk infused with locally collected, dried mushrooms. Bruce cures his cheeses at the cool ambient temperature of his home. "My approach is to create processes and environments that maximize the opportunity for beneficial indigenous molds and bacteria." He emphasizes that his operation is not commercial. "I do not want to compromise tradition or innovation," which commercial food safety regulations would require.

Left, the incredible platter of homemade cheeses, cured meats, bread, and summer vegetables that Bruce shared with us.

Right, more of Bruce's aging cheeses.

A CHEESE STORY

The homemade cheese I've been eating most often lately is made by my beloved partner Shoppingspree3d/Daniel, who lives within walking distance down the road, and participates in milking the descendants of the same herd of goats I wrote about in *Wild Fermentation*. He loves those goats dearly, and he talks reverentially about "their alchemy of transforming elements of the forest into rich nourishment." With a large group of people sharing one kitchen with very limited refrigeration, it is not uncommon for the community to run out of space to refrigerate milk. Sometimes making cheese is the solution to an urgent problem.

Generally, Shoppingspree makes fresh, unaged, acid-curdled cheeses. He was discouraged from aging cheeses because rodents repeatedly got into the cheeses he was trying to age, and he found that fresh cheeses are delicious and easy to make. He has explored different traditional fresh cheeses, such as Indian paneer and Mexican queso fresco, but he's taken to calling each of his cheeses "a cheese story." "People are always asking what kind of cheese it is," he says. Rather than try to replicate any specific traditional style, he likes to embrace the differences in each batch. "This is the one I accidentally scalded, this is the one I made when we had too much milk; each cheese comes with a story. The story is what the cheese is; perfection has no place in the cheese story, and each cheese is a unique manifestation of the miracle of mammary glands."

You can use pasteurized milk from the supermarket for this recipe, but avoid ultrapasteurized, as the high-temperature processing can prevent effective curd formation. Shoppingspree generally starts with raw milk, and he prefers older milk to fresher milk, because it is prefermented. The older, more acidic milk forms tighter curds and a firmer, more cohesive cheese. For this style of cheese, you can curdle the milk with various acids. Shoppingspree's favorite curdling agent is sauerkraut juice, followed by lime juice, lemon juice, then vinegar. Often he blends a few of these.

This cheese lends itself to frying. Shoppingspree's favorite breakfast is a wilted salad he calls a "back-to-the-land breakfast cheese story." He melts butter, fries small chunks of cheese seasoned with some Special Sauce (page 211), then pours the fried cheese and hot butter over fresh garden greens. To complete the circle, he uses the whey from his cheesemaking process to fertilize the greens in the garden.

TIMEFRAME

6 hours or longer

EQUIPMENT

Cheesecloth

INGREDIENTS

for roughly 2 pounds of cheese

1 gallon/4 liters milk,
ideally raw milk that's already
fermenting and starting to
taste sour

About ¼ cup/60 milliliters
sauerkraut juice, lime juice,
lemon juice, or vinegar
(less if your milk is sour)

Salt (to taste)

PROCESS

Heat the milk slowly and gently. If you scald the milk, you will taste it, and that will be the most prominent feature of your cheese story. Use moderate heat, and stay with it. "Stir, stir, stir, stir, stir," advises Shoppingspree. He likes to make a vortex in the milk as he stirs, and says, "This is when you sing to the milk and do woo," adding that "cheese is highly susceptible to woo."

Bring the milk to a slow boil, then turn off the heat and let the hot milk cool for a few minutes.

Dilute the curdling agent with a couple of tablespoons of water. Add it slowly to the hot milk, as you gently stir. "Every step of this process benefits from slowness," he emphasizes. Try not to break apart the fragile, cloudlike curd. Add only as much of the acid solution as it takes to curdle the milk. As soon as the acid reaches sufficient concentration in the hot milk, the curdling will be visible and obvious. More acid than necessary for curdling imparts an acidic flavor, and can give the cheese a gluey texture. Once the milk curdles, it's fine to leave the curds resting in the whey for a while.

Line a colander with cheesecloth, and gently scoop the curds out of the whey and into the cheesecloth. Try not to break the curds in this process. Add a sprinkle of salt after each scoop.

Gather the corners of the cheesecloth, and hang the cheese over a bowl or pot for the whey to continue to drain. Leave it hanging in a cool spot for at least 6 hours, if possible.

The resulting cheese will have a rounded, irregular shape, which Shoppingspree describes as "brain-like," and will be firm enough to slice.

TEN BELLS CHEESE

My friend Soirée-Leone makes really wonderful aged cheeses. She does not raise milking animals herself. Instead, she accesses raw milk from local farmers, for which she barters cheese and her other culinary creations, mostly fermented. When I asked her if she would share a couple of cheeses for this book, this is one that she suggested immediately. "These cheeses are easy; you can unleash your cheesemaking creativity in terms of shaping, culturing, spices and additions; they can be aged over 60 days [the US Food and Drug Administration's threshold for legal sale of raw milk cheeses] if you are concerned about the safety of raw milk cheeses; and importantly, they do not require specialized equipment."

Ten Bells is a raw cow's milk cheese inspired by Swiss cheesemaker Herr Glauser's Belper Knolle, which is flavored with garlic, formed into balls, coated with black pepper, and aged. The finished cheese "looks a bit like a truffle and shaves like a truffle," observes Soirée. "Belper Knolle and my own Ten Bells are seemingly impossible, as they become hard cheese after just a few short weeks." The aging can be done in a small plastic tub in your refrigerator, no special aging space required. Here is Soirée's method:

Ten Bells Cheese.

TIMEFRAME

A month or longer; the initial ripening requires 12 to 16 hours, so a nice schedule is to start this cheese in the late afternoon or early evening and drain it in the morning.

EQUIPMENT

Crock or pot with a capacity of at least 1 gallon/4 liters

Cheesecloth

Small plastic storage container with lid

Bamboo mats or cheese mats

INGREDIENTS

for two small cheeses weighing together about a ½ pound/225 grams

1 gallon/4 liters whole milk, ideally raw (you can use pasteurized milk from the supermarket, but avoid ultrapasteurized); typically, this cheese is made with cow's milk, but Soirée has also made it with goat's milk

¼ cup/60 milliliters ripe kefir to introduce cultures ✳

⅛ to ¼ teaspoon calcium chloride diluted in ⅛ cup/ 30 milliliters unchlorinated water (if using pasturized milk) †

PROCESS

If you are using cold milk, heat the milk to lukewarm, about 85°F/29°C. Use moderate heat and stir frequently. If you overheat the milk, pull it off the burner and allow it to cool. If you are using fresh, warm milk, simply pour it into a pot or crock. A crock is a bit more insulating, but if using a pot, you can wrap it in towels.

If you are using kefir, stir it in gently. If you are using a commercial culture, sprinkle it on top of the milk and allow it to hydrate for a few minutes before using an up-and-down motion with a mixing spoon to distribute it thoroughly.

If you are using pasteurized milk, add the diluted calcium chloride. Allow to stand for a few minutes before adding the rennet.

If you are using kefir or other cultures that do not include rennet, you will need to add rennet. Add the dissolved rennet to the milk and stir gently for a few minutes.

Cover the pot or crock and wrap it in towels. Allow the milk to ripen and the curd to form for 12 to 16 hours.

Place a cheesecloth over a colander above a pot or bucket. (It's best not to pour the rich whey down the drain; drink it, ferment and cook with it, or feed it to animals, plants, or compost.) Spoon the curds into the cheesecloth and allow to drain until the whey is no longer draining quickly. Then, mix the curds around a bit, to allow more whey to drain. Grab three corners of the cheesecloth and wrap the fourth corner around the three and pull the end up through the bit you just wrapped. Hang the cheese to drain for 8 to 12 hours. If flies are a problem, consider protecting the draining curd. My favorite way is to use a small board wedged in a bucket with the draining curd hanging by a string from it, with the lid on the bucket. It can be helpful to open the cheesecloth and move the cheese around to allow for more even draining; with such a small batch, rearranging the curds once while draining is adequate.

✳ if you prefer to use a pure-culture starter, Soirée recommends 1 packet of C20G or C20 direct-set cultures that include rennet, or other mesophilic cultures such as ⅛ teaspoon MA4001 or Flora Danica, which will require the addition of rennet

† Soirée recommends adding calcium chloride before adding rennet if you are using store-bought pasteurized milk

continued on following page

¼ tablet rennet dissolved in ¼ cup (60 milliliters) water ✳

1½ tablespoons salt †

2 garlic cloves, crushed (to taste)

4 tablespoons whole black peppercorns, toasted until fragrant, then coarsely ground (to taste)

Add the salt to the drained curd, gently working it in with your hands.

Gently work the crushed garlic cloves into the drained curd. Add other seasonings if you like.

Though the Belper Knolle that inspired this cheese is traditionally made into truffle-like lumps, I have found that it ages and stores more easily when formed into patties. Divide the curd in half and form each half into a patty roughly 1-inch/2.5-centimeters thick. Press and smooth the top, bottom, and sides. Or experiment with other shapes.

Coat each cheese in the toasted and crushed black pepper.

Place the cheeses on a bamboo mat or cheese mat on a tray and allow to dry at room temperature. Dry for 1 to 2 days, until the exterior looks dry and is dry to the touch. A fan can expedite the process. If flies are a problem, improvise a protective environment that excludes insects while allowing for good air circulation.

Arrange the cheeses with air space between them on a bamboo mat in a lidded plastic container, and place the container in the refrigerator. Check after a couple of days and if the container has condensation, remove the lid and air it out, then punch a few holes in the lid of the container. (Sometimes no holes are required and other times lots of holes.) The trouble with employing a refrigerator without added humidity is that cheeses can really dry out and crack. I prefer to start with no holes or just a few holes and air out as needed. Flip the cheeses about once a week, so that they lose moisture evenly. No brushing or other care is required.

This cheese can be enjoyed after just a month, or aged for several months. I've aged it as long as 8 months; eventually it will dry out in an unfavorable way.

✳ Soirée recommends using non-GMO WalcoRen rennet tablets, which have a longer shelf life than liquid rennets

† Soirée generally uses Himalayan pink salt or Celtic gray, but any salt will do; no special "cheesemaking salt" is required

SHANKLEESH

Shankleesh rolled herbed cheeses in the jar, ready for oil.

Soirée introduced me to this wonderful, easy-to-make cheese. In her own words: "This cheese is simply well-drained yogurt, salted, formed into balls, coated with seasonings of your choice, and tossed in oil. Put the jar full of oil and cheese balls in the fridge to enjoy later. I have lost jars of this cheese in the refrigerator for nearly two years . . . and they were still delicious. The key is that the yogurt cheese must be well drained, and you must keep the container of oil and cheese sufficiently cool . . . a refrigerator will do. You can make this cheese with homemade yogurt or store-bought."

TIMEFRAME

About 24 hours to make the cheese; then the longer it ages, the better it gets

EQUIPMENT

Finely woven cheesecloth

INGREDIENTS

for about ½ pound/250 grams

1 quart/1 liter live-culture whole milk yogurt

1 teaspoon salt, or a bit more if you prefer

Za'atar blend, or seasoning blend of your choice (to taste) ✳

About 16 ounces/500 milliliters olive oil, or another oil you like

PROCESS

Place the yogurt in cheesecloth over a bowl. Tie up the cheesecloth and hang to drain for about 12 to 14 hours.

Work the salt into the cheese.

Hang the cheese in the cheesecloth for another 12 hours or so, at which point it should be firm, dry, and ready for the next step.

Form the cheese into balls of any size you like. Spices and herbs can be added into the cheese by mixing them into it before forming balls, and/or rolling the balls in a seasoning blend after forming.

Carefully pack the balls into a jar. Pour the olive oil over the balls to cover. Store in the refrigerator.

The cheese can be eaten immediately, but it is so much better after a couple of months.

The residual oil is terrific to cook with or blend into other dishes after all the cheese is eaten.

✳ a dry harissa blend of cumin, caraway, coriander, ancho chili powder, fennel, smoked paprika, garlic, cinnamon, cayenne, and sumac is my current favorite

RICOTTA "MISO"

One of the most dramatic and unexpected applications of koji that I have tried is this ricotta cheese. The resulting product has the soft, spreadable texture of ricotta, but rather than a fresh, mild flavor, it (relatively) quickly develops the funkiness of a long-aged cheese. I was inspired to try this by *Koji Alchemy*, the wonderful book about koji written by Rich Shih and Jeremy Umansky.

TIMEFRAME

2 to 6 months

VESSEL

Wide-mouth jar with a capacity of 1 quart/1 liter, or a little smaller

INGREDIENTS

for a 1-quart/1-liter jar, but the proportions work at any scale

15 ounces/425 grams koji

3 tablespoons/1.5 ounces/ 45 grams salt (5 percent of the combined weight of ricotta and koji)

15 ounces/425 grams ricotta cheese

PROCESS

Combine the koji with the salt and mix them together with clean hands, using the abrasive salt to partially break down the koji.

Add the ricotta and continue mixing with your hands until the ingredients are fully combined.

Pack the mixture into a jar, trying to eliminate air spaces as you go. If the jar is not full and has a lot of airspace, protect it from oxidation by covering the surface with plastic wrap. Secure the lid on the jar loosely so pressure can release.

Age the koji ricotta in the refrigerator. It develops faster at typical ambient temperatures, but can also become rancid.

Taste after about 2 months. It should taste like a well-aged cheese, such as Parmesan. Enjoy it then, or continue aging it in the refrigerator.

Use this rich, flavorful ricotta "miso" as a spread, in salad dressings or sauces, or in casseroles, stews, or other dishes.

Rushan

It came as something of a surprise to me to find that there are places in China with cheesemaking traditions, because cheese is so often specifically cited as being absent from Chinese cuisine. My brief time in China revealed to me the incredible diversity of geography, cultures, and traditional practices across that vast land. We visited a village in Yunnan called Dung Chang, not far from Dali, where a local specialty is a cheese called *rushan*. Cheesemaker Yang Qun Qun walked us through the process. (You can see the video of this process on YouTube in *People's Republic of Fermentation*, episode 7.)

Fermentation is the first step. The curdling agent for the cheese is whey from a previous batch, which is highly acidic after a month-long ferment. Mrs. Yang calls this "sour sauce," and she starts with about 2 cups/500 milliliters of it in her wok. Once the whey comes to a boil, she

Cheesemaker Yang Qun Qun with a piece of the rushan cheese she makes.

"Sour sauce," the curdling agent, is the whey from a previous batch of cheese, fermented for a month.

Working and straining
the curd.

Using big chopsticks
to stretch the curd.

Rushan outside
drying.

adds cold, fresh cow's milk, or "sweet sauce." As it heats, the milk curdles.

Mrs. Yang uses a pink plastic fan, which looks something like a fly swatter, to strain the curds and then press them together and work them into a rubbery, mozzarella-like state. Next, she squeezes the curd in her hand to press out the whey, then she uses thick chopsticks to roll and stretch the cheese in order to make it as thin as possible. She wraps the stretched cheese between two wooden poles to dry. Once the initial drying firms it, she moves it outside the shop to dry in the sun and wind.

Once ready, rushan has a chewy, leathery texture. It's usually cut into flat slices and deep-fried. As soon as the cheese touches the oil, it sizzles and turns golden as it inflates with pillow-like air pockets. After frying, it is sprinkled with sugar. Ultralight, crispy, warm fried cheese. Yum!

Fried rushan.

Rows of rushan drying in the sun.

Yogurt Starters

At the University of Gastronomic Sciences in Pollenzo, Italy, I met Andrea Pieroni, an Italian ethnobotanist whose research focuses on fermentation and other food and botanical medicine traditions in Eastern Europe. He works with a team of collaborators who cast a wide net, seeking to document all sorts of regional practices in danger of disappearing. In one article, they write:

> A common theme noted for production of these foods and beverages was the reliance on natural starter cultures available in the local environment, or more frequently, arising from microbes growing on the primary ingredients themselves (autochthonous "wild type" starter cultures). However, these unique sets of local knowledge are at risk as trends in the displacement of these food traditions by products of the large-scale industrialized agriculture and food industry on the market prevail, even in rural areas. This trend, combined with declines in the transmission of traditional knowledge concerning local microbial refugia, fermented food ingredients and fermentative processes, has resulted in the marginalization and even disappearance of many such practices today.[1]

One tidbit of Andrea's research that he shared was especially interesting to me: The range of plants, insects, and objects that people talked about using as yogurt starters is very consistent with an idea articulated in the research findings, namely that there is a "reliance on natural starter cultures available in the local environment." In another research project titled "The Disappearing Wild Food and Medicinal Plant Knowledge in a Few Mountain Villages of North-Eastern Albania," Andrea and his collaborator Renata Sõukand record many varied yogurt starters, including:

- the cambium (tender inner bark) layer of beech trees
- unripe fruits of crab apple, grape, plum, and wild strawberry
- fresh aerial parts of St. John's wort
- leaves of sorrel and *Sedum album* (white stonecrop)
- ants
- clarified butter
- buttermilk
- rain-water[2]

This calls to my mind the variety of botanical starters used across Asia to start koji-like fungi (see "*Faf* and Koji's Many Other Cousins" on page 176). It also reminds me how many different plants (and other elements of nature) can function as starters in any realm of fermentation. As we were discussing this via email, Andrea added that he had heard elsewhere about "(dirty) broken pieces of glass" used as a starter for yogurt!

When I asked Andrea whether he had photographs I could use of people using any of these starters to make yogurt, he was quick to point out that he hadn't witnessed any of them in action. Rather, they were reported to him by people he interviewed as starters that they had seen used in the past. Now, most people buy commercial yogurt or, if they make yogurt at home, rely on backslopping.

I, too, make yogurt by backslopping—that is, using my previous batch as the starter. Most mass-produced yogurts use pure-culture starters rather than the broader evolved communities found in traditional, heirloom yogurts, and so they only function as effective starters for one generation, or possibly two. Lacking the protection of an evolved community structure, these pure-culture starters are highly vulnerable to random environmental bacterial exposure and viral phages that can attack bacteria, analogous to the vulnerability of monocultures compared to the resilience of biodiverse systems in agriculture. Once you find a good heirloom culture that can effectively perpetuate itself over time, it's easy to keep using it, and refrigeration makes it easy to maintain over long periods.

My starter is very well traveled. It came from Romania to New York City in the nineteenth century, and it has been used in a small knish restaurant in New York City, called Yonah Schimmel Knish Bakery, ever since. But although I have enjoyed Yonah Schimmel's yogurt, and wrote about it in *Wild Fermentation*, I didn't have any of it to use as a starter in my kitchen. Some readers of *Wild Fermentation* sought it out, like Eva Bakkeslett, a Norwegian woman who went to Yonah Schimmel on a trip to New York and brought some of the yogurt home with her. She organized a workshop that we co-taught in the U.K. in 2014, and that was the yogurt she brought to use as a starter.

I decided to try a technique I had read about that was used by some European immigrants to the United States to bring their starters with them: drying the starter on a cloth. I dipped a clean cloth into the yogurt, saturated it, then dried it in the window until it was a crusted cloth, which I packed among my clothes in my luggage. When I got home, it remained buried and forgotten for a few months. But when I eventually found it, I heated a cup of milk and cooled it to about 110°F/43°C, then dipped the crusty cloth into the warm milk, broke off the flakes of dried yogurt into it, and squeezed residual milk absorbed by the cloth back into the milk. After eight hours at 110°F/43°C, my milk had transformed into a thick, tart, delicious yogurt. I made that single cup into more, and I have backslopped from that starter for years now, ever since.

Continuity like this makes the process easy, but it is a luxury easily interrupted. Jars can break, there can be power failures, accidents eventually happen. This is why I find Andrea's research so compelling. If for some reason we lose our dependable starters, it's important to have some ideas for plan B.

TARHANA

I first met Turkish food writer Aylin Öney Tan in 2010 at the Oxford Symposium on Food and Cookery, when I watched her deliver a wonderful paper on the many Turkish foods derived from yogurt. At the conference, she shared small pieces of hard, dried yogurt for us to taste, which were a flavorful and wholesome snack. Aylin and I have stayed in touch, and as I began working on this book, she invited me to attend the online 2020 edition of the Dublin Gastronomy Symposium, at which she and her colleague Nilhan Aras were presenting a paper on a Turkish yogurt-derived food called *tarhana*.

Aylin and Nilhan describe tarhana as an instant soup, a fusion of nomadic and agrarian Anatolian traditions that served to preserve food from seasons of plenty for sustenance during seasons of relative scarcity. The heavy summer flow of milk, turned into yogurt; the summer wheat; and the summer vegetables and herbs, all processed together into a dried and easily storable form that requires nothing more than hot water to reconstitute into a meal.

Tarhana is very closely related to *kishk*, which I wrote about in *Wild Fermentation* and *The Art of Fermentation*, only tarhana is even more versatile. Wheat (in whole grain, cracked, or flour form), is mixed with yogurt, as in kishk; but unlike kishk (so far as I know), tarhana often incorporates legumes, vegetables, herbs, and even fruits. "It is a hearty, umami-rich, nutritious winter soup full of the goodness and bounty of summer months," Aylin and Nilhan write.[3]

They document variations in regional tarhana styles, including different forms of wheat; different legumes, vegetables, herbs, and fruits, and whether these are used cooked or raw; and the varying forms of the final product, from a wet paste, to thin wafers, to dried donuts, balls, and crumbles. All in all, it is an extremely versatile food. It can be used as an instant soup, or as a flavoring and thickener in a more elaborate soup, stew, or sauce. This recipe is my take on tarhana. Use this as a starting point, but experiment with what is abundantly available!

TIMEFRAME

1 to 2 weeks, typically in summer when the sun is shining and the days are long

EQUIPMENT

Blender or food processor (optional)

Dehydrator (optional)

INGREDIENTS

for about 4 cups/750 grams

1 pound/500 grams tomatoes, okra, sweet and/or chili peppers, and/or other vegetables, coarsely chopped

1 small onion

A few garlic cloves

1 pound/500 grams whole wheat flour, more if needed

1 cup/250 milliliters yogurt

1 tablespoon/15 grams salt

PROCESS

Cook the vegetables, including the onion and garlic, in a pot over medium heat, without oil, for 20 minutes or longer, until they are soft and melded together into a stew. If you are not using tomatoes, add a little bit of water if the vegetables seem dry and at risk of burning. Once cooked, allow the vegetables to cool. (Alternatively, use raw vegetables.)

Purée the vegetables using a blender or food processor, or mince them by hand, then transfer to a mixing bowl.

Add the flour, yogurt, and salt, and knead into a smooth dough. If it seems too wet, add additional flour until the dough is dry enough to handle.

Ferment the mixture in a bowl for 1 to 2 weeks. Cover with a cloth to keep out flies and dust.

Knead daily, working the exposed outer surface to the interior. If you neglect to do this, the surface of the tarhana will become covered with mold. As the days go by, the aroma of the tarhana will evolve as it goes through different stages of fermentation, each with its own distinctive metabolic by-products. The longer you ferment it, the stronger and the funkier it will get.

Form the fermented tarhana into cookies on a baking tray.

Dry the tarhana cookies in the sun if possible, or at a low temperature in a dehydrator.

As they dry, gradually break the cookies into smaller pieces to create more surface area, and move them around a couple of times a day to expose different edges to the air and sun. In the end, the tarhana will be a crumble.

USING TARHANA

Soak the tarhana for about 10 minutes before using. For each portion, soak about ¼ cup/50 grams crumbs in ½ cup/120 milliliters of water. As it soaks, stir the tarhana and break up any big clumps.

Add boiling water for the simplest soup. Or prepare a more elaborate soup and add tarhana to flavor and thicken. Tarhana can also be used as the basis of a gravy or sauce. Sauté soaked tarhana, then add hot water, just a little at a time, until it reaches the desired consistency.

Eating My Way through Conferencelandia

I cannot possibly overstate my love for cheese. The most unremarkable cheese can satisfy me quite contentedly, but certain cheeses really excite me. The cheeses that I find most alluring now—the stinkiest and moldiest ones—are the ones that disgusted me as a kid. They smelled so strong and wrong, and looked so ugly; they seemed to be decaying. Now, I can see that it is that edge between ripeness and decay, where deliciousness inches toward putrefaction, that I find so exciting. Certain cheeses, like certain fruits or certain wines, get better and better . . . until they get worse. Over the course of my life, the line separating these states has shifted for me, and I enjoy an awful lot of foods that are on the other side of the dividing line for many people.

Almost as much as the flavors of cheese, I love its varied textures. Nothing tops a runny, gooey, creamy, funky, ripe soft cheese—until I bite down on a crunchy crystal of flavor in a dry aged cheese. Crumbled, melted, spread, stretched, and more, cheese brilliantly illustrates the versatility of milk as transformed via human cultural tradition and imagination.

My work as a fermentation revivalist has brought me to a great many events where opulent food has been served, and almost always features cheese. In situations like this, my love of cheese can easily lead me to excess. The conference circuit I have found myself on offers plentiful opportunities for top-notch cheese gorging.

Certain events have been epic in their scale, such as Terra Madre, the biennial Slow Food event in Torino (Turin), Italy, billed as "the biggest international event dedicated to food, the environment, agriculture, and food politics." This event, which I attended in 2008 and 2018, hosts thousands of people who represent every part of the world. There is a huge marketplace area, showcasing traditional foods, and also the Slow Food Presidia, a designation to promote foods at risk of extinction.

Cheeses at Terra Madre.

The Presidia and the marketplace were full of tantalizing sights and smells. I was particularly blown away by the diversity of cheeses that I saw and tasted there. Cheesemaking (like all aspects of food production) has evolved in so many quirky particular ways suited to the resources and conditions from which they arose. Some of these unique methods have survived, adapting to the demands of larger markets and distribution, while others have disappeared altogether. But some very quirky traditional cheeses, not at all suited to easy distribution, somehow manage to persist. What an awesome sight it was to see the skin of an entire sheep as an enclosure for a huge mass of cheese, and the bark of a tree used similarly (I wish I had taken photos of those!). I also saw the most luxuriant mold growth I've ever seen on cheeses at this event.

- - -

Some events have featured impeccably curated cheese buffets; others have featured just a few special local cheeses. Sometimes people have presented me with their fermented experiments. At the Ballymaloe Literary Festival of Food and Wine, which takes place in County Cork, Ireland, butter makers Patrik Johansson and Margit Richert—who call themselves the Butter Vikings—had come a few months before the festival to bury some butter in the peat bog at the farm, which they dug up as part of their presentation. Many people were horrified at the idea of eating the buried butter, or put off by the strong cheesy smell of it. I loved its funky cheesiness, at first, but then the pleasure was challenged by the flavor of rancidity. Since then, a onetime student of mine, Dr. Johnny Drain, has written provocatively about rancidity in butter in ways that have forced me to reconsider my judgment. "The chemical processes responsible for rancidity in butter, and the flavours and aroma compounds they produce, are common to and characterise many much-loved cheeses," he points out. "The perception of rancidity and oxidation in foods and fats are culturally elastic and context-dependent." Mild rancidity, he proposes, adds richness and complexity to butter's flavors.[4]

The climax of my conference cheese gorging had to be when I spoke at the American Cheese Society's annual conference. In addition to educational programming and networking, this particular conference features a cheese competition. Cheesemakers submit their best cheeses, which are sorted into dozens of different categories. I was not privy to the judging process, but evidently the judges barely nibble at each cheese, because the finale of the conference is a reception with all the submitted cheeses, arranged on tables by tasting category, and in some cases piled high. I tried to modestly nibble, as I flitted from the tables of blue molded cheeses to the tables full of soft-ripened cheeses, and finally lost myself in the smoked cheeses. Thanks to the sheer number of cheeses, even tiny nibbles quickly added up to fullness. Cheese vehicles such as bread and crackers were the only respite from the cheese. I drank beer to dilute all the cheese in my stomach. Maybe I should have brought a jar of kraut to balance things out?

The endless cheese spread at the American Cheese Society Conference's Festival of Cheese.

SEVEN

MEAT AND FISH

For the most perishable of foods, namely meat and fish, fermentation has been an important part of a multipronged strategy for preservation. Only rarely is fermentation alone used to preserve them. More commonly, fermentation is combined with drying, salting, smoking, or some combination thereof. Each technique contributes to preservation, and in their compounding, the total preservation value becomes greater than the sum of the parts.

Methods of preservation vary according to climate. Drying is the simplest. In places with a lot of sun, food can easily be dried. Bacalao, dried salted cod, an early and still important food commodity in international trade, is caught and dried primarily in sunny North Atlantic locations. At markets in Burma (Myanmar), I saw the most amazing variety of dried fish I have ever seen. Where it is not easy to dry fish or meat in the sun, people have often smoked it instead. Sometimes a series of different preservation methods are applied. In Japanese *katsuobushi*, skipjack tuna (bonito) are gutted and trimmed, then cooked, repeatedly smoked, inoculated and grown with a mold (*Aspergillus glaucus*), then sun-dried. The end product feels as dry as a chunk of light wood, and shavings are taken from the fish with a

tool similar to an old hand wood planer. These shavings are used as a seasoning.

The only places I know of where meat and fish are fermented without other compounding preservation methods are in the Far North, where the cold temperatures themselves constitute a compounding preservation method. In this chapter, we visit Alaska and learn about how stinkheads and some other local delicacies are prepared. Greenlander microbiologist Aviaja Lyberth Hauptmann describes some of the fermentations of her homeland, as well, and how they have been misunderstood and misrepresented.

Then, we delve into a range of Asian fermentation processes in which meat or fish are fermented with rice and/or some form of koji. The rice provides carbohydrates, which enable bacteria to produce lactic acid and thereby contribute to the preservation of the meat or fish. I elaborate on different styles of *narezushi* I tried in Japan and describe how to make a couple of them. I also describe how the women in the village of Qinfen, in rural China, fermented an yu and an rou, carp and pork, respectively, fermented in a rice and spice paste. I share recipes for *naem*—a Thai style of fermenting pork in a paste of rice, garlic, and salt—and recount

Different kinds of dried
fish at a market in Burma.

Katsuobushi shaving
tool and drawer full of
katsuobushi shavings,
with the katsuobushi they
were shaved from laying
across the drawer.

my experience learning about *sobrasada*, Mallorcan sausages fermented with lots of powdered sweet peppers as a carbohydrate source.

It makes the most sense to undertake fermentation in this realm if you have a source for fresh and local fish or meat. One impressive home meat curer I met in Australia, Bruce Kemp (see "Passion Cheesemaking" on page 265) told me, "I'm on a mission to increase the consumption of both feral and indigenous species that are culled to protect agricultural crops." Bruce served me delicious salamis of possum and wallaby, in addition to his creative cheeses. "I've also recently made a salami focused on feral animals in Australia. Think horse, hare, goat, and boar. All cause significant environmental damage here." He says many people reject the idea of eating these meats cooked, but he reports that fermentation seems to make them more palatable to all meat eaters.

Stinkheads

As in other far northern regions of the world, where summer is short and the long winters are intensely cold and dark, habitation of Alaska has been possible thanks to ingenious food preservation techniques. I have visited Alaska twice now, both times in the summer. In summer, Alaska is a land of plenty. Many people fish, and the ones who don't, get fish from their friends who do. Even though the growing season is relatively short, certain vegetables reach jumbo sizes during the very long summer days. There are lots of berries! Yet as lush as the summer is, in winter food is scarce. Preservation is a way of life. The Indigenous peoples of Alaska have longstanding traditions of fermenting and drying food for winter, and waves of settlers have all brought traditions of their own.

I have had the opportunity to learn about a few traditional Alaskan food practices from Indigenous Alaskan people. In Sitka, I met a Tlingit elder named Bertha Karras, who excitedly told me about traditional preserved foods of the Tlingit people. She described the process for making stinkheads, or fermented salmon heads. The salmon heads were placed in a burlap sack, then buried under rocks at the beach for 8 to 10 days for the salt water to rinse over them. According to Bertha, eating these fermented salmon heads "cleanses the body." She also talked about venison corned beef; smokehouses in every community; fermenting salmon roe in jars; and drying salmon until it was "dry like a bone," for winter storage, then soaking it for a day to reconstitute it before cooking. She recalled collecting wild celery, usnea, Labrador tea, and salmonberry shoots.

What was sad about our conversation was that Bertha talked about these food traditions in a nostalgic way, recalling them as memories from her youth. "The traditional foods are nearly all gone," she lamented. When I asked her why she thought they had disappeared, she blamed it on "mixed culture." We might imagine that, in a place where people had worked out ways to sustain themselves well from the bounty of the land and

Bertha Karras and her granddaughter Cayla at their home in Sitka, Alaska.

sea, those traditions would be cherished and continued by newcomers. But when cultural mixing is propelled by the forces of colonialism and capitalism, these forces dominate and, in some cases, destroy the existing cultures with a barrage of new products and tastes that are driven by insidious marketing. The cumulative effect displaces and marginalizes traditional ways. Bertha's adult granddaughter, Cayla, who lives with her, chimed in that she thought there was great interest among her generation in learning about traditional Tlingit foods, but since hardly anyone is carrying on the traditions, there is a lack of knowledge and learning opportunities. Now is the time to revive these traditions, while people like Bertha are here to share them in living memory, before they disappear altogether!

In Juneau, I met another Tlingit elder, Leona Santiago, who learned traditional Tlingit foodways from her grandparents. She talked about a variety of ways that they used to preserve fish, including drying, smoking, canning, and fermenting. I was introduced to Leona by Marc Wheeler, who owns a café called Coppa in the heart of downtown Juneau and wowed me with his culinary imagination (years later, I'm still thinking about candied salmon ice cream). In Coppa's kitchen (after hours), Leona showed us how she prepares stinkheads, and also how to make a beautiful foam from soapberries.

Leona's stinkheads are just as Bertha had described, except they are not buried at the beach. "Before, heads were buried on the beach under rocks, and the tide would come over the heads," Leona explained. "This was done with sacks and the heads were placed in the sack for a week." Now, she says, very few people ferment the salmon heads at all, and those who do mostly use barrels and store them in outdoor smokehouses. We made ours in ceramic pots (inserts from electric slow cookers). Leona used the heads of coho salmon, which she calls *gink*. She washed the heads, then she cut through the bottom of the jaw and neck on each one so they could be opened with their sides flayed outward. Then she arranged the flayed heads looking up in the vessel, neatly stacking them. She sprinkled a handful of salt on top, covered the salted salmon heads with water, loosely covered the vessel, and stored them in a cool place to ferment.

Leona preparing coho salmon heads for fermentation.

Salmon heads splayed open after cutting.

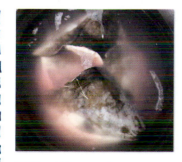

Stinkheads fermented.

Leona emphasized not to ferment the heads wrapped in plastic or tightly sealed. "We don't age anything in plastic, nor do we place a lid on top that is screwed on." This is to guard against the possibility of botulism, which can only develop in the complete absence of oxygen, and has been associated with some traditional Alaskan ferments made using plastic rather than traditional air-permeable materials. As for length of fermentation, Leona said she usually ferments stinkheads for about a week. "Until the eyes turn red," was the guidance she offered. When they are available, she does the same thing with sacs of salmon eggs (called stink eggs after they have been fermented).

The next day I was off to teach in a few other south-eastern Alaska communities. But my route home a week later included a several-hour layover in Juneau, so Marc came to the airport and took me to a field just outside for a stinkhead tasting and farewell toast. I really wish Leona had been there. There we were—Marc and I; my partner, Shoppingspree3d/Daniel; and Marc's friend Jennifer—four uninitiated white people, tasting this food completely outside our experience and palates, without having any idea of what to expect or knowing whether the process had gone as it should. We all tasted a little bit. The flavor was not offensive but not especially appealing to me, either. I later asked Marc whether Leona had gotten to eat any of it, and he replied, "Yes, and how!" He told me that Leona's friend Marie, another Tlingit elder, had joined her in eating the stinkheads. "She and Leona ate the heads with such relish, it was magical to watch." I think that if I had been there to witness that, I would have been able to approach the stinkheads with greater relish, myself.

IQALLUK

One of my Kodiak, Alaska, hosts, Bonnie Dillard, teaches art at Kodiak High School, doing art projects with her students using an overabundant local resource: marine debris, the trash from the sea that washes up onto beaches, marinas, and other coastal areas. At the downtown Kodiak marina, she showed us this marine debris sculpture her students made, called *Iqalluk*, or "fish" in the local Alutiiq language.

Hooligans

While in Alaska, I kept hearing about small oily fish known as hooligans (or eulachons). They are generally plentiful and easy to catch at riverheads at spawning time, when they are especially fatty. Native peoples of coastal Alaska have traditionally used hooligans as a source of oil, which they extract using fermentation. The hooligans spontaneously decompose for a week, and are then covered with boiling water so their oil floats to the top and can be skimmed off. Unfortunately, I did not get to witness this process, but I did get to taste some hooligans.

When I expressed interest in trying hooligans, people in Haines pointed me toward John Svenson, an artist with a gallery outside of town, who excitedly shared them with me when I showed up. John and his wife, Sharon, harvest buckets of hooligans every year at spawning time, and they can them, lots of them. When I emailed John with some questions as I was writing this, he told me that he and Sharon had canned 10 cases of hooligans, 12 jars to a case, from about four, 5-gallon/20-liter buckets full of fish, which they catch in nets. It takes mere minutes to catch the fish, but it takes days to process them all, which involves removing the organs and head of each fish, smoking them, packing them into jars, and pressure canning. But preserving that abundance of rich, luscious fish is so worth it! When they saw how much I loved the hooligans, they sent me home with a jar. The oily, fishy flavor made me miss Alaska big-time. I used up every drop of precious oil in that jar.

John Svenson excitedly sharing hooligans with me.

Kiviaq and other Greenland Fermentation Traditions

By Aviaja Lyberth Hauptmann

Aviaja Lyberth Hauptmann is a Greenlander microbiologist studying many different facets of fermentation in traditional Greenland diets. She very generously agreed to describe the process for making kiviaq, *and introduce other aspects of her important work, for this book.[1] She wrote this section.*

It has been called everything from "one of the most impressive meat fermentation tours de force" to "the world's most disgusting meat dish." To those who make this fermented food, it is simply called kiviaq. Kiviaq, seabirds preserved in a seal skin, is a heritage food for Greenlandic Inuit living in Avanersuaq, North Greenland, which encompasses the northernmost permanently populated places on Earth. Needless to say, food resources here are not always abundant. So when they are, as when the little auk (*Alle alle*) arrives in the thousands in northern Greenland in May, there is great sense in catching and preserving as many of these tiny birds as you possibly can before they disappear in late July.

To do this, all you need is your *kallut*—a net with a 3-meter-long handle—and a seal skin. You bring your kallut to the cliffside from whence the birds fly in and out of their nests. You need to catch between 300 and 600 birds, depending on the size of your seal skin. The birds are picked by hand from the net. You lock the bird's wings on its back, and then you push its chest with your thumb in a specific way so that the heart stops beating. Next, the birds must be cooled down, out of direct sunlight. After cooling down, you stuff the birds into a sealskin, from which the rest of the seal has been carefully cut out whole, leaving a hollow skin with four holes where the head, the tail, and the two flippers were. As you put the birds into the skin, you must occasionally press out the air, either by hand or by standing on the kiviaq.

Catching auks using a kallut.

Once the skin is full and the air has been thoroughly pressed out, you sew the holes in the skin tightly. You seal the seams with leftover seal blubber to protect the kiviaq from flies, and squeeze the sealed kiviaq in between carefully placed rocks in the ground. Finally, you cover the kiviaq with smaller and then larger rocks, and leave it to transform.

Over the coming months, the aroma of the kiviaq will change from something that is indistinguishable from the surrounding rocks to something much stronger that might resemble what some know to be the aroma of fermenting olives, letting the fermenter know that it is ready. In warmer years, the kiviaq might be ready sooner, within three months. Once done, it will be put in the freezer alongside fermented eider eggs, fermented mussels from the walrus stomach, narwhal intestines, and other delicacies of northern Greenland. Some might think an animal-based diet to be unvaried. But the diversity of dishes and flavors that can arise from animals is well illustrated by a northern Greenlandic freezer: eider eggs with yellow and green colors and flavors of aged cheese; narwhal intestines with the consistency of caramel and flavors that can hardly be described with words.

Stuffing auks into a seal skin.

Sewing holes in the seal skin.

Stuffed seal placed in rocks to ferment.

Kiviaq after fermentation. The bird pictured is a guillemot, another bird sometimes used in the process.

In stark contrast to the plant-based diets promoted as universal panaceas to solve almost all our global crises, Inuit foods present a very different vision of eating from and for the land. They are, to many, difficult to understand. Different cultures have different notions about where the boundaries between fermented and rotten lie. In most cultures, fermentation requires human action and control to avoid the rotten. To Inuit, fermentation does not always require human agency. Ferments can also be created by nonhuman forces, whether it be a caribou fermenting vegetation in its rumen, or the sun fermenting a seal left on the shore. Danish colonizers observing Inuit leaving seals to ferment for later use have misunderstood this practice as wasteful behavior. This misunderstanding has created devastating narratives about the wastefulness of Inuit that continue to inform natural resource management in the Arctic. Such management policies and practices have illegalized foods such as the eider egg, an important fermented food in North Greenland.

Understanding Inuit fermented foods requires appreciating the geographical, political, and cultural context in which these foods have evolved and continue to develop. The high Arctic presents its inhabitants with a highly nutritious animal-sourced diet, which has been the foundation of Inuit lives and cultures in Greenland for a thousand years. From the onset of colonization, diets in the Arctic have changed to include increasingly high amounts of imported foods. The public health consequences of this shift are felt daily by many Inuit now suffering from a host of diseases once rare in the Arctic. But the consequences are not just physical. Hunting, gathering, and fermenting in Greenland are family efforts—efforts that require families to interact, to teach and learn between generations, to spend time on the land, to move, to collaborate, and finally to be able to eat and celebrate together. These activities are fundamental to human well-being. In this way, Inuit fermentation practices resemble those of other peoples around the world, in that they are a treasured, important, and complex part of our culture.

Sobrasada

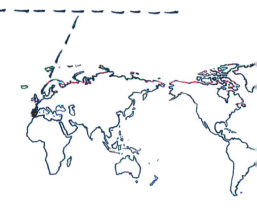

When I taught in Mallorca at a farm called Son Moragues (see "Olives" on page 86), my hosts, Bruno Entrecanales and his wife, Aina, had me over for dinner the evening I arrived. They served me wonderful olives from the farm and a beautiful meal of local specialties. My most vivid food memory of the evening is of sobrasada, the softest, creamiest cured pork I have ever tasted. It was served as an hors d'oeuvre; we spread it like soft butter on bread and enjoyed it with wine.

Bruno and his family make the sobrasada each year from a single pig that they raise and slaughter on the farm, using roughly half meat and half fat. Bruno specified that they do not use the prime cuts for sobrasada, and that they use only meat with no blood in it (meat with blood is separated to make *butifarrons*, another type of sausages made with spiced minced meat). They grind the meat and fat together, then they mix it with a blend of spices: 5 percent of its combined weight in dried sweet paprika—a specific local variety called *pebre bord*—which gives the sobrasada its characteristic bright color;

Left, Bruno's daughter, also named Aina, eating sobrasada.

Right, Bruno, his son Balti, and another helper, mixing sobrasada to stuff into casings.

Sobrasada, in different sizes, hanging to cure in Bruno's cellar.

2.5 percent of the weight in salt; chili pepper and black pepper to taste; and 0.25 percent of the weight in ascorbic acid. The antioxidant properties of the paprika (supplemented by ascorbic acid) play an important protective role during fermentation. Bruno told me that one year's sobrasada was ruined because he had used paprika that had lost its antioxidant qualities, "probably due to drying the peppers too hot and fast," he says.

The sobrasada is made in cool weather, and it is cured in the cool, humid conditions characteristic of a Mallorcan cellar. Bruno makes different sausage sizes of sobrasada, using different internal membranes of the pig, each with its own name. Smaller ones cure faster. The thinnest one, made from the small intestine and called *longaniza*, takes about a month. The largest ones, from the large intestine and the bladder, take at least a year and can continue to cure for much longer. "The bladder, called *bufeta*, is by far my favorite," says Bruno, who describes how it "turns from red to orange when two years old and tastes even better than before."

Using Rice to Ferment Meat and Fish

Generally, when fermentation is used for preservation purposes, the primary preservative is lactic acid, along with acetic acid and alcohol. These are all produced by different organisms, but they all consume the same macronutrient: carbohydrates. Meat and fish have extremely limited amounts of carbohydrates as compared to plant materials. This characteristic makes the fermentation of meat and fish very different from that of plant materials, which are relatively rich in carbohydrates.

One way to enable fermentation to preserve meat and fish is to add plant-source carbohydrates. Doing so facilitates lactic acid fermentation. In most salamis, this is accomplished with sugar and/or seasonings, such as the sweet paprika in sobrasada (see "*Sobrasada*" on page 295). In the Asian traditions I have learned about, rice is typically used, although other grains can be used similarly. The following recipes and stories elaborate this fermentation technique.

Pieces of pork, prepared for fermentation by coating them with a mixture of rice and spices, in the village of Qinfen in Guizhou, China.

Narezushi

In my lifetime, I have witnessed sushi become a globalized food. It is available almost everywhere now. I love sushi and sashimi, but I never thought much about their broader context until I started writing about fermentation and thinking about traditional methods of food preservation. Would you eat sushi at a restaurant without a refrigerator? The sushi that has gone global is really only possible thanks to refrigeration. Fish can be (relatively) safely eaten raw anywhere where it is fresh—that is, killed on-site—and served quickly. However, beyond that context, eating raw fish relies upon refrigeration to keep the fish fresh by slowing decomposition and pathogenic growth.

From reading, I learned that, traditionally, sushi consumed outside of coastal areas was frequently fermented. It is known as *narezushi*. Rather than being served on rice seasoned with vinegar, narezushi is fermented in rice, and the resultant lactic acid preserves the fish. This was fascinating to me, but I had never encountered narezushi in a Japanese restaurant in the United States or anywhere else. So when I went to Japan, narezushi was at the top of my tasting agenda.

I was able to try three different forms of narezushi while I was in Japan. The first was *kabura zushi*, yellowtail fish sandwiched between turnip slices and fermented with rice and rice koji. I was served kabura zushi when I visited cookbook author Nancy Singleton Hachisu and her husband, Tadaaki, at their home in Saitama. While Nancy and I knew each other from conferences in the United States, all Tadaaki knew about me was that I wrote about fermentation, and so he wanted to share a lesser-known Japanese ferment with me. The kabura zushi was absolutely delicious. There was nothing extreme or challenging about its flavor. The fermentation period was short—about a week. Tadaaki explained his simple process to me, which appears in the recipe that follows.

One style of narezushi I had read about long before I went to Japan was *funazushi*. Made from a particular fish from Lake Biwa, not far from Kyoto, it is fermented for

Tadaaki Hachisu with kabura zushi (*next to wine glass*) and other food he and his wife, author Nancy Singleton Hachisu, served me.

Funazushi, carp fermented for a year or longer, served with the mostly decomposed rice it was fermented in.

Hatahata zushi, sandfish fermented with rice, koji, and vegetables.

at least a year (often longer) in rice. In Kyoto, I was able to find and try funazushi thanks to the help of Australian travel writer and tour organizer Jane Lawson. Funazushi is tart, almost lemony, and after more than a year of fermentation, the rice is decomposed while the fish is still firm. It was so good that we ordered a second plate of it.

The final style of narezushi that I was able to try is *hatahata zushi*, fermented sandfish. Hatahata zushi is a local specialty in Akita, a coastal city in the north of Japan. The fish is salted and left to sit for a few days, then it is rinsed and fermented with rice, koji, carrot, kombu, and turnip. Though traditionally made for winter preservation, I would guess that the one I tried had been fermenting for a relatively short time. It wasn't especially sour, and it reminded me of sweet pickled herring, which I have always loved. The fish was still quite firm, though the rice was pretty well broken down.

MAKING FUNAZUSHI IN ITALY

By Maria Tarantino

Maria Tarantino is an Italian fermentation experimentalist and educator I've gotten to know in my travels. This is her funazushi story.

Back in 2007, I met Hiroshi Tanaka. He lives near Lake Biwa, in Shiga prefecture, and he is one of the last artisanal producers of funazushi. When I returned home to Europe, I decided to try and make the first European funazushi. I contacted Hiroshi, and he was happy to assist. He provided me with a detailed description of the procedure.

First, I had to procure a fish similar to *funa*. I used tench (*Tinca tinca*) bred in organic rice fields not far from Pavia. I took a bag of tench in the breeding season. They were alive and splashing around in my car as I drove back to Milan. I scaled them and gutted them via the throat, leaving the rest of the fish intact, and I stored them in layers with a large amount of salt (20 percent of their weight) in a wooden bucket for 40 days.

After that, I removed the fish from the salt, rinsed them, and air-dried them for 24 hours. To prevent flies from laying their eggs in the fish, I had to surround them with a fine mesh.

I cooked rice and salted it (15 percent of its dry weight). I prepared a small bowl on the side with a mix of sake and vinegar. I dipped each fish head in the sake/vinegar mix (this helps to soften the head bones), and carefully filled the body with salted rice. Then I layered the leftover salted rice beneath, between, and above the layers of stuffed fish in the bucket.

I topped the whole thing with a braid of rice straw, a wooden lid, and a heavy weight. At first, I thought the braid was just traditional decoration. Luckily, I wrote and asked Hiroshi about it. It turned out that this was the starter of the fermentation! This was one of the most powerful moments in my learning about fermentation, revealing how the most crucial elements in a process can seem irrelevant at a first glance. The experience of preparing the funazushi was also a powerful instance of cross-cultural work, a bridge across distant culinary traditions, an effort to understand the other . . .

A few months later, I extracted my fermented tench from the wooden bucket and vacuum-packed two or three to send to Japan for Hiroshi's verdict on the experiment: "Yes, it smelled something like funazushi when it was delivered onto the table. Yes, I opened the pack together with my wife and found it good! We both clapped our hands. It really smells like genuine funazushi, Maria!"

KABURA ZUSHI

I was first served this delicious fermented sushi by Tadaaki Hachisu at his home in Japan. This recipe is adapted from the one that appears in his wife Nancy Singleton Hachisu's book, *Preserving the Japanese Way*.

TIMEFRAME

About 2 weeks

EQUIPMENT

Large nonmetallic bowl with drop lid (such as a plate) that fits inside and can sit on the turnips inside the bowl

Weights: one roughly 1¾ pounds/800 grams; the other roughly 3 pounds/1.5 kilograms (improvise with household objects)

Resealable freezer bag

Steamer

INGREDIENTS

for 6 to 8 servings of a few kabura zushi sandwiches each

1¾ pounds/800 grams small turnips

3½ tablespoons/55 grams salt, divided

¾ pound/350 grams yellowtail fillets

1½ cups/350 grams uncooked rice ✳

4 ounces/100 grams rice koji

PROCESS

Scrub the turnips and slice into ¾-inch-/2-centimeter-thick rounds.

Slice into each round, from one edge toward the opposite edge, but not all the way through, to create a clamlike shape.

Toss the slit turnips with 1½ tablespoons/24 grams of the salt (3 percent of the weight of the turnips) and layer in a large nonmetallic bowl. Add a drop lid and place a 1¾-pound/800-gram weight on top. Store in a cool, dark spot for 1 week.

After 4 or 5 days have elapsed, pack the yellowtail fillets with 2 tablespoons/31 grams salt (10 percent of the weight of the fish) in a resealable freezer-style bag. Roll up the bag, squeezing out all the air, and refrigerate for 2 or 3 days.

After the turnips and fillets have sat for the prescribed period, rinse the rice and soak it for a few hours.

Line a bamboo or other steamer with a cloth and steam the rice above the water, not in it, for 30 minutes, until soft.

Fluff the rice and cool to body temperature.

Crumble or sprinkle the koji onto the rice, and mix in.

Drain the salted turnips in a sieve.

Blot the yellowtail fillets with a clean kitchen towel, then slice the fillets diagonally into ¼-inch/6-millimeter pieces of sashimi.

✳ Nancy specifies "Japanese rice"

Sandwich a slice of yellowtail into the slit of each turnip slice.

Press a ½-inch/1-centimeter layer of the rice mixture into the bottom of the nonmetallic bowl (washed and dried) that had held the turnips. Arrange the turnip "sandwiches" on top of the rice in one layer. Cover with more rice, then repeat. The last layer should be rice.

Cover the surface with plastic wrap or muslin cloth and set a drop lid and a 3-pound/1.5-kilograms weight on top. Ferment for 1 week in a cool, dark corner of your kitchen.

Reverse the bowl onto a roasting pan to drain for 4 hours before cutting and serving.

Kabura zushi is best fresh but can be stored in the refrigerator for a couple of weeks, ideally prior to draining, and well packed to protect it from oxygen. It will get increasingly sour in the fridge, which may make it less appealing to some, but only enhances safety.

Kabura zushi
ready to serve.

AN YU AND AN ROU

An yu, fermented carp, served whole . . .

Quite analogous to narezushi in Japan, an yu is a Chinese preparation of river carp stuffed with and buried in a paste of rice and spices, and fermented for months. This delicious fish was served to us, either raw or gently warmed, every day that we were in the village of Qinfen (the remote Dong village I visited in southwestern China). It appeared to be quite a staple food. It was served with scissors. We cut off pieces of fish with scissors, using our fingers to pull the tender, tasty flesh from the delicate bones. An rou is a very similar preparation made with pork. We were never served an rou, but we did get to observe it being made. (You can see a video of this process in *People's Republic of Fermentation*, episode 4.)

. . . and in pieces.

TIMEFRAME

2 to 5 months, in cool weather and an unheated space

EQUIPMENT

Steamer

Ceramic crock with lid

Improvisational objects to keep the fermenting fish elevated, to enable liquid to drain from it. In the village, they placed aluminum cans into the ceramic crock, covered in a layer of cotton. I recommend using a few unfinished hardwood blocks and a bamboo mat if you have access to them. Whatever you choose to use, make sure that it is nonreactive.

INGREDIENTS

3 whole freshwater fish, ideally carp

About 1 cup/200 grams sea salt, divided

1 cup/200 grams uncooked sticky rice *

1 cup/250 milliliters jiu niang (unstrained fermented rice), *amazake* (Japanese koji-fermented sweet rice porridge), or kasu

¼ cup/60 milliliters mijiu or sake or other rice alcohol

½ cup/60 grams dried chili flakes, divided

3 slices fresh ginger, finely chopped

¼ teaspoon Sichuan peppercorns, ground

PROCESS

Prepare the fish. The women who showed us how to do this had a very specific technique: Cut each fish lengthwise along the top, leaving it attached at the bottom, so each fish can be opened like a book. Make the cut from just behind the head to just above the tail. Cut carefully from one side of the spine downward. Make another intersecting cut crosswise, just above the tail. Try not to pierce the internal organs. Cut above and below the organs until the fish can be opened. Carefully remove the guts (in the village they removed the gall bladder to discard, and cooked the rest, which we ate). Rinse the fish with water, gently scrubbing with your fingers along the spine to remove any dried blood there.

Coat the fish generously, with about ¼ cup of the salt per fish, on all sides. Use even more salt if necessary to coat all surfaces. This heavy salting does not flavor the fish or stay with it; it draws moisture from the fish and firms it up. Lay flat, cover, and set aside in a cool spot no warmer than 55°F/12°C, or in the refrigerator, for 3 days. Before proceeding to the next steps, rinse the curing salt off the fish.

Soak the sticky rice for several hours or overnight.

Steam the rice, held above water as it cooks. Use at least twice as much water by volume as rice. I use a bamboo steamer for this, lined with cotton cloth. If the steamer is above a wok, be sure to check the water level as it boils and add additional hot water as necessary. Steam the rice for 20 to 30 minutes, until cooked through but still keeping the shape of rice. (Don't overcook it into mush.)

Cool the rice to body temperature.

Mix the rice with the jiu niang, mijiu, half of the chili flakes, ginger, and Sichaun pepper, forming it all into a paste.

In a separate container, mix the remaining ¼ cup chili flakes with ¼ cup/60 grams salt.

First, dust all sides of the fish with the chili-salt mixture. Then cover all sides with the paste, sandwiching some inside the open fish.

Prepare the fermentation vessel. Improvise appropriate non-reactive objects to keep the fish and paste elevated and draining.

* also called sweet rice or glutinous rice

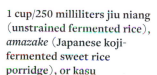

AN YU AND AN ROU *CONTINUED*

Layer the fish in the vessel, and use paste to fill any space between and around the fish. Cover the top with paste.

Ferment in a cool spot for a minimum of 2 months, and up to 4 or 5 months for best flavor.

When the fermentation is complete, scrape off and reserve most of the rice mixture. Warm the fish on both sides in a pan, serve with scissors, and enjoy picking the tasty fish from the bones. Serve with the fermented spiced rice paste on the side.

AN ROU

For an rou, fermented pork, follow exactly the same process as the an yu, replacing the fish with 2 pounds/1 kilogram of fatty pork, skin-on if possible. Belly or shoulder is ideal, but any pork could work.

Cut pork into 4- to 6-inch chunks.

Coat the pork generously with salt on all sides, cover, and set aside in the refrigerator or a cool spot for 3 days.

Rinse or scrape the curing salt off the pork, then proceed as for an yu, above.

Slice the cured pork to use in cooking like bacon. Reportedly well cured, an rou is also eaten raw, sliced thin like prosciutto, but I have not tried this.

Cleaning and salting fish.

Coating fish with chilies and salt before stuffing with paste.

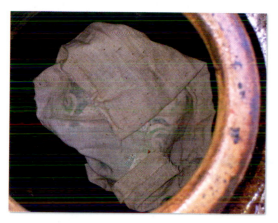

The aluminum cans were wrapped in a cotton cloth.

Placing fish in the crock.

The crock filled with fish to ferment.

Butchering pork for an rou.

Pork pieces after salting.

Pork coated with seasoned rice paste, ready to ferment.

NAEM

Ribs coated with a paste of rice, garlic, and salt, fermenting to become naem.

Naem is a Southeast Asian variant on fermenting meat with rice. This is a ferment I learned about, not in my travels, but right at home. At one of my residency programs, a Thai American student from New York, Justin Ruaysamran, showed up with a big sealable plastic bag full of pork ribs fermenting in a paste of rice, garlic, and salt. It smelled better with each passing day, and after a couple of days Justin fried them for us to eat. How incredibly succulent they were, their flavor deepened and compounded by the fermentation. I've made them many times since then, and I've taught people how to make them. Once, when my hosts in tropical Panama fermented them for five hot days, they smelled so funky that I wondered whether the flavor would be too much. But after cooking, everybody raved about how amazing they were.

Justin's parents are both from Thailand, but he was born in the US and grew up in Houston, Texas, at a time when there were few other Thai families there and no Thai restaurants or markets. "Any version of fermented meat was difficult to find," he told me. "My recipe was the result of missing Thailand, and because I was only able to go back every two or three years, I had to find a way to make things for myself." Justin learned how to make naem and related meats from market vendors in Thailand, where he told me that "oftentimes the line between home and store (in the physical sense) is blurred, as the store may simply be an outside extension or pop-up of their kitchen. More than just asking questions, I observed how they prepared, stored, and cooked their meats."

TIMEFRAME

3 to 5 days

VESSEL

Mortar and pestle, or food processor

Sealable plastic bag

INGREDIENTS

for 6 to 8 servings

2 garlic heads, broken into cloves and peeled

2 tablespoons/30 grams salt

1 cup/175 grams cooked and cooled rice

3 pounds/1.5 kilograms pork ribs ✳

PROCESS

Using a mortar and pestle, starting with the garlic and salt, then adding the rice, blend into a smooth paste. Justin uses a food processor.

Spread the paste on the ribs, making sure to coat the entire surface of each rib. Then pack the paste-coated ribs into a sealable plastic bag, removing as much air as possible.

Ferment 3 to 5 days, depending on temperature (longer if cooler) and desired flavor (longer for stronger).

The ribs can be stored in the refrigerator, after fermentation and before cooking, for up to several weeks, stabilized by acids and salt.

Cook the ribs any way you like. Justin deep-fried them that first time, which was amazing. He also likes to grill them. I've also oven-roasted them.

Variations: Justin says, "The same recipe works well with beef ribs and, surprisingly, steamed (and cooled) mushrooms. I've added small amounts of herbs, such as cilantro, with success. I've tried brown, red, and black sticky rice, but plain white jasmine rice is my favorite."

Also, the bones left over after eating the naem ribs make a rich flavorful stock. Cover with water, add a little vinegar, and gently simmer, covered, for a few hours.

✳ if possible, ask the butcher to cut each rib in half, to create more surface area for the rice and garlic paste to latch on to the meat

GROUND MEAT NAEM

Naem can also be made with ground or minced meat, traditionally pork, with the mix wrapped and fermented in banana leaves. Generally, I have used a jar or a sealable plastic bag as a vessel. The characteristic sour-salty-garlicky-funky flavor of naem can be achieved with a variety of meats and grains. I have enjoyed experimenting with beef, and with grains other than rice, with excellent results. After the fermentation, I like to cook the ground meat naem with vegetables. Beef and kasha naem was so perfect sautéed with a little onion and cabbage! You can also sauté it with other vegetables or form into burgers.

TIMEFRAME

3 to 5 days

VESSEL

Mortar and pestle, or food processor

Jar or sealable plastic bag

INGREDIENTS

for about ¾ pound/340 g

½ cup/85 grams cooked grain

3 garlic cloves (to taste)

1 heaping teaspoon/
5 grams salt

½ pound/250 grams ground
or minced meat

PROCESS

Start with cooked grain, cooled to body or refrigerator temperature.

Grind the garlic and salt together using a mortar and pestle, food processor, or other tool.

Add the grain and garlic-salt paste to the meat and mix thoroughly.

Pack the mixture into the jar or sealable plastic bag for fermentation.

Ferment at room temperature for 3 to 5 days. Mix in the jar or massage the sealable plastic bag each day. The smell and flavor will get stronger with the passing days.

The naem is now ready to cook.

A WHOLE WORLD IN A JAR

Because you are a human being on planet Earth—wherever you are from, and wherever you live—fermentation is part of your birthright and cultural inheritance. Practices around the world vary quite a lot, as you can see from the diversity of foods and beverages described in these pages. What and how people ferment are integral elements of culture. Fermentation follows from what people grow, harvest, raise, hunt, and fish; and the climate and terrain that dictate each of these. However, so many traditional practices have disappeared altogether, and so many more are on the brink of extinction unless people carry them on.

Carrying on and spreading fermentation practices does not require you to traverse the globe. While it has been incredibly fun and interesting to visit so many places, meet so many people, and taste and learn about so many different fermented foods, most of what I learn on these journeys reinforces and reaffirms the same basic fermentation concepts.

Specific fermentation traditions vary from place to place, but the foundations are the same everywhere: people ferment what is abundant, and they generally rely upon organisms that are naturally present on those foods or nearby. Fermentation is not precious, and it does not require exotic ingredients or obscure starters.

I hope this book leaves you excited to experiment with some of the ferments that I have written about. You will learn from investigating varied traditions, organisms, and substrates. But my most earnest desire is that you will draw inspiration from the ferments documented here to work with whatever food resources are abundant around you. Let's reclaim fermentation in the context of reclaiming food more broadly. Participate in expanding and strengthening local food systems however you can, and use your fermentation passion, skills, and experience to enhance local food resources, as people everywhere do and have done for longer than anyone can remember.

ACKNOWLEDGMENTS

This book has involved a huge amount of collaboration. Of course, the journeys I document have all involved hosts and organizers, without whom I would not have had these experiences. But in writing about these adventures, I have again turned to many of them, and many others who I have met along the way, to fill in gaps in my memory and provide me with details, contacts, and photographs.

With apologies in advance to anyone I may have neglected to include, I thank: Etain Addey, Darina Allen, Neal Applebaum, Jordan Aversman, Ana de Azcárate, Johann Li Boscán, Ahren Boulanger, Justin Bullard, Marie T. Cameron, Stephanie Cameron, Javier Carrera, Antonio De Valle Castilla, Nora Chovanec, Sadie Chrestman, Beth Conklin, Hernan Correa, Liz Crain, James Creagh, Felipe Croce, Jennifer De Marco, Bernie Deplazes, Brian Dolphin, Naomi Duguid, Jenna Empey, Bruno Entrecanales, Kevin Farley, Sharon Flynn, Michelle O. Fried, Paulina Garcia, Nerea Zorokiain Garin, Douglas Gayeton, Raquel Guajardo, Bernat Guixer, Nancy Singleton Hachisu, Aviaja Lyberth Hauptmann, Valerie Herrero, Maya Hey, Jennifer Holmes, Alex Hozven, Asha Ironwood, Patrick Ironwood, Paul Iskov, Adam James, Felipe Janicsek, Leticia Janicsek, Bruce Kemp, Dolly Kikon, Judy King, Mara Jane King, Karmela Kis, Galia Kleiman, Kris Knutson, Matteo Leoni, JoAnn Lesh, Pao Liu, Justin Lubecki, Yuri Manabe, Harry Mangat, Holly Marban, Melissa Mills, Gordon Monahan, Esteban Yepes Montoya, Ramón Perisé Moré, Anna Mulé, Shinobu Namae, Sean Nash, Donna Neuworth, Misa Ono, Lola Osinkolu, Fabian Pacheco, Joel Pember, Andrea Pieroni, Lynne Purvis, Joel Rodrigues, Tim Root, Joshua Pablo Rosenstock, Justin Ruaysamran, Mattia Sacco Botto, Anand Sankar, Leona Santiago, Malcolm Saunders, Sasker Scheerder, Soirée-Leone, Alejandro Solano, Michael Stusser, Hiroshi Sugihara, John Svenson, Aylin Öney Tan, Maria Tarantino, Satomi Terada, Dana Thompson, Michael Twitty, Anton van Klopper, Mirjam Veenman, Willem Velthoven, Tara Whitsitt, Todd Weir, and Marc Wheeler. With all this help filling in gaps in my memory, any errors or misunderstandings are mine alone.

For reading my evolving manuscript and offering feedback, I am grateful to my dear friends Shoppingspree3d/Daniel Clark, MaxZine Weinstein, Soirée-Leone, Spiky, and Mara Jane King.

I thank my agent, Valerie Borchardt, my editors, Ben Watson and Natalie Wallace, and the rest of the team at Chelsea Green Publishing.

从土地出发
向农民学习!!!

Let's bow in gratitude
to land, nature and
Farmers

IMAGE CREDITS

Front cover and page vi	Jessica Tezak, jesstezak.com
Page x	Todd Weir
Page 18	Michael Cannon
Page 19, *middle*	Jeison Castillo, courtesy of El Taller de los Fermentos
Page 26, *top*	Mara Jane King
Page 32	Nerea Zorokiain Garín
Page 34	Jessica Tezak
Page 48, *bottom*	Yuri Manabe
Page 50, *bottom*	Yuri Manabe
Page 52, *bottom*	Adam James
Page 71, *top*	Antonio De Valle Castilla
Page 77, *all*	Kevin Farley
Pages 78 and 79	Photo collage by Douglas Gayeton as part of his Lexicon of Sustainability
Page 88	Nerea Zorokiain Garín
Pages 92 thru 95	Sasker Scheerder
Page 103	Jessica Tezak
Page 108, *top*	Mattia Sacco Botto
Page 124, *top*	Poster by Pico de Pajaro Zurdo
Page 136	Francesca Cirilli, courtesy of the Slow Food Archive
Page 157	Illustration by Misa Ono
Page 164	Vine Collective @vinecollective
Page 165, *top*	Hiroshi Sugihara
Page 169, *bottom*	Mattia Sacco Botto

NOTES

CHAPTER 3:
GRAINS AND STARCHY TUBERS

1. Renata Sõukand et al., "An Ethnobotanical Perspective on Traditional Fermented Plant Foods and Beverages in Eastern Europe," *Journal of Ethnopharmacology* 170 (July 2015): 284–96, https://doi.org /10.1016/j.jep.2015.05.018.

2. Sõukand et al., "An Ethnobotanical Perspective," 291.

3. Genevieve Bardwell and Susan Ray Brown, *Salt Rising Bread: Recipes and Heartfelt Stories of a Nearly Lost Appalachian Tradition* (Pittsburgh: St. Lynn's Press, 2016), ix.

4. Personal communications with author.

5. Bardwell and Brown, *Salt Rising Bread*, 63.

6. Personal communications with author.

7. Personal communications with author.

8. Santiago Ospina, *Tucupí: El legado de la Yuca Brava*, Vimeo video, 4:50, October 5, 2018, https://vimeo.com/293652067.

9. Jane Ryan, "Indigenous Australia's Fermented Beverages," Diffords Guide, accessed December 28, 2020, https:// www.diffordsguide.com/en-au /encyclopedia/2709/au/bws.

10. Lynne Purvis, "Way Before Daffodil Meadow," self-published.

11. Robin Wall Kimmerer, *Braiding Sweetgrass: Indigenous Wisdom, Scientific Knowledge, and the Teachings of Plants* (Minneapolis: Milkweed Editions, 2013), 9.

CHAPTER 4:
MOLD CULTURES

1. Rich Shih and Jeremy Umansky, *Koji Alchemy: Rediscovering the Magic of Mold-Based Fermentation* (White River Junction, VT: Chelsea Green, 2020), 108.

2. René Redzepi and David Zilber, *The Noma Guide to Fermentation* (New York: Artisan, 2018), 363.

3. Jeff Gordinier, "Better Eating, Thanks to Bacteria," *The New York Times*, September 17, 2012, https://www.nytimes.com/2012 /09/19/dining/fermentation-guru-helps -chefs-find-new-flavors.html.

4. Gordinier, "Better Eating, Thanks to Bacteria."

5. Bernat Guixer, Michael Bom Frøst, and Roberto Flore, "Tempeto—Expanding the Scope and Culinary Applications of Tempe with Post-Fermentation Sousvide Cooking," *International Journal of Gastronomy and Food Science* 9 (October 2017): 1–9, https://doi.org/10.1016/j.ijgfs .2017.03.002.

6. Bernat Guixer, "The Interphase between Science and Gastronomy, a Case Example of Gastronomic Research Based on Fermentation—Tempeto and Its Derivates," *International Journal of Gastronomy and Food Science* 15 (April 2019): 15–21, https://doi.org/10.1016/j.ijgfs .2018.11.004.

CHAPTER 5: BEANS AND SEEDS

1. Naomi Duguid, *Burma: Rivers of Flavor* (New York: Artisan Books, 2012), 41.
2. Dolly Kikon, "Fermenting Modernity: Putting *Akhuni* on the Nation's Table in India," South Asia: Journal of South Asian Studies 38, no. 2 (2015): 320–35, http://doi.org/10.1080/00856401.2015 .1031936.
3. Kikon, "Fermenting Modernity," 320–35.
4. Kikon, "Fermenting Modernity," 320–35.
5. Kikon, "Fermenting Modernity," 320–35.
6. "Promoting Origin-Linked Quality Products in Four Countries (GTF/ RAF/426/ITA): Mid-Term Progress Report," Slow Food, accessed April 21, 2021, http://www.fao.org/fileadmin /templates/olq/documents/documents /Midtermreport3.pdf.
7. Fuchsia Dunlop, "Rotten Vegetable Stalks, Stinking Bean Curd and Other Shaoxing Delicacies," in *Cured, Fermented and Smoked Foods: Proceedings of the Oxford Symposium on Food and Cookery 2010*, edited by Helen Saberi (Totnes, U.K.: Prospect Books, 2011), 92.
8. Holly Davis, *Ferment: A Guide to the Ancient Art of Culturing Foods, from Kombucha to Sourdough* (Sydney, AU: Murdoch Books, 2017), 251.
9. Miin Chan, "Lost in the Brine," Eater, March 1, 2021, https://www.eater .com/2021/3/1/22214044/fermented -foods-industry-whiteness-kimchi -miso-kombucha.

CHAPTER 6: MILK

1. Renata Sõukand et al., "An Ethnobotanical Perspective on Traditional Fermented Plant Foods and Beverages in Eastern Europe," *Journal of Ethnopharmacology* 170 (July 2015): 284–96, https://doi.org /10.1016/j.jep.2015.05.018.
2. Andrea Pieroni and Renata Sõukand, "The Disappearing Wild Food and Medicinal Plant Knowledge in a Few Mountain Villages of North-Eastern Albania," *Journal of Applied Botany and Food Quality* 90 (2017): 58–67, https://doi.org/10.5073 /JABFQ.2017.090.009.
3. Nilhan Aras and Aylin Öney Tan, "Tarhana: An Anatolian Food Concept as a Promising Idea for the Future," Dublin Gastronomy Symposium 2020, page 1, https://arrow.tudublin.ie/cgi/viewcontent .cgi?article=1198&context=dgs.
4. Johnny Drain, "Aged Butter Part 2: The Science of Rancidity," Nordic Food Lab Archive, January 29, 2016, https:// nordicfoodlab.wordpress.com/2016/01 /29/2016-1-29-aged-butter-part-2-the -science-of-rancidity.

CHAPTER 7: MEAT AND FISH

1. Aviaja Lyberth Hauptmann adds: "I am indebted to the community of Siorapaluk, especially the Hendriksen family, who taught me everything I know about kiviaq and other ferments of Avanersuaq. And also to my kind and helpful colleague Joshua Evans for feedback."

INDEX

Note: Page numbers in *italics* refer to photographs. Page numbers in **bold** refer to recipes.

hair rinse, from fermented rice
   starch water, 113
Hakko Shokudo Kamoshika
   (café), 25–26
hatahata zushi, 300, *300*
Hauptmann, Aviaja Lyberth,
   285, 292–94
Hawai'i, coffee production, 250
heads (first distillates), 107
Hill, Bernice, 68
Himalayan Fermented Foods
   (Tamang), 180, 181
honey
   fermentation of, 1
   mead from, 27–31
   t'ej from, 27–28
honey process for coffee
   fermentation, 252
hooligans, 291
Hozven, Alex, 76, 78–79, *78*, 80–81
Huang, H. T., 181
Hulst, Iris van, 190

I
India
   akhuni, 216–19
   molded starter traditions,
      176–181
   natto-like seasonings, 207
   water-powered community
      grain mill, 99, *99*
Indigenous Food Lab, 135, *135*, 136
indigenous practices
   in Alaska, 287–290
   appropriation by white people,
      260–61
   Bribri chicha, 182–85
   cacao production and
      consumption, 246–47
   chicha making, 117, *118*
   colonialist displacement of,
      xiii, 74, 136–37, 294
   Greenland fermentation
      traditions, 292–94
   guarapo de piña ceremony, 19
   need for celebration and
      preservation of, xiii, xiv–xx,
      134–37, 287–88, 311

replacement by factory
   production, 4, 225
shifting meanings of, 218–19
El Taller de los Fermentos
   outreach, 119–121
Indonesia
   palm wine, 2–3
   tapè, 166, **167**
   tempeh, 186–89
insects
   consumption of grasshoppers
      and ants, 71
   fermentation by leafcutter
      ants, 201
   sautéed crickets, 108, *109*
   worldwide consumption of, 74
Insects: An Edible Field Guide
   (Gates), 74
Inuit fermentation traditions,
   292–94
"Iqalluk" (sculpture), 290, *290*
Ireland, Ballymaloe Literary
   Festival of Food and Wine, 282
iru (fermented African locust
   beans), 226, 227
Iskov, Paul, 163
Italy
   farinata, 257, **258**, 259
   funazushi making in, 301
   Terra Madre event, 29, *29*, 56–57,
      135, *135*, 136, 280–82, *281*
   winemaking in Umbria, 15–17

J
jaiyaju (tucupí starter), 133
James, Adam, 51–53, *51*
Janicsek, Leticia, 254–55
Japan
   fermented tofu, 234
   fruit enzymes, 25–26
   funazushi, 298, 299, 300
   kabura zushi, 298, 299, **302–3**
   kasu, 151–55
   katsuobushi, 285, 286
   koji traditions and
      innovations, 141–43
   mirin, 159, **159–160**
   narezushi, 298–300

natto, 204–7, **208–10**
persimmon pickling medium,
   24, **24**
persimmon vinegar, 22, **23**
Satomi Terada's Sake Lees
   Bagna Càuda, **153**
Satomi Terada's Sake Lees
   Gratin, **152**
shio-koji, 156–58, **158**
sunki, 47–50
tofu misozuke, 240, **241**
Jared (friend), 25
Jessieca (friend), *16*
jiu niang (unstrained
   fermented rice)
   from rice alcohol, 112
   as starter for whole grain
      bread, 102
   in an yu and an rou, 305
jiu qu (rice alcohol starter),
   111, *111*
Johansson, Patrik, 282
Jones, Brandon, *76*
jora (malted corn), 122, **122**
jualapa (grating tool), 19
justice and diversity concerns,
   xiv–xx, 260–61

K
kabura zushi, 298, 299, **302–3**
kahm yeast, 46
Kaida turnips, sunki from, 48, *50*
Kajiwara, Shiori, 165
Kalap village, India, molded
   starter traditions, 176–181
kallut (net), 292, *293*
Karmela (friend), 54–55, *54*, 58, 59,
   62, 63
Karras, Bertha, 287, 288
Karras, Cayla, 288, *288*
kasu (sake lees)
   ideas for using, 155
   kasuzuke from, 78, 80–81
   overview, 151
   in an rou, 305
   Sake Lees Crackers, **154**
   Satomi Terada's Sake Lees
      Bagna Càuda, **153**

ABOUT THE AUTHOR

Sandor Ellix Katz is a fermentation revivalist. A self-taught experimentalist who lives in rural Tennessee, his explorations in fermentation developed out of his overlapping interests in cooking, nutrition, and gardening. He is the author of four previous books: *Wild Fermentation*, *The Revolution Will Not Be Microwaved*, *The Art of Fermentation*—which won a James Beard Foundation Award in 2013—and *Fermentation as Metaphor*. These books, and the hundreds of fermentation workshops he has taught around the world, have helped catalyze a broad revival of the fermentation arts. *The New York Times* calls Sandor "one of the unlikely rock stars of the American food scene." For more information, check out his website: www.wildfermentation.com.

the politics and practice of sustainable living

CHELSEA GREEN PUBLISHING

Chelsea Green Publishing sees books as tools for effecting cultural change and seeks to empower citizens to participate in reclaiming our global commons and become its impassioned stewards. If you enjoyed *Sandor Katz's Fermentation Journeys*, please consider these other great books related to food and drink.

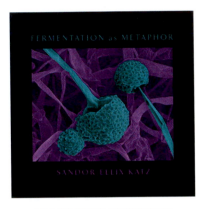

FERMENTATION AS METAPHOR
SANDOR ELLIX KATZ
9781645020219
Hardcover

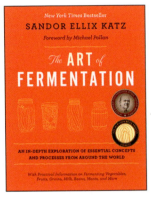

THE ART OF FERMENTATION
An In-Depth Exploration of Essential Concepts and Processes from around the World
SANDOR ELLIX KATZ
9781603582865
Hardcover

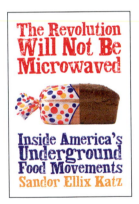

THE REVOLUTION WILL NOT BE MICROWAVED
Inside America's Underground Food Movements
SANDOR ELLIX KATZ
9781933392110
Paperback

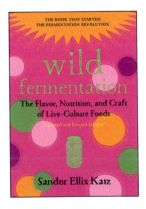

WILD FERMENTATION
The Flavor, Nutrition, and Craft of Live-Culture Foods, Updated and Revised Edition
SANDOR ELLIX KATZ
9781603586283
Paperback

the politics and practice of sustainable living

For more information,
visit **www.chelseagreen.com**.